CHAGALL

CHAGALL

A RETROSPECTIVE

Edited by Jacob Baal-Teshuva

BEAUX
ARTS
EDITIONS

Frontispiece: The last photograph of Marc Chagall, 1985.
© Cinquini.

CONTENTS

Chagall on Art and Life

The Circus, the Ballet, and the Opera

Chagall's Graphic Work

Chagall's Ceramics, Sculpture, and Stained Glass

Homage to Chagall

The Tapestries and Mosaics

The Biblical Message

Chagall and Israel

Remembering Chagall

To my wife, Aviva, with love

ACKNOWLEDGMENTS

First and foremost, I am indebted to Marc Chagall, for his friendship through the years and for the many hours spent in his midst. He was a complex man who was full of inspiration, energy, and dedication to his art.

To my wife, Aviva, my best critic, for her continued patience and constructive criticism, I am also especially grateful.

Ms. Meret Meyer, Chagall's granddaughter, was most kind and cooperative, in part on behalf of her late mother Ida Chagall, in supplying early photographs of the master as well as of the wonderful works that make up her mother's extraordinary collection. Also great sources for visual material were the Musée National d'Art Moderne, Centre Georges Pompidou in Paris and the Réunion des Musées Nationaux, Paris, both of whom supplied numerous photographs for this book. Thanks also to Mrs. Christina Burrus, for her assistance obtaining photographs of Chagall's early work for the Jewish Theater; Mme. Yvette Cauquil Prince, who wove more than twenty-five Chagall tapestries and was kind in lending visual material of these unique pieces; Mr. Marcus Diener, one of the greatest of Chagall collectors; Mr. Charles Marq, for the historical photos from his personal collection; Mr. Alexander Liberman, for his wonderful photographs of Chagall; Mr. James Goodman of the Goodman Gallery, New York; Ms. Nancy Whyte of Christie's, New York; Mr. David Nahmad; Mr. Jose Mugrabi; Mr. and Mrs. Dov Gottesman; Ms. Bertha Katz; Mrs. Raja Edelman of Kaller Kimche, Inc.; Ms. Linda Breitel for her kind and efficient help in Moscow; Mr. Leon Leneman in Paris; and to all of the private collectors of Chagall's work.

I am grateful to the Solomon R. Guggenheim Foundation for their permission to use material from their catalogue and especially to Professor Benjamin Harshav of Yale University for his rare translations from the Russian and Yiddish of many early documents by and about Marc Chagall. I thank also all of the authors—scholars, curators, friends, and admirers of Chagall—whose work appears in this volume; theirs is a great contribution.

Special thanks are also due Hugh Levin, who commissioned this book and remained supportive throughout this large undertaking; to Denise Magidson, for tirelessly typing portions of the text; and to Deborah T. Zindell, for her precise copyediting and her assistance in preparing the manuscript. And last but not least thanks to Jeanne-Marie P. Hudson of Hugh Lauter Levin Associates for her dedication and long hours, her good judgement and enormous work in bringing this volume to fruition.

—Jacob Baal-Teshuva

BIBLIOGRAPHICAL INDEX

Marc Chagall, *My Life*. Da Capo Press, New York. © ARS, N.Y./ ADAGP, Paris.

Alfred Werner, *Chagall Watercolors and Gouaches*. © 1970 by and reprinted with permission of Watson-Guptill Publications.

Edouard Roditi, "Chagall's Early Years," *Encounter*, Issue 54, vol. X, no. 3, March 1958.

Bella Chagall, *First Encounter*. Original Yiddish text and German version © 1945 by Ida Chagall. English translation © 1983 by Ida Chagall. Reprinted by permission of Schocken Books, published by Pantheon Books, a division of Random House, Inc.

Marc Chagall, *My Life*. Da Capo Press, New York. © ARS, N.Y./ ADAGP, Paris.

Marina Bessonova, "The Master from Vitebsk," originally published in *Chagall Discovered: From Russian and Private Collections*. © 1988 Sovietskii Khudozhnik Publishers, Moscow. Reprinted by permission of the author.

Irina Antonova, Foreword, *Chagall Discovered: From Russian and Private Collections*. © 1988 Sovietskii Khudozhnik Publishers, Moscow. Reprinted by permission of the author.

Marc Chagall, "Why Did I Go to Paris?" *Chagall by Chagall*. Published by Harry N. Abrams, New York, 1979. © ARS, N.Y./ADAGP, Paris.

Marc Chagall, *My Life*. Da Capo Press, New York. © ARS, N.Y./ADAGP, Paris.

Guillaume Apollinaire, *Chroniques d'Art*. © 1960 Editions Gallimard, Paris.

Jean-Jacques Lévêque, "Chagall and the Poets," *XXe Siecle Review, Special Issue: Homage to Marc Chagall*. © 1982 Leon Amiel Publishers, New York and Paris.

Pierre Schneider, from *The Louvre Dialogues*. © 1991 Editions Adam Biro, Paris.

Marc Chagall, letter to Kandaurov, November 14, 1911. Russian State Archives of Literature and Art; fund 769, catalogue #1, unit 210. © ARS, N.Y./ADAGP, Paris.

Marc Chagall, letter to Pavel Ettinger, April 2, 1920. The Pushkin State Museum of Art; fund 29, catalogue III, unit 4675. © ARS, N.Y./ADAGP, Paris.

Anatoly Lunacharsky, "Young Russian in Paris: Marc Chagall," *Chagall: The Russian Years, 1907–1922* by Aleksandr Kamensky. Rizzoli, New York, and Editions du Regard, Paris, 1989.

Iakov Tugendhold, "A New Talent," *Chagall: The Russian Years, 1907–1922* by Aleksandr Kamensky. Rizzoli, New York, and Editions du Regard, Paris, 1989.

Alain Jouffroy, "Theatre and Revolution," *XXe Siecle Review, Special Issue: Homage to Marc Chagall*. © 1982 Leon Amiel Publishers, New York and Paris.

Osip Mandelshtam, "The Moscow State Yiddish Theater," *Marc Chagall and the Jewish Theater*. Translated from the Russian and Yiddish by Benjamin and Barbara Harshav. © 1992 by and reprinted with permission of The Solomon R. Guggenheim Foundation, New York.

Avram Kampf, "Art and Stage Design: The Jewish Theatres of Moscow in the Early Twenties," *Tradition and Revolution: The Jewish Renaissance in Russian Avant Garde Art, 1912–1918*, edited by Ruth Apter-Gabriel. Reprinted by permission of the author and The Israel Museum, Jerusalem.

Alexandre Benois, "On the Exhibition of 'Jewish Art,'" *Chagall: The Russian Years, 1907–1922*. Rizzoli, New York, and Editions du Regard, Paris, 1989.

Abram Efros and Iakov Tugendhold, "The Emperor's Clothes," "Chagall," "The Artist Marc Chagall," *Marc Chagall and the Jewish Theater*. Translated from the Russian and Yiddish by Benjamin and Barbara Harshav. © 1992 by and reprinted with permission of The Solomon R. Guggenheim Foundation, New York.

E. Tériade, "Chagall and Romantic Painting," *XXe Siecle Review, Special Issue: Chagall Monumental*. © 1973 Leon Amiel Publishers, New York and Paris.

Raissa Maritain, *Chagall: A Selection of Paintings from American Museums and Private Collections*. Reprinted by permission of Galerie Chalette, New York.

Jacques Maritain, *Art and Poetry*. © 1943 Philosophical Library, Inc.

Katharine Kuh, "The Art of Marc Chagall," published in *WFMT Chicago Fine Arts Guide*, April 1961, vol. 10, no. 4. Reprinted with permission.

Marc Chagall, letter to Benois, March 1935. Russian State Archives of Literature and Art; fund 938, catalogue #2, unit 311. © ARS, N.Y./ADAGP, Paris.

André Breton, published in *XXe Siecle Review, Special Issue: Homage to Marc Chagall*. © 1982 Leon Amiel Publishers, New York and Paris.

René Berger, "Chagall and the Presence of the Myth," *XXe Siecle Review, Christmas 1961*. © 1961 Leon Amiel Publishers, New York and Paris.

James Johnson Sweeney, *Marc Chagall*. © 1946 by and reprinted with permission of The Museum of Modern Art, New York.

Gilbert Lascault, "Monumental Paintings," *XXe Siecle Review, Special Issue: Homage to Marc Chagall*. © 1982 Leon Amiel Publishers, New York and Paris.

Marc Chagall, "Leaves from My Notebook," *Marc Chagall and the Jewish Theater*. Translated from the Russian and Yiddish by Benjamin and Barbara Harshav. © 1992 by and reprinted with permission of The Solomon R. Guggenheim Foundation, New York.

Marc Chagall, letter to Ettinger, August 29, 1936. The Pushkin State Museum of Art; fund 29, catalogue III, unit 4684. © ARS, N.Y./ADAGP, Paris.

Marc Chagall, letter to Benois, February 6, 1940. The Russian State Archives of Literature and Art; fund 938, catalogue #2, unit 311. © ARS, N.Y./ADAGP, Paris.

Marc Chagall, Afterword, *First Encounter* by Bella Chagall. Original Yiddish text and German version © 1945 by Ida Chagall. English translation © 1983 by Ida Chagall. Reprinted by permission of Schocken Books, published by Pantheon Books, a division of Random House, Inc.

Louis Aragon, *Recent Paintings: 1966–1968*. © 1968 Pierre Matisse Gallery, New York. Reprinted by permission of the estate of Louis Aragon.

Marc Chagall, *Le Cirque: Paintings 1969–1980*. © 1981 Pierre Matisse Gallery, New York. Reprinted by permission of the estate of Pierre Matisse.

Virginia Haggard, *My Life with Chagall*. © 1986 by Virginia Haggard. Reprinted by permission of Donald I. Fine, Inc.

John Martin, "Decor by Chagall Dominated Ballet." © 1945 by *The New York Times*. Reprinted by permission.

Edwin Denby," Chagall in Wonderland." *Dance Index-Ballet Caravan, Inc.*, vol. IV, no. 11, November 1945.

Abram Efros, "He Has No Theatre Blood at All." *Dance Index-Ballet Caravan, Inc.*, vol. IV, no. 11, November 1945.

Sir Rudolf Bing, *Chagall at the Met* by Emily Genauer. © 1971 by and reprinted with permission of The Metropolitan Opera Association, New York, and Leon Amiel Publishers, New York and Paris.

Emily Genauer, *Chagall at the Met*. © 1971 by and reprinted with permission of The Metropolitan Opera Association, New York, and Leon Amiel Publishers, New York and Paris.

Marc Chagall, remarks at the unveiling of the murals at the Metropolitan Opera House, Lincoln Center, September 8, 1966. Translated by Lincoln Center. © Lincoln Center for the Performing Arts, Inc.

Ambroise Vollard, "How I Came to Publish La Fontaine's *Fables*," *XXe Siecle Review, Special Issue: Chagall Monumental*. © 1973 Leon Amiel Publishers, New York and Paris.

Sylvie Forestier, "Autour de l'oeuvre grave," *L'oeuvre Grave*. © 1987 Museé

National Message Biblique Marc Chagall, Nice. Reprinted by permission of the author.

Marc Chagall, *Chagall Lithographs*. © 1960 by and reprinted with permission of George Braziller, Inc.

Robert Marteau, "Chagall as Engraver," *XXe Siecle Review, Special Issue: Homage to Marc Chagall*. © 1982 Leon Amiel Publishers, New York and Paris.

Charles Sorlier, *Marc Chagall Lithographe*, Galerie Enrico Navara. Reprinted by permission of the estate of Charles Sorlier.

Jacques Thirion, "Marc Chagall's Sculpture and Ceramics," *XXe Siecle Review, Special Issue: Chagall Monumental*. © 1973 Leon Amiel Publishers, New York and Paris.

Charles Marq, "When Chagall Hears the Angels Singing," *XXe Siecle Review, Special Issue: Homage to Marc Chagall*. © 1982 Leon Amiel Publishers, New York and Paris.

Marc Chagall, remarks at the dedication of the *Peace* window at the United Nations. Translation © The United Nations, New York.

Carlton Lake, "Artist at Work: Marc Chagall," Originally published in *The Atlantic Monthly,* July 1963.

Virginia Haggard, *My Life with Chagall*. © 1986 by Virginia Haggard. Reprinted by permission of Donald I. Fine, Inc.

Françoise Gilot and Carlton Lake, *Life with Picasso*. © 1964 by and reprinted with permission of McGraw Hill, Inc.

Henry McBride, "Chagall at the Museum of Modern Art," *The Flow of Art: Essays and Criticisms of Henry McBride*. Published by Atheneum Publishers, New York. © 1975 by and reprinted with permission of the estate of Henry McBride.

Marc Chagall, letter to Ettinger, November 22, 1947. Pushkin State Museum of Art; fund 29, catalogue III, unit 4692. © ARS, N.Y./ADAGP, Paris.

Louis Aragon, Marc Chagall, *Recent Paintings, 1966–1968*. © 1968 Pierre Matisse Gallery. Reprinted by permission of the estate of Louis Aragon.

Alfred Werner, *Chagall Watercolors and Gouaches*. © 1970 by and reprinted with permission of Watson-Guptill Publications.

René Huyghe, "Chagall ou la Réalite Interieure." Originally published in *French Vogue, Special Issue on Marc Chagall,* 1985.

James Johnson Sweeney, "An Interview with Marc Chagall." First published in *Partisan Review,* vol, XVI, no. 3, 1949.

Louis Aragon, "The Admirable Chagall," *XXe Siecle Review, Special Issue: Homage to Marc Chagall*. © 1982 Leon Amiel Publishers, New York and Paris.

Guy Weelen, "Monuments of a Return to the Land of the Prophets," *XXe Siecle Review, Special Issue: Homage to Marc Chagall*. © 1982 Leon Amiel Publishers, New York and Paris.

Marc Chagall, "Speech at the Unveiling of the Tapestries in the Knesset, Jerusalem," *Marc Chagall and the Jewish Theater*. Translated from the Russian and Yiddish by Benjamin and Barbara Harshav. © 1992 by and reprinted with permission of The Solomon R. Guggenheim Foundation, New York.

Marc Chagall, "Letter to the President of Israel," *Marc Chagall and the Jewish Theater*. Translated from the Russian and Yiddish by Benjamin and Barbara Harshav. © 1992 by and reprinted with permission of The Solomon R. Guggenheim Foundation, New York.

Marc Chagall, "Le Message Biblique," *Marc Chagall: 1887–1985*. © 1985 Réunion des Musées Nationaux, Paris.

Dora Vallier, "From Memories to Myth," *XXe Siecle Review, Special Issue: Homage to Marc Chagall*. © 1982 Leon Amiel Publishers, New York and Paris.

André Verdet, "Eternity Recaptured," *XXe Siecle Review, Special Issue: Homage to Marc Chagall*. © 1982 Leon Amiel Publishers, New York and Paris.

Benjamin Harshav, "Jewish Art and Jesus Christ," *The Role of Language in Modern Art: On Texts and Subtexts in Chagall's Paintings*. Published in *Modernism/Modernity*, vol. 1, no. 2. © 1994 by and reprinted with permission of The Johns Hopkins University Press.

Marc Chagall, "My Land," *Marc Chagall and the Jewish Theater*. Translated from the Russian and Yiddish by Benjamin and Barbara Harshav. © 1992 by and reprinted with permission of The Solomon R. Guggenheim Foundation, New York.

Bernard Berenson, *Marc Chagall: A Biography* by Sidney Alexander. © 1978 Sidney Alexander. Reprinted by permission of G.P. Putnam's Sons.

Jacob Baal-Teshuva, "Chagall in a Reminiscent Mood." First published in *The Jewish Forum,* September–October 1962.

Marc Chagall, Summary, in English, of Chagall's Letter to President Weizman, *Marc Chagall and the Jewish Theater*. Translated from the Russian and Yiddish by Benjamin and Barbara Harshav. © 1992 by and reprinted with permission of The Solomon R. Guggenheim Foundation, New York.

Marc Chagall, "A Word at the Celebration in Jerusalem," *Marc Chagall and the Jewish Theater*. Translated from the Russian and Yiddish by Benjamin and Barbara Harshav. © 1992 by and reprinted with permission of The Solomon R. Guggenheim Foundation, New York.

Marc Chagall, "On the First Day of the War," *Marc Chagall and the Jewish Theater*. Translated from the Russian and Yiddish by Benjamin and Barbara Harshav. © 1992 by and reprinted with permission of The Solomon R. Guggenheim Foundation, New York.

Marc Chagall, "To Israel," "The Ship," *Marc Chagall and the Jewish Theater*. Translated from the Russian and Yiddish by Benjamin and Barbara Harshav. © 1992 by and reprinted with permission of The Solomon R. Guggenheim Foundation, New York.

Aleksandr Kamensky, Chagall: *The Russian Years, 1907–1922*. Rizzoli, New York, and Editions du Regard, Paris, 1989.

Alexander Liberman, *The Artist in His Studio*. © 1988 by Alexander Liberman. Reprinted by permission of Random House, Inc.

André Malraux, "Homage to Marc Chagall," *The Ceramics and Sculpture of Chagall*. © 1972 Editions Sauret, Monaco.

Andrei Voznesensky, *Chagall Discovered: From Russian and Private Collections*. © 1988 Sovietskii Khudozhnik Publishers, Moscow. Reprinted by permission of the author.

John Russell, "Art View; Farewell to Chagall, The Great Survivor." © 1985 by *The New York Times*. Reprinted by permission.

André Verdet, "Farewell to Marc Chagall," © *Artforum,* Summer 1985 issue.

Charles Marq, "Pour Mémoire," *Centenaire 1887–1987*. Published by Association des Amis du Musée National Message Biblique Marc Chagall. Reprinted by permission of the author.

Charles Sorlier, *Centenaire 1887–1987*. Published by Association des Amis du Musée National Message Biblique Marc Chagall. Reprinted by permission of the estate of Charles Sorlier.

CHRONOLOGY

1887

JULY 7. Marc Chagall, born Moyshe Segal, in Vitebsk, White Russia, the first of nine children to Zahar and Feiga-Jta Segal, workers of modest means.

1889

Attends the *cheder*, the Jewish primary school, for seven years. He is then sent to the official upper school of Vitebsk.

1906

Enters the studio of painter Yehuda Pen, where he is introduced to a more prosperous circle of people in Vitebsk. Remains at Pen's studio for two months, then takes a job with a local photographer as a photo retoucher.

1907

WINTER. Goes to St. Petersburg to become a sign painter. He is unsuccessful and tries to make a living again as a photo retoucher. He lives in virtual poverty.

SPRING. Chagall is taken under the wing of lawyer and art patron Goldberg. Lives in Goldberg's house and gets a residence permit.

APRIL 17. Chagall enters the school founded by the Imperial Society for the Protection of the Fine Arts.

SEPTEMBER. His work is soon noticed and he receives a one-year scholarship.

1908

JULY. Leaves the Imperial School and works for several months in a private school run by the painter Pavel M. Saidenberg. Meets influential patrons, including Max Vinaver.

FALL–WINTER. Enrolls at Svanseva School and studies under Leon Bakst, the director of the school.

1909

Continues his studies with Leon Bakst. Makes frequent trips to Vitebsk to visit his family, and there meets Bella Rosenfeld, his future wife.

1910

Continues his studies at the Svanseva School.

APRIL. Exhibits *The Wedding, The Dead Man,* and *Peasant Eating* (a work since lost) in St. Petersburg.

Is offered a grant by his patron Max Vinaver and leaves St. Petersburg for Paris. Lives in a studio in the Impasse du Maine and attends several academies, including La Palette, La Grand Chaumiere.

1911

Moves into a studio in La Ruche, at 2 Passage Danzig, near the slaughterhouses. Among his neighbors are poets and artists from all over the world: Léger, Laurance, Archipenko, Modigliani, Soutine. Befriends poets Blaise Cendrars, Max Jacob, André Salmon, and Guillaume Apollinaire.

Vitebsk. 1912. Collection Ida Chagall, Paris.

Paints his first great masterpiece, *To Russia, Asses, and Others.* Also paints *The Carter Sight, I and the Village,* and *Homage to Apollinaire.*

1912

Exhibits three canvases at the Salon des Indépendants: *The Black Musician, Half Past Three (The Poet),* and *Pregnant Woman.* By invitation exhibits *Golgotha* at the Salon d'Automne.

1913

Exhibits the large-scale paintings *Birth* and *Adam and Eve* at the Salon des Indépendants. Also exhibits *Maturity, The Painter and his Fiancée,* and *A Musician,* which are acquired by the Regnault Collection.

1914

Exhibits *The Fiddler* and *Self-Portrait* at the Salon des Indépendants.

JUNE 15. His first one-man show opens at the Galerie der Sturm in Berlin. In the same month he takes a trip back home to Russia, intending a brief visit. The outbreak of World War I prevents him from returning to Paris.

1915

Attempts, without success, to return to Paris.

MARCH. Exhibits twenty-five of his 1914 paintings at the official Moscow Art Exhibition.

JULY 25. Marries Bella Rosenfeld in Vitebsk.

He is employed in a war economy office in Petrograd, in lieu of military service. Meets some of the great Russian poets: Alexander Blok, Essenine, Mayakowsky, Pasternak.

1916

His daughter Ida is born.

Exhibits sixty-three paintings in the Contemporary Russian Art show at the Dobitchine Gallery.

NOVEMBER. Forty-five paintings are exhibited at the Knave of Diamonds Gallery in Moscow.

1917

Continues to exhibit in Russia.

The October Revolution erupts. The Ministry of Cultural Affairs is established, and Chagall is asked to head the department of fine arts. Bella advises him to refuse and they return to Vitebsk to live with her parents.

1918

The first monograph of his work is published, written by Abram Efros and Iakov Tugendhold.

AUGUST–SEPTEMBER. A school of fine arts is opened in Vitebsk, and Chagall becomes its director and the state's Commissar for Arts.

The state buys twelve of his paintings at a very low price.

1919

JANUARY 28. The inauguration of the Vitebsk Academy takes place. Among its teachers are Ivan Pougny, El Lissitzky, Kazimir Malevich, and Yehuda Pen. Differences arise between Chagall and Malevich and El Lissitzky, and Chagall ends up leaving the academy to establish himself in Moscow.

1920

MAY. Leaves Vitebsk for good and settles in Moscow.
Executes several sets for the Yiddish theater in Moscow.

1921

Begins his autobiography, *My Life*.

1922

SUMMER. Chagall leaves Russia with his paintings and goes to Berlin. He is later joined by his wife and daughter.

1923

While in Germany, attempts to locate some of his canvases lost during the war. Recovers only three.

SEPTEMBER 1. Returns to Paris on a visa.

FALL. Meets with art dealer Ambroise Vollard, who gives him several commissions, including a chance to illustrate Gogol's *Dead Souls*.

1924

Moves to a new studio at 101 Avenue d'Orleans. Meets artists Sonia and Robert Delaunay, Marcoussis, and Juan Gris. Witnesses the birth of Surrealism and is invited to join circles frequented by Max Ernst, André Breton, and other Surrealists. Chagall refuses.

DECEMBER. First retrospective at the Galerie Barbazanges-Hodebert, where he meets André Malraux, who is later to play an important role in Chagall's career.

1925

Finishes the plates for *Dead Souls*.

1926

JANUARY. Has his first exhibition in the United States, at the Gallery Reinhardt in New York.

Chagall's family. c. 1910. His parents seated in the center, Chagall standing upper left. Collection Ida Chagall, Paris.

At Ambroise Vollard's request, paints one hundred large gouaches that form the basis of his work for engravings to illustrate *The Fables* of La Fontaine. Spends most of the year away from Paris, which begins his long attachment to the Côte d'Azur. Meets the publisher Tériade.

1927

Takes up the theme of the circus, upon Vollard's request.

1928

Spends the summer alone in Ceret. Starts work on the engravings for *The Fables*. Bella translates his autobiography into French.

1929

Travels to Ceret with Bella. Buys a house in Montmorency near the Porte d'Auteuil.

1930

APRIL. Goes to Berlin for the opening of the exhibition of his gouaches for *The Fables* at the Flechtheim Gallery.

Vollard commissions Chagall to do illustrations for the Bible.

1931

FEBRUARY–APRIL. With Bella and Ida visits Cairo and the pyramids, and then spends several months in Palestine at the invitation of Meir Dizengoff, the mayor of Tel-Aviv.

His autobiography, *Ma Vie*, is published in France.

1933

Visits Holland, Italy, Spain, and England. Studies Rembrandt and El Greco.

NOVEMBER–DECEMBER. Large Chagall retrospective at the Kunsthalle Basel. The Nazis have a public burning of Chagall's work in Mannheim.

1936

Moves into a new studio in Paris, at #4 in the Villa Eugene-Manual.

1937

Does fifteen engravings for the Bible in Tuscany. The Nazis order all of Chagall's work removed from German museums, renouncing it as decadent art. Chagall becomes a French citizen.

1938

Exhibition at the Palais des Beaux-Arts in Brussels.

1939

Shortly before the declaration of World War II, Chagall and his family take refuge in Saint-Dye-Sur-Loire, where he has already hidden his canvases. Chagall is awarded the Carnegie Prize.

1940

Meets Picasso. Is advised to take his family to the free zone, south of Loire. They spend a year in Gordes, a little village in the Luberon.

MAY 10. The Germans invade Belgium.

Toward the end of the year, Chagall is visited by Varian Fry, head of the Emergency Rescue Committee, and Harry Bingham, United States General Consul in Marseilles, with an invitation to come to the United States.

1941

JUNE 23. Lands in New York the same day the Germans invade Russia. Chagall finds old friends Mondrian, André Breton, and others already in New York. Meets Pierre Matisse, later to become his dealer.

1942

SUMMER. Visits Mexico to do sets and costumes for the ballet *Aleko,* with music by Tchaikovsky and choreography by Léonide Massine.

1943

Spends time with his family in Cranbury Lake, New York. News of war-torn Europe greatly saddens Chagall, and his feelings are expressed in his paintings, especially *War Obsession* and *Yellow Crucifixion.*

1944

World War II ends.

SEPTEMBER. Bella falls ill and is taken urgently to the local hospital, where she dies within thirty-six hours due to lack of proper care. Overwhelmed by grief over Bella's death, Chagall is unable to paint for almost a year.

1945

SPRING. Starts to work again. Spends time on the shore of Lake Beaver in Krumville, New York, and in Sag Harbor, Long Island.

SUMMER. Beginning of Chagall's relationship with Virginia Haggard McNeil, who bears him a son. He executes the sets and costumes for the American Ballet Theater's production of Stravinsky's *Firebird.*

1946

APRIL–JUNE. The Museum of Modern Art in New York holds its first large Chagall retrospective, exhibiting more than forty years of Chagall's work. The retrospective later travels to the Art Institute of Chicago.

MAY. Chagall travels to Paris for a three-month stay.

SEPTEMBER. Returns to his home in High Falls, New York, and begins color lithographs for *The Arabian Nights.*

1947

FALL. Chagall returns to Paris for a retrospective organized for the occasion of the reopening, after German occupation, of the Musée National d'Art Moderne.

Retrospectives open in various European cities: the Stedelijk Museum, Amsterdam; the Tate Gallery, London; the Kunsthaus, Zurich; Kunsthalle, Bern.

1948

AUGUST. Chagall returns to France for good and settles in Orgeval.

Makes the acquaintance of Aimé Maeght, who becomes his dealer. *Dead Souls* is published by Tériade.

1949

Begins to work in ceramics for the first time.

1950

MARCH. First exhibition at the Galerie Maeght, Paris.

Moves to Vence. Spends time with Matisse and Picasso, who live in Nice and Vallauris respectively. Devotes time to graphic work. Meets master lithographer Charles Sorlier and executes lithographs with him in Mourlot.

DECEMBER. Exhibition at the Kunsthaus, Zurich.

1951

Visits Israel for an opening of his work in Jerusalem.

1952

JUNE. Visits the cathedral in Chartres to study the conception and technique of its medieval stained glass windows.

JULY 12. Meets and marries Valentina (Vava) Brodsky.

SUMMER. Visits Greece, Rome, Naples, and Capri.

Tériade commissions Chagall to do original color lithographs for *Daphnis and Chloe,* by Longus. Tériade publishes La Fontaine's *Fables* with Chagall's etchings, begun in 1926.

1953

APRIL. Visits Turin for the opening of a retrospective at the Palazzo Madama.

1954

Revisits Greece, Florence, and Venice, where he renews his acquaintance with the works of Titian and Tintoretto.

1955

Begins work on the series of paintings *The Biblical Message.*

1956
Completion and publication of the Bible, with 105 etchings by Chagall.

1957
Retrospective exhibition of his engravings at the Bibliothèque National in Paris. Chagall does his first mural mosaic, *The Blue Cock.* Begins work on his illustrations for *Daphnis and Chloe.*

1958
FEBRUARY. Lectures at the University of Chicago.
Back in France, meets and befriends Charles Marq, master glassmaker and director of the Jacques Simon Glass Works in Reims, at whose atelier all of Chagall's stained glass windows are produced. Begins stained glass windows for the Metz Cathedral.

1959
Receives an honorary doctorate from the University of Glasgow. Appointed an honorary member of the American Academy of Arts and Letters.
JUNE. Opening of a retrospective at the Musée des Arts Decoratifs, the Louvre, Paris.
Completes three stained glass compositions for the Metz Cathedral: *Moses Receiving the Tablets of the Law; David and Bathsheba; Jeremiah and the Exodus of the Jewish People.*

1960
Begins work on stained glass windows for the Hadassah Medical Center in Jerusalem. Receives an honorary doctorate from Brandeis University. Is awarded, jointly with Oskar Kokoschka, the Erasmus Prize of the European Cultural Foundation, Copenhagen.
First exhibition of stained glass windows intended for the Metz Cathedral opens at the Museum of Reims.

1961
Exhibition of the stained glass windows *The Twelve Tribes of Israel* at the Musée des Arts Decoratif and, later that year, at the Museum of Modern Art, New York.

1962
Continues work on the stained glass windows for the Metz Cathedral.
FEBRUARY. Unveiling and dedication of The *Twelve Tribes of Israel* at the Hadassah Hospital Synagogue, Jerusalem.

1963
Retrospectives at the National Museum in Tokyo and the National Museum in Kyoto. At the invitation of General de Gaulle and André Malraux, Chagall begins work on a new ceiling for the auditorium of the Paris Opera House.
MAY. Visits Washington, D.C.

1964
MAY. The Musée des Beaux Arts, Rouen, exhibits the stained glass windows for the Metz Cathedral.
Completes *The Good Samaritan* in stained glass for the

Self-Portrait. 1914. The Philadelphia Museum of Art. The Louis E. Stern Collection.

chapel of Pocantico Hills in New York State, as a memorial for John D. Rockefeller, Jr.
SEPTEMBER 17. Unveiling of the stained glass window, *Peace,* at the United Nations, New York.

1965
Receives an honorary doctorate from the University of Notre Dame.

1966
Leaves his home in Vence and moves into a house in Saint-Paul-de-Vence. Begins work on two large murals for the Metropolitan Opera in New York: *The Sources of Music* and *The Triumph of Music.* Does eight stained glass windows entitled *The Prophets* for the chapel in Pocantico Hills.

1967
FEBRUARY 19. Inauguration of the new Metropolitan Opera House and opening of the Metropolitan Opera's production of Mozart's *The Magic Flute,* with decor and costumes by Chagall.
JUNE. Chagall and Vava donate the series of paintings *Biblical Message* to the Louvre, where they are exhibited. In 1973 the paintings are transferred to the Musée National Message Biblique Marc Chagall in Nice.
Publication of *Le Cirque,* with text and thirty-eight lithographs by Chagall. Chagall retrospectives in Zurich and Cologne in honor of the painter's eightieth birthday.

1969
Laying of the foundation stone for the Musée National Message Biblique Marc Chagall in Nice.
JUNE. Attends the inauguration of the new Parliament building in Jerusalem, for which he has created floor mosaics, a mural mosaic, and three large tapestries.

1970
Retrospective of Chagall's work in engraving at the Bibliothèque National, Paris.

1972
Begins work on illustrations for Homer's *Odyssey*.

1973
JUNE. At the invitation of the Russian Minister of Culture, Chagall and Vava travel to Moscow and Leningrad. Chagall is reunited with two of his sisters, whom he has not seen since his departure from Russia fifty years earlier. Chagall refuses to visit Vitebsk.
JULY 7. On this day, the painter's birthday, the Musée National Message Biblique Marc Chagall is opened in Nice.

1974
Exhibition at the National Gallery in West Berlin.
JUNE 15. Unveiling of the stained glass windows for Reims Cathedral.
Chicago welcomes Chagall for his *Four Seasons* mosaic.

1975
Begins work on lithographs for Shakespeare's *The Tempest*.

1977
JANUARY 1. Chagall is awarded the Grand Cross of the French Legion of Honor.
Visits Israel and is declared an honorary citizen of Jerusalem.

1978–1979
Continues work in stained glass, and begins work on copperplate engravings to illustrate the Psalms. The *America Windows*, a three-paneled stained-glass work, is unveiled at the Art Institute of Chicago.

1980–1982
Numerous exhibitions of his work, worldwide.

1984
Chagall visits Paris for the last time.

1985
Major retrospectives at the Royal Academy, London, and the Philadelphia Museum of Art, both of which he is unable to attend.
MARCH 28. Chagall dies at his home in Saint-Paul-de-Vence at the age of ninety-seven.
He is buried in the local Christian cemetery.

Pregnant Woman. 1912–13. Oil on canvas. 76 3/8 x 45 1/4 in. (194 x 115 cm). Stedelijk Museum, Amsterdam.

INTRODUCTION

"If I create from the heart, nearly everything works;
if from the head, almost nothing." —Marc Chagall

Ten years after his death Marc Chagall is the most popular artist of this century. From Tokyo to Budapest, from Mexico City to Bejing, his works with their shimmering colors are collected worldwide. Chagall was one of the most original of the giants of twentieth-century art. He was the last great survivor of the School of Paris. On the last day of his life in 1985 at the ripe-old age of ninety-seven Marc Chagall was hard at work on a lithograph depicting the artist in his studio. He finished the lithograph, but never signed it. Chagall, the first living artist to exhibit at the Louvre, and one of the most beloved, admired, and sought after artists of the twentieth-century, had a love affair with life, love, art, and the whole world. Little wonder that a man so impassioned lived so long.

Chagall's genius sprang from the fertile soil of his homeland of Vitebsk in Czarist White Russia, was nurtured in the glow of the "Paris light," soared against the background of the world events of his lifetime, and, enriched by a deeply spiritual awareness, matured into a magnificent expression of his dreams, fantasy, and poetry in images that cause even the most earthbound observer to be transported into the dizzying realm of color and form. Ambroise Vollard, the famous French art dealer and publisher, said of Chagall's work: "No work was ever so resolutely magical. Its splendid prismatic colors sweep away and transfigure the torment of today, and at the same time preserve the age-old spirit of ingenuity in expressing everything which proclaims the pleasure principle, flowers and expressions of love." Chagall must have been pleased with Vollard's description of his art; Chagall was truly a singular artist who remained true to himself and his creativity and whose work defied the limitations of classification. His motivation was simply the expression of his unbridled imaginings, and the result is an oeuvre that is comprised of invented symbols of feeling and emotions, coming from the heart in a sophisticated and captivating playfulness.

Chagall's output was prodigious and immense. He was not afraid to tackle the most monumental work, whether it be large murals as on the ceiling of the Paris Opera or his scores of stained glass windows that shimmer with the color and light of his later genius. Chagall's work for the stage, the ballet, and the opera, his large mosaics, as well as the huge tapestries that hang in the Israeli Knesset (Parliament), brought him equally great acclaim and admiration as did his paintings, gouaches, watercolors, pastels, ceramics, sculptures, and graphic arts. Volumes have been devoted to Chagall's prolific career, to this lover of life whose suspended lovers, rooftop fiddlers, winged clocks, churches and houses, weddings and funerals are the images that make up his "dreamscape."

I first met Chagall in 1951 on the occasion of a retrospective in Jerusalem and Tel Aviv that was a great triumph and gave the artist much pleasure. Our friendship lasted up to his death in 1985. We met through the years in his Paris apartment, in Vence, in Saint-Paul-de-Vence in the south of France, in Reims while he was working on the Jerusalem stained glass windows, and whenever he visited New York for exhibitions, the inaugurations of his stained glass windows at the Rockefeller Church in Tarrytown, New York, the *Peace* window at the United Nations in New York City, the murals at the Metropolitan Opera, his stage designs at the Met for Mozart's opera *The Magic Flute,* or when he gave lectures and received honors.

Whenever I met Chagall I always addressed him, as is the custom in France, as *Maitre* (Master), which sounds like the French word *metre,* for meter. Chagall

COLORPLATE I. *The Dead Man.* 1908. Oil on canvas. 26 7/8 x 33 7/8 in. (68.2 x 86 cm).
Musée National d'Art Moderne, Centre Georges Pompidou, Paris.

COLORPLATE 2. *Self-Portrait with Seven Fingers* (detail). 1913–14. Oil on canvas. 50 ³/₈ x 42 ¹/₈ in. (128 x 107 cm).
Stedelijk Museum, Amsterdam. Photograph: Giraudon/Art Resource, New York.

COLORPLATE 3. *My Fiancée in Black Gloves.* 1909. Oil on canvas. 34 ⁵/₈ x 25 ⁵/₈ in. (88 x 65 cm).
Kunstmuseum Basel. Photograph: SCALA/Art Resource, New York.

COLORPLATE 4. *The Wedding*. 1910. Oil on canvas. 39 1/8 x 74 in. (99.5 x 188.5 cm)
Musée National d'Art Moderne, Centre Georges Pompidou, Paris.

COLORPLATE 5. *To Russia, Asses and Others.* 1911. Oil on canvas. 61 7/8 x 48 in. (157 x 122 cm).
Musée National d'Art Moderne, Centre Georges Pompidou, Paris. Photograph: Art Resource, New York.

COLORPLATE 6. *The Studio*. 1910. Oil on canvas. 23 5/8 x 28 3/4 in. (60 x 73 cm).
Musée National d'Art Moderne, Centre Georges Pompidou, Paris.

COLORPLATE 7. *Calvary*. 1912. Oil on canvas. 68 3/4 x 75 3/4 in. (174.6 x 192.4 cm).
The Museum of Modern Art, New York. Acquired through the Lillie P. Bliss Bequest.
Photograph © The Museum of Modern Art, New York.

always replied, "I am only a centimeter" or at times, "I am only a millimeter." I played his "modest" game and replied, "You are a kilometer." Clowning and acting was part and parcel of his life. Some thought that he even resembled Harpo Marx of the famed Marx Brothers. He was a great mime and injected his humor into many of his paintings. Many of Chagall's creations defy the laws of gravity. When I once asked Chagall to explain certain aspects of his work he answered, "I often do not understand them myself." When he painted a couple with the girl's head upside down, he said to me, "It is very simple. In Yiddish there is an expression that the man turned the girl's head, so I painted it this way." Literally.

Chagall was a very complex man, shy and mischievous, simple and shrewd, naive and sophisticated, canny and stingy, although at times generous. He was emotional, but also precise, sensitive, and sentimental. He could be very witty, but also malicious, acerbic, and melancholic. He was very sensitive to criticism, but did not hesitate to criticize and demolish others. He never liked to discuss his contemporary artists, preferring to talk about the Old Masters. One of the only exceptions was Picasso, of whom Chagall made a drawing he called *Thinking of Picasso* (1914). He was obsessed with Picasso. Chagall thought that Picasso, who he always called "the Spaniard," had "more head than heart," that he was "sly and dangerous." Picasso on Chagall? "When Matisse dies Chagall will be the only painter left who understands what color really is. I am not crazy about those cocks and asses, and flying violinists and all the folklore, but his canvases are really painted, not just thrown together. Some of the things he's done in Vence convince me that there's never been anybody since Renoir who has the feeling for light that Chagall has."

I remember well joining Chagall on his daily walk in Vence, before he moved to Saint-Paul. He would become instantly annoyed when tourists who did not know him would stop him and ask for directions to the Matisse Chapel. He always gave the impression that he did not care about money, fame, or being a celebrity, but quite the opposite was true. He was passionate about his work and his life, and enjoyed all the acclaim that accompanied both. When the painter Mané-Katz was asked what he thought of Chagall, he replied: "A great artist and a wonderful human being." When Chagall was asked his opinion of Mané-Katz he answered: "A terrible artist and an awful man." Mané-Katz, when asked how he could praise Chagall when Chagall clearly damned him, replied: "All artists are liars . . ." Chagall's genius seemed to excuse a multitude of indiscretions.

Chagall's formative years in the town of Vitebsk in White Russia were shaped by the combination of Russian folk art and icons, a sophisticated naivete, and the enthusiasm and verve of his Hasidic community. These early years exerted a powerful influence on Chagall for the rest of his life. Chagall never abandoned the Russian motifs of his youth—they kept reappearing in one form or another throughout his life, and he remained true at all times to the impressions of his childhood in Vitebsk. In his work there was always a mixture of Jewish-Hasidic traditions, customs, and rituals, and of the Russian tradition found in literature, poetry, and the theater. Chagall used Hebrew calligraphy in many of his drawings and illustrated books, and his early training as a sign painter also influenced his work. He said, "In all my pictures there is not one centimeter free from nostalgia for my native land." Chagall's world view was grounded in Vitebsk. In his foreword to *Marc Chagall: 100th Anniversary of His Birth—The Marcus Diener Collection* (Tel Aviv Museum of Art), Marc Scheps, past director of the Tel Aviv Museum of Art, writes: "Chagall more than any other artist in the twentieth century succeeded in turning the local into the universal. For Chagall, Vitebsk was the whole world and the whole world was Vitebsk. Throughout his career his Vitebsk roots remained a part of him wherever he went, and it was for this reason that he was so beloved by many who had never even heard of this Russian town. They sensed that his universality grew out of a deep love for his fellow men."

The Jewish population of Vitebsk was less than forty thousand. Most of the townsfolk were traders and manufacturers. Chagall's father worked in a herring warehouse and his mother had a little grocery store, the income of which helped feed their family of eight children, six girls and two boys. (A seventh daughter died in infancy.) Marc was the eldest child. He was very handsome with soft blue eyes. His family counted on him to contribute to the upkeep of the family. Since Jews did not have equal rights and were therefore not admitted to the local school, Chagall's mother had to give a generous tip of fifty rubles to the school master to have her son admitted. There he learned Russian, while at the Jewish School (the *cheder*) he studied Hebrew and the Bible. It was at that time that he showed a talent for drawing. Chagall's mother agreed to let him join the art school of Yehuda Pen, a Jewish academic portrait artist. At the same time he worked for a local photographer as a retoucher. He hated the job and eventually went to St. Petersburg where he earned his living as a sign painter. He could not rent a room and had to share a bed with a workman. He finally found an art patron, entered the school founded by the Imperial Society for the Protection of the Fine Arts, and secured a scholarship for a year while at the same time post-poning his military service. "It was at this time," said Chagall, "that I was intro-duced to a cluster of art patrons, everywhere; in their drawing rooms, I felt as though I'd just come out of the bath, my face red and overheated." Among them was the very influential Maxim Vinaver, who became his patron. Of Vinaver, Chagall said: "I remember his shining eyes, his eyebrows that went slowly up and down his finely shaped mouth, his light chestnut beard, that whole noble profile which I, alas, always shy, did not dare to paint. He was a man who was very close to me, almost like a father."

Chagall enrolled in the Svanseva School where he studied under its director, Leon Bakst, a Russian artist who specialized in designing sets and costumes for the ballet. Recalling Bakst, Chagall said: "I don't know why, but his fame, fol-lowing the Russian season abroad, turned my head. Would he grant that I had tal-ent or not? Leafing through the studies that one by one I lifted from the floor where I had stacked them, he said, drawing the words with his lordly accent, 'Yes, yes, there is some talent, but you've been spoiled, you are off to a bad start, spoiled.'"

In 1910 Vinaver gave the twenty-three-year-old artist a grant to go live and work in Paris for four years. It was Chagall's first trip outside Russia, his first sojourn to Paris, the city of lights and the center of art. Paris in 1910 was a great revelation to the young Chagall. He was intoxicated with the sights and sounds, the tempo and spirit, of Paris. He was in a constant state of excitement. He visited Montmartre and the Latin Quarter and was thoroughly carried away with the magnificence of the Louvre. In the galleries he saw the Impressionists; he discov-ered the work of Bonnard, Matisse, and de La Fresnay; he became lost in the scenery of Manet, Seurat, Van Gogh, and Pissarro. After visiting the museums he would paint all night, happy to be in the center of world art.

France became his "second motherland," his real roots and background remaining deeply imbedded in the soil of Vitebsk. In Paris, Chagall was suddenly exposed to Cubism, Expressionism, Surrealism, and Fauvism, and although he was comfortable with these movements and was invited to join some of them, he always remained uniquely true to himself, refusing to ally with any of the recog-nized schools. He discovered French sophistication, culture, literature, and poet-ry, but he remained nostalgic for Vitebsk. In *Paris Through the Window* (1913), now hanging in the Solomon R. Guggenheim Museum in New York, besides painting the Eiffel Tower and the Paris Metro upside down, Chagall included a head with two faces, one looking at Paris, the other turned towards his birthplace.

Paris was a world full of wonder for Chagall, and he marveled at its charms, from the bakeries with their fresh crispy bread to the cafés where artists and stu-dents gathered to sip wine or drink coffee. It was in La Ruche, "the Beehive," where artists of many different countries lived and worked, that Chagall at age twenty-five painted his first masterpieces: *I And the Village, Homage to Apollinaire,* and *To Russia, Asses, and Others,* among others. About his studio in La Ruche, Chagall remembered: "The studio hadn't been cleaned in a week.

Stretchers, eggshells, cans of cheap soup, long empty, lay around in a mess . . . on the shelves, reproductions of El Greco and Cezanne lay next to the remains of a herring that I had cut in two, the head for the first day, the tail for the next, and thank God, some crusts of bread." While his fellow artists slept until noon, Chagall worked and painted away with his famous blues. To Chagall, blue was not only a color, it was a state of the soul. Blue was the color of melancholy and nostalgia, the color of longing for his home and his loved ones, especially his fiancée Bella. Cubism was the dominant art movement at this time and while it influenced Chagall it did not ultimately sit well with his emotions. Cubism was analytical and synthetic, with monochromatic colors and architectural structures; Chagall's work was lyrical and emotional. To him a painting was an invented symbol of feeling and emotion coming from the heart.

Chagall, at twenty-seven in Paris, was very lonely. He missed his fiancée, Bella, whom he had left back in Vitebsk. He decided to go back home by way of Berlin, marry Bella and then return to the West. After obtaining a Russian passport on June 15, 1914, a day after the opening of his exhibition in Berlin that was to assure his future fame, Chagall boarded a train for Vitebsk. On July 25, 1915, he married Bella in Vitebsk, despite the objections of her well-to-do family.

The outbreak of World War I prevented Chagall's return to France. Instead, he enlisted in the army and was assigned to a camouflage unit in Petrograd, where he worked as a clerk until 1917. This period was for Chagall one of the most artistically productive in his life. Not only was the number of paintings he produced staggering, but the quality and originality therein was astonishing. Some of his favorite subjects were his family—his brother David and several of his sisters—and the familiar people and places that characterized Vitebsk. In the spring of 1916 Chagall's only daughter, Ida, was born. This blessed event in his life was celebrated in the painting *Double Portrait with Wineglass* (1917), showing Chagall suspended in the air on his wife's shoulders, holding up a cup of wine.

Chagall and Bella were back in Vitebsk in 1917 after a brief stay in St. Petersburg, and in September 1918 Chagall became Commissar for Arts in Vitebsk for the new Soviet republic. Disappointment and deception followed as his Academy of Art, embraced with love by the artist turned director, ultimately was taken over by the Suprematists, including Kazimir Malevich and El Lissitzky, both of whom Chagall had hired to teach at the academy. Enraged and betrayed, Chagall left Vitebsk for good in May 1920 and moved to Moscow with his wife and child. Here he was approached to design sets for the Jewish Theater in Moscow. Relatively new to set design, he nevertheless undertook this challenge with his typical enthusiasm, especially since Bella had ambitions as an actress. Among the characters that ended up floating on the monumental murals for the theater auditorium was the famous Jewish actor Shlomoe Michoels, as well as another familiar face, that of the artist himself. He conceived the panels to symbolize music, dance, literature, and comedy in the figures of a jester, a dancing woman, a poet, and a musician-violinist with his face painted green. Later, when the Jewish Theater moved to larger quarters the murals were placed in the foyer.

Chagall was at the height of his energy and enthusiasm, and all the people around him were hypnotized by his work. The actors loved Chagall and his magic. But there were those who did not understand his work and found it outrageous. Some even saw his figures as caricatures of Jewish life. But the negative criticism did not impress Chagall; he knew with what love he painted his figures and that his art spoke what was truly in his heart. The new Soviet republic was three years old and starving, but in the theater a group of actors danced and sang with great enthusiasm, fervor, and joy. The theater stage had become Chagall's canvas.

Tragically, Chagall's murals were rolled up during the Stalin era and stored beneath the theater's stage where they were subject to moisture and damaging conditions. It was not until 1950 that the murals were acquired by the state Tret'iakov Gallery in Moscow. Chagall himself did not know the fate of his murals until the late 1960s. In 1973, while visiting the Soviet Union at the government's invitation, after an absence of more than fifty years, during which period his paintings were never exhibited, he was received with great acclaim. The murals were unrolled in front of his eyes and he wept like a child, full of emotion. The Russians asked him to sign them and he obliged. It was only in 1989 that the murals were restored and readied to be exhibited in the West. They were shown in Switzerland, Germany, Finland, Israel, Austria, and the United States. In his autobiography *My Life* Chagall describes his work for the Jewish Theater as a visual manifesto for the new theater: "I thought, here is an opportunity to do away with the Old Jewish Theater, its psychological naturalism, its false beards. There on these walls I shall at last be able to do as I please and be free to show everything I consider indispensable to the rebirth of the National Theater." Without doubt, these works rank among the best produced by Chagall. Some say that if Chagall never produced another painting he would have remained a great artist.

In 1922 Chagall went to post-war Berlin, where, as he described, "one had the impression of living in a nightmare." He and his family returned to Paris in 1923 after securing the necessary visas. Commission upon commission followed as Vollard asked Chagall to execute etchings for Gogol's *Dead Souls,* La Fontaine's *Fables,* and the Bible. His commissions took him to Palestine, Italy, Holland, England, and Spain. While his contemporaries like Picasso, Braque, and Matisse always stayed in France, Chagall was constantly on the move—the embodiment of "the Wandering Jew"—traveling from place to place due to wars and revolutions, visiting museums and especially looking for the Old Masters. "I am sure Rembrandt would have loved me," Chagall remarked.

At the outbreak of World War II in 1939, Chagall took all of his canvases and left Paris for south of the Loire. At the end of 1940 Chagall, like many other artists, was invited to seek a safe haven in the United States. Chagall said: "I lived and worked in America during part of the universal tragedy that touched all mankind. I did not get any younger as the years passed. But I was able to draw strength in a hospitable atmosphere without my art having to deny its origins." In 1942, because of union problems in the U.S., Chagall traveled to Mexico where he executed the sets and costumes for the ballet *Aleko*, performed in New York. Personal tragedy struck in 1944 when Chagall's beloved Bella died suddenly in upstate New York; the bereaved artist could not work for nearly a year.

Nine months after Bella's death, Virginia Haggard McNeil, an attractive thirty-year-old French-speaking English woman, was hired by Chagall's daughter, Ida, to be his housekeeper, cook, and domestic helper. After a while, a relationship developed and Chagall asked her to pose for him. Virginia was married at the time to an English painter and had a five-year-old daughter. However, soon Chagall and Virginia became lovers. She became pregnant and gave birth to Chagall's son, David McNeil, who never took his father's name. Virginia left her husband and moved in with Chagall—a romance that lasted seven years.

Chagall was never happier than when he shared his life with a beloved partner, and during the years he spent with Virginia he was once again very productive, full of love and joy. His gouaches and lithographs burst with Chagall colors; his passion and satisfaction could be seen in his paintings *Pont Neuf* and *The Madonna of Notre Dame,* among many others. It was also during this time that Chagall's renewed fervor and enthusiasm allowed him to execute his sets and costumes for the American Ballet Theater's production of Stravinsky's *Firebird.* Nineteen curtain calls on opening night testified to its soaring success, and critics hailed Chagall's designs as the predominant factor.

But eventually the relationship with Virginia became strained. She was involved with a natural-cure group, and the attention she paid to it made Chagall extremely jealous. At the same time a Belgian photographer named Charles Leirens came to photograph the artist. While Chagall was in Paris to work on his lithographs, Virginia and Charles became lovers. Upon discovering this Chagall became furious and went into a rage. The tension intensified and Virginia decided to leave, taking their son David with her, and leaving behind eighteen gouaches and oils Chagall had given to her through the years. Her departure, she said, was "a logical conclusion to an unhappy situation. Looking back on our seven years together I have nothing but loving and grateful memories. I had to leave, I had to find out who I was, not go on simply as the wife of a famous artist, the charming hostess to important people."

Once again, it was Chagall's daughter Ida who introduced her father to a woman with whom he fell deeply in love and with whom he was to spend the rest of his long life. Chagall married Valentina (Vava) Brodsky, a dark-haired Russian woman twenty-five years his junior, on July 12, 1952. And, once again, love gave Chagall renewed energy, happiness, and inspiration.

Chagall had many passions. His love affair with life, love, and art was deep enough to cross many barriers. Throughout his life, Chagall resisted others' attempts to label him as part of any recognized art movement. He also never wanted to be classified as a Jewish painter. Although his beloved Vitebsk was never far from his art, he was truly a citizen of the world, and his deep spiritualism allowed him to appreciate the many voices that spoke outside of the Jewish tradition. This fact sometimes put him at odds with his Jewish admirers and followers. Chagall often painted Christ on the Cross, and these paintings were always highly controversial in the Jewish community. The artist asserted that the Crucifixion represents the suffering of the Jewish people through the ages, including the atrocities suffered during the Holocaust. His critics dismissed all excuses and explanations and accused Chagall of catering to Christian symbols in almost all of his religious commissions. While scores of European and American churches boast Chagall stained glass windows, there is only one synagogue in Jerusalem that can claim that distinction.

From an early age, Chagall was fascinated with the theme of Jesus as told in the Gospels: he painted the *White Crucifixion* in 1938, *The Descent From the Cross* in 1941, and *Yellow Crucifixion* in 1943. Many others followed in later years. Chagall tried to "sweeten the pill" by adding at times a Menorah, a Prayer Shawl, and some other Jewish symbols, but that only fueled the critics' fire. It seems that Chagall regarded Jesus as one of the great Jewish prophets, in direct contradiction to Jewish teachings. He failed to convince his fellow Jews that Jesus was a universal symbol. They clearly did not see the relevance of the inclusion of a crucifix, for example, in the paintings of *Jacob's Ladder* or *The Creation of Man*, which hang in the Chagall museum in Nice. Knowing that he would be severely criticized, Chagall added the following inscription at the Church of Assy in France: "In the name of the freedom of all religions." What Chagall failed to understand, according to his critics, was that a church is not a museum, but is instead a place where religious dogma rather than abstract artistic truth exists. What Chagall's critics failed to understand was that the artist's vision was grounded in an abiding love that was broad enough to embrace all people and passionate enough to celebrate the love of God everywhere.

The most important moment in the life of Chagall the artist was the opening of his museum, Message Biblique, on July 7, 1974. He was awarded the highest degree of the French Legion of Honor and also became an honorary citizen of Jerusalem. His last major exhibition was held in 1985 at the Royal Academy in London, and later traveled to the Philadelphia Museum of Art. Old and weakened, Chagall was unable to attend. On March 28, 1985, he died in his house in Saint-Paul-de-Vence at age ninety-seven. Upon hearing of the death of Marc Chagall, the Chief Rabbi of Nice, Joseph Pinson, contacted Chagall's wife Vava and invited her to bury Chagall at the Jewish cemetery there. Vava, who had no Jewish background and was neither involved nor versed in Jewish life, refused by saying she wanted him buried in Saint-Paul-de-Vence, where he had lived. "But there is no Jewish cemetery there," said the Chief Rabbi. It was sad to see Marc Chagall buried in a Roman Catholic cemetery surrounded by hundreds of crosses. Teddy Kollek, Jerusalem's mayor at the time, said: "I think it a great lack of sensibility on the part of his family to do this."

At Chagall's funeral, Jewish mourners brought pebbles to the grave site, symbolizing enduring memory. Christians brought flowers. In the film *Chagall's Journey* (produced by the Jewish Theological Seminary in New York) author Chaim Potok remarked: "In his life and his work he was not committed to any denomination, or even to preconceived secular values. For his personal visions of the world, he drew from all the cultures in which he found himself—from Russia and France, from his Jewishness and from Christianity. He expressed himself, a free inventor, restricted only by his conscience. In that he found serenity."

I saw Chagall for the last time at his ninety-seventh birthday celebration held at his museum in Nice. He looked frail and fragile. Several months later he was gone. But his magic, his color, and his simplicity continue to excite and electrify the art world, the public, and his many admirers. In 1994 his work had its first exhibition ever in Peking, China. It was a huge and unprecedented success, evidence that Chagall's oeuvre has a worldwide audience who yearns to hear the "voices" his "angels speak." His great fantasy, legacy, and contributions to twentieth-century art will always be with us.

—Jacob Baal-Teshuva
New York and Paris
1995

CHAGALL

THE RUSSIAN YEARS

MARC CHAGALL

From *My Life*

1922

BIRTH

The first thing I ever saw was a trough. Simple, square, half hollow, half oval. A market trough. Once inside, I filled it completely.

I don't remember—perhaps my mother told me—but at the very moment I was born a great fire broke out, in a little cottage, behind a prison, near the high-road, on the outskirts of Vitebsk.

The town was on fire, the quarter where the poor Jews lived.

They carried the bed and the mattress, the mother and the babe at her feet, to a safe place at the other end of town.

But, first of all, I was born dead.

I did not want to live. Imagine a white bubble that does not want to live. As if it had been stuffed with Chagall pictures.

They pricked that bubble with needles, they plunged it into a pail of water. At last it emitted a feeble whimper. But the main thing was, I was born dead.

I hope the psychologists have the grace not to draw improper conclusions from that!

THE BIRTHPLACE

However, that little house near the Pestkowatik road had not been touched. I saw it not so long ago.

As soon as he was a little better off, my father sold the cottage. The place reminds me of the bump on the head of the rabbi in green I painted, or of a potato tossed into a barrel of herring and soaked in pickling brine. Looking at this cottage from the height of my recent "grandeur," I winced and I asked myself:

"How could I possibly have been born here? How does one breathe?"

However, when my grandfather, with the long, black beard, died in all honor, my father, for a few roubles, bought another place.

In that neighborhood, no longer near an insane asylum as at Pestkowatik. All about us, churches, fences, shops, synagogues—simple and eternal, like the buildings in the frescoes of Giotto.

Around me come and go, turn and turn, or just trot along, all sorts of Jews, old and young, Javitches and Bejlines. A beggar runs towards his house, a rich man goes home. The cheder boy runs home. Papa goes home.

In those days there was no cinema.

People went home or to the shop. That is what I remember after my trough.

I say nothing of the sky, of the stars of my childhood.

They are my stars, my sweet stars; they accompany me to school and wait for me on the street till I return. Poor dears, forgive me. I have left you alone on such a dizzy height!

My town, sad and gay!

As a boy, I used to watch you from our doorstep, childishly. To a child's eyes you were clear. When the walls cut off my view, I climbed up on a little post. If

Self-Portrait with Parents in Profile. 1911. Pen drawing on paper. 8 1/4 x 5 1/8 in. (21 x 13 cm). Musée National d'Art Moderne, Centre Georges Pompidou, Paris.

My Life, Chagall's autobiography, recreates with highly individual style Chagall's early childhood in Vitebsk in the 1890s and his struggle to become an artist in the face of opposition, antisemitism, and poverty. It presents an intimate look at Chagall's formative years in Russia and in Paris prior to World War I, and paints a colorful picture of village life in Russia at the turn of the century.

Giotto (c. 1266–1337), Florentine painter who, with Cimabue, is generally regarded as the founder of modern painting.

Our Dining Room. 1911. Pen and ink on paper. 7 1/2 x 8 5/8 in. (19 x 22 cm). Musée National d'Art Moderne, Centre Georges Pompidou, Paris.

then I still could not see you, I climbed up on the roof. Why not? My grandfather used to climb up there too.

And I gazed at you as much as I pleased.

Here, in Pokrowskaja Street, I was born a second time.

FATHER AND MOTHER

Have you sometimes seen, in Florentine paintings, one of those men whose beard is never trimmed, with eyes at once brown and ash-gray, with the complexion the color of burnt-ochre and all lines and wrinkles?

That is my father.

Or perhaps you have seen one of the figures in the Haggadah, with their sheeplike expressions (Forgive me, dear father!).

You remember I made a study of you. Your portrait was to have had the effect of a candle that bursts into flame and goes out at the same moment. Its aroma—that of sleep.

A fly buzzing around—curse it!—and because of it I fall asleep.

Must I talk about my father?

What is a man worth if he is worth nothing? If he is priceless? That is why it is difficult for me to find the right words for him.

My grandfather, a teacher of religion, could think of nothing better than to place my father—his first-born son—still in childhood, as a clerk in a herring plant, and his youngest son with a hairdresser.

No, my father was not a clerk but, for thirty-two years, simply a laborer.

He lifted heavy barrels and my heart used to twist like a Turkish bagel as I watched him lift those weights and stir the herring with his frozen hands. His huge boss would stand to one side like a stuffed animal.

34

My father's clothes sometimes shone with herring brine. Farther off, light from above would fall into reflections on every side. Alone, his face, now yellow, now white, would faintly smile from time to time.

What a smile! Where did it come from?

It whispered of the street where dim passers-by roamed about, reflecting the moonlight. Suddenly, I saw his teeth shine. They made me think of a cat's teeth, of a cow's teeth, of any teeth.

Everything about my father seemed to me enigma and sadness. An image inaccessible.

Always tired, always pensive, his eyes alone gave forth a soft reflection of a grayish-blue.

In his greasy, work-soiled clothes, a handkerchief of dull red showing at one of the big pockets, he would come home, tall and thin. The evening came in with him.

From his pocket he would draw a pile of cakes, of frozen pears. With his brown and wrinkled hand he'd pass them out to us children. They were more delicious, more savory and more ethereal than if they had come from the dish on the table.

And an evening without cakes and without pears from Papa's pockets was a sad evening for us.

*   *   *

I shall always have a sinking feeling in my heart—is it from sleep or from a sudden memory on the anniversary of her death?—when I visit her grave, the grave of my mother.

I seem to see you, Mama.

You come slowly towards me. So slowly that I want to help you. You smile my smile. Ah! that smile, mine.

My mother was born in Lyozno, where I painted the priest's house, the fence in front of the house and in front of the fence, the pigs.

Pope or no pope, he smiles as he passes by, his cross glistening; he is about to make the sign over me. His hand slides down along his hip. The pigs, like little puppies, run to meet him.

My mother was the eldest daughter of the grandfather who lay half his life on top of the stove, a fourth in the synagogue and the rest in the butcher shop. He rested so much that grandmother gave up and died in the prime of life.

That was when my grandfather began to stir. The way cows and cattle move.

Was my mother really so very short?

My father paid no attention to that when he married her. But that is a mistake.

In our eyes, our mother had a style that was rare, as rare as was possible in her workaday surroundings.

But I don't want to praise, to overpraise my mother who is no more! Can I speak of her at all?

Sometimes I would rather weep than speak.

At the cemetery, at the entrance, I rush forward. Lighter than a flame, than an airy shadow, I hasten to shed tears.

I see the river disappearing in the distance, the bridge farther off and, close at hand, the eternal barrier, the earth, the tomb.

Here is my soul. Look for me over here, here I am, here are my pictures, my origin. Sadness, sadness!

That is her portrait.

It does not matter. Am I not there myself? Who am I?

You will smile, you will be surprised, you are going to laugh, you passer-by.

Lake of sufferings, hair gray too soon, eyes—a city of tears, soul almost non-existent, brain that is no more.

What is there, then?

I see her managing the household, ordering my father about, always building little dream houses, setting up a grocery shop, supplying it with a whole wagonload of merchandise, without money, on credit. With what words, by what means can I show her smiling, seated for hours at a time in front of the door or at

My Life abounds with the same richness and fantasy that are found in Chagall's paintings. Here are his family, his fiddler uncle playing on the roof, flying lovers, musicians, weddings, funerals, and daily life. The text ends in Moscow in 1922 and describes the collapse of Czarist Russia, which Chagall witnessed upon his return from Paris at the outbreak of World War I.

the table, waiting for some neighbor or other to whom, in her distress, she may unburden herself?

At night when the shop was closed and all of us children were home, Papa dozed off to sleep at the table, the lamp rested and the chairs grew bored; out-of-doors we couldn't tell where the sky was, where Nature had fled; not that we were silent, but simply that everything was quiescent. Mama sat in front of the tall stove, one hand on the table, the other on her stomach.

Her head rose to a point at the top where her hair was held in place by a pin.

She tapped one finger on the table that was covered with an oilcloth, tapped several times and that meant:

"Everyone is asleep. What children I have! I have no one to talk to."

She loved to talk. She fashioned words and presented them so well that her listener would smile in embarrassment.

Like a queen, erect, motionless, her pointed coiffure in place, she asked questions through closed lips that scarcely moved. But there was no one to answer her. At a distance I was the only one to follow her.

"My son," she said, "talk to me."

I am a little boy and Mama is a queen. What shall I say?

She is angry, her finger taps the table repeatedly.

And the house is enveloped in quiet sadness. . . .

So many years have gone by since she died!

Where are you now, dear little mother? In heaven, on earth? I am here, far from you. I would feel happier if I had been nearer you; at least I would have seen your monument, touched your tombstone.

Ah! Mama! I can't pray any more and I weep more and more rarely.

But my soul thinks of you, of myself, and my thoughts are consumed in grief.

I don't ask you to pray for me. You know yourself what sorrows I may have. Tell me, dear mother, from the other world, from Paradise, from the clouds, from wherever you are, does my love console you?

Can my words distill for you a little sweetness, tender and caressing?

Father. 1911. Oil on canvas. 31 ¹/₂ x 17 ³/₄ in. (80 x 45 cm). Musée National d'Art Moderne, Centre Georges Pompidou, Paris.

ALFRED WERNER

The Young Artist
1970

Dr. Alfred Werner, author, critic, lecturer, and art historian, wrote more than twenty books that include monographs on Modigliani, Degas, Dufy, Barlach, and Chagall.

Modigliani died with "Cara Italia!" on his lips, and Picasso has remained Spanish to the core despite sixty years of residence in Paris; but there is no vestige of Livorno in the pictures of the one, nor of Málaga in those of the other. To Londoners and Parisians, the expatriate Whistler may have appeared very American, yet the artist became angry upon being reminded of his native Lowell, Massachusetts, and even claimed to have been born in St. Petersburg, Russia. A biography of the eminent *Blauer Reiter* painter August Macke begins, "He was born in Meschede, which played no further role in his life."

By contrast, the enormous impact that Vitebsk and, in particular, its Jewish quarter has had on Chagall cannot be stressed sufficiently. His capital is invested in his childhood; he has managed to make his nostalgic memories last a full lifetime! Chagall is aware how strongly the Jewish milieu of his native Vitebsk has influenced all his work. True, he has scoffed at attempts to appropriate him for nationalism's sake. Firmly believing in the internationality of art and in the brotherhood of all artists, whatever their religious beliefs or ethnic origins, he once explained: "If a painter is Jewish and paints life, how can he help having

Amedeo Modigliani (1884–1920), born in Livorno, Italy, to an Italian Jewish family, arrived in Paris in 1906 and spent the rest of his life there.

Pablo Picasso (1881–1973) made Paris his home for more than forty years.

James Abbott McNeil Whistler (1834–1903).

Blaue Reiter (Blue Rider) was the name given to a group of Munich artists in 1911 by two of the most important members of the group, Wassily Kandinsky and Franz Marc. According to Kandinsky, they invented the name because they both liked blue and Marc liked horses.

Jewish elements in his work? But if he is a good painter, there will be more than that. The Jewish element will be there, but his art will tend to approach the universal." . . .

Most of the Jews of Vitebsk were poor, and none felt comfortable in the oppressive milieu of Russian authoritarianism. To survive, they needed their religion, their separate identity. Unfortunately, this self-contained Jewish civilization also deprived them of aesthetic stimuli. Eastern European Judaism was more fundamentalist than that of the West and it was inimical to the plastic arts; in accordance with the Second Commandment, "Thou shalt not make unto thee any graven image," the depiction of any figure was considered improper by rabbinic authorities. Yet the ordinary Jew went further in his suspicions of any manifestation of painting, let alone sculpture.

Within the context of the ghetto attitudes, it was erratic enough that Marc wanted to become a singer, then a violinist, thereafter a dancer, and finally a poet; one had to be practical, above all, in a culture of poverty. But to become a painter! What induced him (and other artists of the ghetto) to take up pencil and brush remains a mystery. In the paternal home, not even a reproduction could be seen on the walls, and if they were decorated at all, it was with no more than a couple of family photographs. To Marc's parents, "art," if it meant anything, meant something both blasphemous and *meshuggah* (crazy). When Marc approached his mother and confessed that he wanted to be a painter, she told him simply not to bother her. One of his uncles refused to even shake hands with the young "sinner."

In his autobiography, Chagall indicates that, although drawing was taught at the non-sectarian school he attended as a teenager, and he was often busy copying illustrations from magazines, he still had only the fuzziest notion of what was preoccupying him:

"I was familiar with all the street slang and with other, more modest, words in current use.

"But a word as fantastic, as literary, as out of this world as the word 'artist'— yes, perhaps I had heard it, but in my town no one ever pronounced it.

"It was so far removed from us!

"On my own initiative, I'd never have dared to use that word.

"One day a school friend came to see me and, after looking at our bedroom and noticing my sketches on the walls, he exclaimed: 'I say! You're a real artist, aren't you?'

"An artist? What's that? Who's an artist? Is it possible that . . . I, too . . . ?"

The Painter in Front of the Vitebsk Cathedral. 1911. Watercolor. 8 x 10 in. (20.3 x 25.4 cm). Musée National d'Art Moderne, Centre Georges Pompidou, Paris.

EDOUARD RODITI with CHAGALL

"Chagall's Early Years"

1957

Edouard D'Israeli Roditi (b. 1910), writer and poet who founded, with poet Stephen Spender, The Oxford University Poetry Club.

I met Chagall for the first time around 1930, at a Montparnasse café, the Dôme. He was that evening in the company of a group of artists and intellectuals from Central and Eastern Europe. . . . Later, I met Chagall again in New York, where he was a refugee during the war years. Again, I have recollections of much coming and going, in an apartment on Riverside Drive.

To-night, however, there are only five of us: Chagall; his wife Vava; the photographer André Ostier; the art-dealer Heinz Berggruen; and myself. On the walls of this Paris apartment in the Ile Saint Louis, which Chagall has recently acquired as a home-away-from-home for occasional visits to the French capital, one is surprised to find as samples of the master's work a few posters of his recent exhibitions. These are pinned up as in the rooms of an art-student who cannot yet afford any original works of the painters whom he admires. After a while, Chagall suggests that I accompany him into the next room where we shall be undisturbed. To be more at ease, he lies down on a big blue divan-bed, leaving me seated almost behind him. As he begins to answer my questions—or to not answer them—I feel as if I were almost psychoanalysing him. The flow of his memories is so torrential that I find it difficult to note all that he says. As he speaks, he stares at the blank white wall ahead of him, a screen on which he seems to project and visualise all that he recounts to me.

*　　*　　*

"At what age did you paint your first picture or first begin to draw?"

"I have never known when I was really born. Officially, I was born in 1887, which explains why my seventieth birthday has now been celebrated—for instance in the New York Museum of Modern Art, which recently staged a special show of my graphic work on that occasion. But am I really a septuagenarian? In spite of my grey hairs, I often feel much younger. Besides, my parents may, as was frequently done in those years in Tsarist Russia, have cheated about the exact date of my birth. If they could manage to prove that I was four years older than my next brother, they could obtain my exemption from military service by claiming that, as the eldest son, I was already contributing to the support of my family."

"Did your family encourage your ambition to become an artist?"

"In our little old provincial ghetto, among the petty traders and craftsmen that my family knew, we had no idea of what it means to be an artist. In our own home, for instance, we never had a single picture, print, or reproduction, at most a couple of photographs of members of the family. Until 1906, I never had occasion to see, in Vitebsk, such a thing as a drawing. But one day, in grade school, I saw one of my class-mates busy reproducing, in drawing, a magazine illustration. This particular boy happened to be my worst enemy, the best student in the class and also the one who taunted me the most mercilessly for being such a *Schlemihl*, because I never seemed able to concentrate or to learn anything in school. As I watched him draw, I was completely dumbfounded. To me, this experience was like a vision, a true revelation in black and white. I asked him how he managed such a miracle. 'Don't be such a fool,' he replied. 'All you need to do is to take a book out of the public library and then try your luck at copying one of the illustrations out of it, as I am doing right now.'

"And that is how," Chagall added after a pause, "I became an artist. I went to the public library and chose there a bound volume of the illustrated Russian periodical *Niwa,* and brought it home. The first illustration that caught my eye in it and that I tried to copy was a portrait of the composer Anton Rubinstein. I was fascinated by the number of wrinkles and lines in his face that seemed to quiver and to live before my eyes, so I began to copy it. But I was still far from thinking of art as a vocation or a profession. At most, it was still but a hobby, though I already began to pin up all my drawings, at home, on our walls."

"One of Soutine's biographers writes that his parents were horrified, and had even beaten him, when he had first expressed his ambition, as a boy, to become a painter. Did your family, in the ghetto of Vitebsk, react as strongly as Soutine's family in their small-town ghetto near Smolensk?"

"My father was a devout Jew and perhaps understood that our religion forbade us to create graven images and, in the opinion of the more orthodox Rabbis, even to reproduce any living creature. But it never occurred to any of us that these little pieces of paper on which I copied what I saw printed on other pieces of paper might be what was thus being so solemnly forbidden. And that is perhaps why nobody, among my relatives and friends, was at all shocked, at first, by my new hobby.

"Then, one day, another classmate of mine, a boy who came of a family that was wealthier than ours and more cultured, dropped by at our home, and chanced

Chaim Soutine (1894–1943), Lithuanian artist influenced by the Expressionists. He arrived in Paris in 1913, where he met Chagall, Modigliani, and others.

The Seated Violinist. 1908. Watercolor and ink on paper. 7 $^{7}/_{8}$ x 5 $^{1}/_{2}$ in. (20 x 14 cm). Musée National d'Art Moderne, Centre Georges Pompidou, Paris.

to see some of my drawings pinned to the wall of the room where I worked and slept. He seemed most impressed by my drawings and proclaimed enthusiastically that I was a real artist. But what did this strange word mean? I had always been somewhat lazy in my studies, a bit absent-minded and unwilling to concentrate or to learn. At home, nobody ever asked me what trade or profession I might want to study. My family was very poor, and the poor cannot afford the luxury of a vocation. On the contrary, boys with a background like mine are generally glad to accept the first job that comes their way, as soon as they are old enough to work. Besides, I could scarcely imagine, at that time, that I would ever be able to do anything very useful in life. At best, I might qualify for some unskilled job, like my father, who found it hard to make both ends meet on his meager salary as a warehouseman for a wholesale dealer in pickled and salted fish. Still, this mysterious word 'artist' might mean a somewhat better opening for me, in my life, and I began to ask my classmate what it meant. He then mentioned the names of the great painters of Tsarist Russia, men like Riepin and Verestchaguine, painters of vast historical scenes that were frequently reproduced at that time in such magazines as those from which I picked the models for my own drawings. But I had never paid any attention to the names of the artists whose works were reproduced in *Niwa,* and nobody in my family had ever mentioned them to me.

Photograph taken in 1928 of Yehuda Pen and neighbors in the backyard of Chagall's parents' house. Collection Ida Chagall, Paris.

"Be that as it may, my madness became apparent for the first time that day. I now knew that I had a vocation, even if my own father still had no idea what this profession that I had chosen really meant. As for me, I already understood that it at least meant my having to attend some school and obtaining some diploma there. That day, my mother was baking bread in the kitchen when I interrupted her to discuss my new plan. But what I said about being an artist made no sense at all to her, and she practically told me to go climb a tree."

"Was it in Vitebsk that you managed to obtain your first training as an artist?"
"Yes, but it was no easy task for me to find a teacher. I had to run all over the city before I found a place where I might study my new trade. After enquiring everywhere, I finally found the studio of Pen, a provincial portrait-painter who also taught a few pupils on the side. I begged my mother to accompany me on my first visit to the master, much as I might have asked either of my parents to come and discuss with some craftsman under what conditions he would accept me as an apprentice. But my mother preferred to consult an uncle of mine beforehand, a man who read newspapers and thus enjoyed, in our family circle, the reputation of being a cultured man of the world. This uncle of mine then mentioned the same names, as examples of all that being an artist could mean, as my classmate. But my uncle also added that men such as Riepin and Verestchaguine also had talent, something that had never yet occurred to any of us. My mother decided, however, on the spot, that she would allow me to study art if Professor Pen, who certainly knew his own business, expressed the view that I had talent. All this must have taken place in 1907 and, if I remember right, I must have then been scarcely seventeen years old."

Yehuda Pen (1870–1937), portraitist and Realist painter who was Chagall's first art instructor. When Chagall became Commissar of Art, he invited Pen to join the staff of the Art College in Vitebsk.

"What were your impressions, on your first visit to Pen's studio?"
"When we got there, my mother and I, the master was out, on some errand downtown. But we were greeted by one of his pupils, who was busy in a corner of the studio, drawing something or other. I had brought along, under my arm, a whole bundle of my own drawings, to show them to the master. When my mother saw, in Pen's studio, so many fine portraits of bewhiskered generals, their chests all bright with medals, and of the wives of local gentry, with their opulent and much bejewelled bosoms, she experienced a moment of hesitation. 'My poor boy,' she sighed, 'you'll never manage to make the grade.' She was indeed ready to turn back and to drag me home again in her wake. I was still so timid that I

COLORPLATE 8. *The Drinker (The Drunk)*. 1911–12. Oil on canvas. 32 $^7/_8$ x 44 $^7/_8$ in. (83.5 x 114 cm). Private collection.

COLORPLATE 9. *The Red Jew.* 1915. Oil on cardboard. 39 ³/₈ x 31 ³/₄ in. (100 x 80.6 cm).
The National Russian Museum, St. Petersburg. Photograph: Agence Novosti.

COLORPLATE 10. *The Newspaper Vendor*. 1914. Oil on canvas. 38 ¹/₂ x 31 in. (97.8 x 78.7 cm).
Musée National d'Art Moderne, Centre Georges Pompidou, Paris.

COLORPLATE II. *Paris Through the Window*. 1913. Oil on canvas. 53 1/2 x 55 3/4 in. (135.8 x 141.4 cm).
The Solomon R. Guggenheim Museum, New York. Gift of Solomon R. Guggenheim, 1937.
Photograph © The Solomon R. Guggenheim Foundation, New York.

COLORPLATE 12. *Poet Reclining.* 1915. Oil on cardboard. 30 ¹/4 x 30 ¹/2 in. (77 x 77.5 cm).
The Tate Gallery, London. Photograph: Art Resource, New York.

COLORPLATE 13. *The Birthday*. 1915. Oil on canvas. 31 3/4 x 39 1/8 in. (81 x 100 cm).
The Museum of Modern Art, New York. Acquired through the Lillie P. Bliss Bequest.
Photograph © The Museum of Modern Art, New York.

COLORPLATE 14. *I and the Village*. 1911. Oil on canvas. 75 ⅝ x 59 ⅝ in. (192.1 x 151.5 cm).
The Museum of Modern Art, New York. Mrs. Simon Guggenheim Fund.
Photograph © The Museum of Modern Art, New York.

COLORPLATE 15. *Over the Village*. 1915. Oil on board mounted on canvas. 19 ¹/₄ x 27 ³/₄ in. (48.5 x 70.5 cm). Tret'iakov Gallery, Moscow. Photograph: Agence Novosti.

held tight to my mother's skirt whenever we left our part of town, as if I were a child and afraid of losing her in the crowd.

"But my mother lingered in Pen's studio, admiring the master's work and questioning his pupil about the chances of a future that this strange trade might offer a promising beginner. The young Bohemian answered her questions somewhat laconically, making a great show of cynicism. Art, he explained, isn't a trade that implies keeping a shop and selling any wares. At this point, Pen returned to his studio from his errands in town. Immediately, I produced my drawings and began to show them to him. My mother asked him if I had any talent. Pen answered evasively that there was 'something' in my work. But his few words of appreciation sufficed and I was thus enrolled on the spot as one of his pupils.

"I did not attend Professor Pen's classes very long, as I soon understood that he could only teach me a kind of art that had little in common with my own aspirations. These were each day becoming more conscious and clear to me, thought they still consisted in knowing what I didn't want to paint rather than what I really wanted to achieve. Still, old Pen was kind enough to realise what sacrifices my studies implied for my poor family, and he soon offered to teach me free of charge. My progress was, however, so rapid that, in 1908, I was already able to move to Saint Petersburg and to enroll there in the Free Academy where Leon Bakst taught." . . .

Leon Bakst (1866–1924), Russian artist and stage designer.

"What was your own style of painting, when you first came into contact with Bakst and his school?"

"All my works of this first period are now lost. I suppose you might have called me, at that time, a Realist Impressionist, as I was still following a trend that had been introduced in Russia by a number of our teachers who, on their return from Paris, had begun to spread among their friends and pupils a few vague notions borrowed from Pissarro and Jules Adler, from Sisley and Bastien-Lepage."

Camille Pissarro (1830–1903); Jules Adler (1895–1949); Alfred Sisley (1839–1899); Jules Bastien-Lepage (1848–1884).

"How did it happen that all your early works of this period are lost?"

"When I first arrived in the Tsarist capital, I was very short of money and, one day, discovered a frame-maker—his name was Antokolsky, like the famous Russian sculptor—whose shop-window was full of photographs and of framed pictures that he seemed to have on sale for various painters who were also his customers. I managed to overcome my natural timidity sufficiently to bring all my work to this man Antokolsky and to ask him if he thought he might be able to sell any of it. He asked me to leave him my paintings and to come back in a few days, allowing him time to think it over. When I returned a week later, it was like a scene from a Kafka novel. Antokolsky behaved as if he had never seen me before and claimed that I had not left him any pictures. As for me, I had of course neglected to ask him for a receipt. I even remember his asking me: 'Who are you?' I have never been able to trace any of the paintings that I left with him, so I often wonder whether he ever sold them."

"Was it in Saint Petersburg that you finally weaned yourself away from your earlier Realist-Impressionist style?"

"Yes, though not at once. One of the first pictures that I painted in the Tsarist capital was a copy of a landscape by Isaac Levitan, the Russian Impressionist master and friend of Chekhov. We all considered Levitan a great man, in those days, and I was fortunate enough to meet in Saint Petersburg several of his friends and patrons, as well as some friends of the painter Serov. I saw many of the works of these two Russian Impressionist masters in private collections. At that time, being a Jew, I needed a special permit to reside in the capital. As I had failed to obtain this permit, I lived there illegally and was unable to register as a student in the National Academy of Fine Arts. That is why I chose to study at the Free Academy, where I studied, among others, under Bakst and Roehrich.". . .

Nikolay Roerich (1874–1947), Russian landscape painter, archaeologist, and stage designer.

"How did you manage your first trip to Paris?"

"Bakst had originally wanted me to take on the job of his assistant Anisfeld,

In the Academy. 1911. Ink drawing on paper. 5 1/8 x 8 1/4 in. (13 x 21 cm). Musée National d'Art Moderne, Centre Georges Pompidou, Paris.

who helped him paint the sets for Diaghilev's ballets and was then about to give up this job. I don't remember how it came about that this plan did not materialise and that I somehow failed to go to Paris with Bakst and the ballet company, but it was finally the lawyer Vinaver, who was also a member of the Russian Parliament or Duma, who offered me the money for my first trip. Vinaver had been, ever since my arrival in Saint Petersburg, my first and most faithful patron. He had several of my paintings in his collection, where I was very proud to see them hang close to works by Levitan and by Serov. It was Vinaver who, one day, suddenly offered to pay my trip to Paris and to transfer to me there, each month, a sum of forty roubles, which I would be able to collect from the Crédit Lyonnais. So I left Russia all alone, and full of misgivings. I was already in love, in those days, with Bella, who lived with her parents in Vitebsk. But her family felt that I was too poor to be considered a desirable son-in-law, and even the German frontier officials, when they boarded our train to inspect our passports and our baggage, viewed me suspiciously and asked me: *'Haben Sie Läuser?'"*

"*What were your first impressions of Paris?*"

"I seemed to be discovering light, colour, freedom, the sun, the joy of living, for the first time. It was from then on that I was at last able to express, in my work, some of the more elegiac or moon-struck joy that I had sometimes experienced in Russia too, the joy that once in a while expresses itself in a few of my childhood memories of Vitebsk. But I had never wanted to paint like any other painter. I had always dreamed of some new kind of art that would be different. In Paris, I now had the vision of the art that I actually wanted to create, in fact an intuition of a kind of new psychic dimension in my painting. Not that I was seeking a new means of expression, in a kind of basically Latin Expressionism like that of a Courbet. No, my art has never been an art of mere self-expression, nor an art that relies on my literary content. On the contrary, it has always been something essentially constructed, in fact a world of forms."

"Haben Sie Läuser" is either an error on Roditi's part, or on Chagall's. The German guard most likely asked, "Haben sie Läuse?" (Do you have lice?).

Gustave Courbet (1819–1877), French Realist painter.

"Is that why you immediately associated with the Paris Cubists?"

"No, the experiments of the Cubists never interested me very deeply. To me, they seemed to be reducing everything that they depicted to a mere geometry which remained a new slavery, whereas I was seeking a true liberation, not a liberation of the imagination or the fantasy alone, but a liberation of form too. If, in one of my pictures, I place a cow on a roof, or a tiny little woman in the middle of the body of a much larger one, all this is anything but literary content. On the contrary, it all seeks to illustrate a logic of the illogical, a world of forms that are *other,* a kind of composition that adds a psychic dimension to the various formulas which the Impressionists and then the Cubists had tried."

"André Breton and the Surrealists have often claimed that you were ten years ahead of their movement and had, as early as 1912, begun to obey the dictates of a kind of automatic painting such as they advocated around 1928 in their earliest manifestos."

"No, this argument is entirely unfounded. On the contrary, I always seek very consciously to construct a world where a tree can be quite different, where I myself may well discover suddenly that my right hand has seven fingers whereas my left hand has only five. Indeed, a world where everything and anything is possible and where there is no longer any reason to be at all surprised, or rather not to be surprised by all that one discovers there."

"One of my friends, the Israeli art-critic Haim Gamzou, claims that you are the Breughel of Yiddish idiom and folklore, and that he has himself identified over a hundred illustrations of popular Yiddish idioms and proverbs in details of your works."

"But I have never set about consciously illustrating these idioms and proverbs as Breughel once did, nor have I ever systematically composed a painting in which every detail illustrates a different proverb. All the idioms and proverbs that I may have illustrated have actually become popular because thousands of ordinary men and women have used them day by day, as I too have done, to express their thoughts. If a carter uses these metaphors and similes, there is nothing literary about his language. And if I, the son of a humble worker of the Vitebsk ghetto, also use them, this is still no reason to argue that my art is literary. Does the mere fact that I have become an artist make my work literary as soon as I express myself, perhaps unconsciously, as did all those who surrounded me in my childhood?"

"And what do you think of all those critics who claim that they have detected in your works the influence of Hassidic mysticism?"

"It is true that all my family belonged to a Hassidic community and that we had even had, in Vitebsk, a famous Hassidic *Wunderrebbe,* a miraculous Rabbi. But I doubt whether anyone can reasonably pretend that my work is essentially an expression of mystical faith or of religious belief. Mysticism and religion, of course, still played an important part in the world of my childhood, and they have left their mark in the work of my mature years too, as much as any other element of the life of the ghetto of Vitebsk. But I have now discovered other worlds too, and other beliefs and disbeliefs. . . ."

"What artistic circles did you choose to frequent when you first came to live in Paris?"

"One of my earliest and closest friends was the poet Blaise Cendrars. With Guillaume Apollinaire, the poet and leading theorist of the Cubists, I was much less at ease, though he was always very friendly and helpful. In those days, I had a studio in La Ruche, that legendary colony of broken-down studios where so many famous artists have lived. Modigliani was one of my neighbours. He was then doing more sculpture than painting. I think I was the only Russian painter there. Soutine moved in later. When I was preparing, in 1914, to go back to

Pieter Breughel the Elder (c. 1525–1569), one of the greatest landscape painters and the most important Dutch satirist after Bosch.

Russia, via Berlin, Soutine came one day to ask me if I would allow him to rent my studio as a sub-tenant while I was away."

"Was Soutine already as odd, as uncommunicative, and as careless of his appearance as he has generally been described?"

"I always found poor Soutine rather pitiful. Anyhow, I was not prepared to sub-let my studio to anyone and, the day I left for Berlin, I tied the door up with a rope, like a parcel, as it had no lock. I had no idea, at the time, that I would see La Ruche again only in 1922."

"What had made you decide to go to Berlin in 1914, just before the outbreak of the First World War?"

"Apollinaire had mentioned my work several times to Herwarth Walden, the organiser of Berlin's Sturm Gallery shows. Walden often came to Paris, in those years, to pick new talents whom he could exhibit in Germany. The German poet Ludwig Rubiner, and his wife Frieda, had also recommended me to Walden. The Rubiners, who were wonderful and devoted friends, were then as frequently in Paris as in Berlin, and many Paris artists owed their German successes to the Rubiners, who were indefatigable propagandists for modern art. Well, one day Walden asked me to let him have some hundred and fifty oils and gouaches of mine. I had already exhibited once in Berlin, in the 1913 Herbstsalon, where the collector Bernard Keller had purchased my *Golgotha* that now hangs in the New York Museum of Modern Art. So I went to Berlin, in 1914, to take a look at my exhibition in Walden's Sturm Gallery. Actually, I stopped in Berlin only a few days, on my way back to Russia, where I planned to see Bella again and hoped to persuade her family to allow her to marry me and to return with me to Paris. We would then have stopped again in Berlin, on the way back, to collect the money that Walden might have obtained for me as a result of sales from my exhibition. But war was declared, and I was able to return to Berlin, and on to Paris, only in 1922, after the Russian Revolution. By that time, Walden had already sold all of my hundred and fifty paintings, but the currency inflation was raging in defeated Germany and the money that Walden had obtained for my work was no longer worth a cent."

Golgotha *refers to* Calvary, *colorplate 7.*

"So this was the second time that you had seen all your work of a whole period sold without your being able to collect any money for it. If I remember right, many of the works that Walden had sold for you are now in important public and private collections. I saw some of them in Amsterdam, among those that the Stedelijk Museum exhibits in a whole room of your works."

"Yes, but the Stedelijk also owns many of my works that come from other sources. Besides, a third unpleasant surprise of this kind awaited me in 1922, when I returned to Paris and tried to go back to my studio in La Ruche. I expected to find it exactly as I had left it, but with the dust of nearly a decade accumulated on all my pictures and other possessions. Instead, I was greeted by new tenants. In my absence, all my belongings and my works had been moved out and sold, and I was never able to salvage anything."

"In a B.B.C. talk that was reprinted in The Listener, *Manya Harari reported, on her return from a trip to Moscow a couple of years ago, that she had still been able to see there quite a number of works which you had painted in Russia between 1914 and 1922. During those years of war and of Revolution, were you able to concentrate much on painting?"*

"Oddly enough, those years were among the most productive of my whole career. On my return from Paris, I found the atmosphere in Russia much more encouraging than before 1910, especially in certain Jewish circles that I had known before my first trip to Paris. Collectors had become far more open-minded, and there were more of them too. In Moscow, I also met at that time an outstanding and very successful engineer, Kagan Chabchay, who bought some thirty paintings of mine, which he planned to donate, with works by other artists too, to a Jewish Museum that he was sponsoring. But the Revolution came before

this project had materialised, and Kagan Chabchay, in 1922, still owned all his private collection, which had not yet been nationalised. He then allowed me to bring back to Paris, so as to exhibit them there, all the paintings he had purchased from me.". . .

"Manya Harari also reports that she met in Moscow a private collector who owns, even today, some thirty of your works, which he has managed to purchase more or less secretly in recent years."

"That is quite possible. I left many works in Russia, most of them in the homes of friends who generally owned small collections that were not nationalised. Many of these collectors or their heirs, I suppose, subsequently sold these paintings on the free market, which is a kind of flea-market in Soviet Russia."

"But your own work has not always been banned in Soviet Russia and, if I remember right, you even enjoyed some official support during the earlier years of the Revolution."

"Yes, I enjoyed the patronage of Lunacharsky, who was the first Soviet Commissar for Education. It was he who nominated me local Commissar for Fine Arts in my native city, in Vitebsk. I was then responsible for all artistic activities in that region, and was thus able to provide Vitebsk with what I had missed there twenty years earlier, I mean a real Fine Arts Academy and Museum."

The Small Salon. 1908. Oil on paper mounted on canvas. 8 7/8 x 11 3/8 in. (22.5 x 29 cm). Private collection.

The Circumcision. 1909. Oil on canvas.
29 7/8 x 25 in. (75.8 x 63.5 cm). Private
collection.

"Were you able to attract to Vitebsk many of your fellow-artists from Moscow and Leningrad?"

"It was fairly easy, and nearly all those whom I approached accepted to come. Food supplies were far more plentiful in Vitebsk than in bigger cities, and I also offered all artists complete freedom. The faculty of my Academy thus acquired many of the great names of the Russian artistic avant-garde. Nearly all schools of modern art were represented there, from Impressionism through to Suprematism."

"But did all these artists representing such different trends co-operate harmoniously in your Vitebsk Academy?"

"On the contrary, our Academy very soon became a veritable hot-bed of intrigue. To begin with, my old friend Pen, who had been my first instructor, was mortally offended because I had neglected to offer him immediately an important position on the faculty. But I was anxious to avoid introducing, at the very start, too academic an element in our teaching. Pen got his revenge by painting a parody of a famous picture of the German Symbolist Arnold Boecklin, the author of the *Isle of the Dead*. In this parody, Pen depicted himself on his death-bed, and gave the devil who had come to fetch his soul a face that was quite recognisably mine. Later, I asked Pen to join our faculty too. But it was with the Suprematists that I had the greatest trouble."

"Was the founder of the Suprematist school, Casimir Malevich, also on your faculty?"

"Yes. At that time, the Constructivists had not yet broken away from the Suprematists, and I had both Malevich and El Lissitzky on the Vitebsk faculty. Even Pougny, who was also a Constructivist before he emigrated to Paris, was there with his wife: they both taught courses in applied art. But Malevich was still

Suprematism was a hyper-orthodox form of Cubism begun in 1913 by Kazimir Malevich as an absolutely pure geometrical abstract art. To the uninitiated it is scarcely distinguishable from analytical Cubism; to the discerning eye it must be distinguished from Constructivism and from the abstract paintings of Mondrian.

Böcklin (1827–1901) was actually Swiss.

Kazimir Malevich (1878–1935), Russian artist who went through phases of neo-Impressionist and Fauve influence and was closely linked with Larionov and the Russian avant-garde movement. He published books on the theory of color and was one of the most influential Russian Cubists.

El (Lazar Markovich) Lissitzky (1890–1941), one of the leading avant-garde Russian artists and a leader (with Kazimir Malevich) of the Suprematist movement.

the leader of this whole group. He had started painting as an Impressionist, until 1905, and had then been one of the first Russian Fauvists. It was Lissitzky, among the Suprematists, who gave me the most trouble. At that time, he was still relatively unknown and, before committing himself exclusively to Suprematism and later to Constructivism, had first attracted the attention of several of my own patrons by handling Jewish themes in a style that was not unlike my own."

"Some of Lissitzky's early works on Jewish themes turn up even to-day in German auctions and, because they are so much like early works of your own and are likewise signed, as you did too at one time, in Hebrew script, are usually listed in German auction catalogues under your name."

"I suppose there are no longer many art experts in Germany who can decipher Hebrew script. But Lissitzky and I were not the only artists in Russia to handle such themes and to sign our works, at that time, in Hebrew script. There was also Issachar Ryback, who died relatively young and has left us some very fine works. He was one of the most gifted in our group of artists who were then seeking to formulate a specifically Jewish style of art. In the early years of the Revolution, the various national groups in Soviet Russia were at first encouraged to develop schools of art of their own, and quite a number of Jewish artists thus happened to pursue, for a while, the same aims. It was thus with Ryback, Nathan Altman, Lissitzky, Rabinowitsch, and Tischler that I came to work in Moscow for the Jewish National Theatre, for the Habbimah, and for the Kamerny Theatre. But most of my theatrical designs were considered too fantastic for use on the stage, and Meyerhold, Tairoff, and Vachtangov never used them. Only Granowsky ever had the courage to use any of my designs. But I also painted some panels to decorate the foyer of the Jewish National Theatre in Moscow."

"One of my American friends who was in Moscow last summer tells me that this Theatre still owns your paintings, but that they are now stored away in the basement and are shown only to foreigners and on request. But how did you manage to find time to found and direct your academy and museum in Vitebsk and to work concurrently for the theatre in Moscow?"

"Well, as they say in Yiddish, you can't be dancing at two weddings at the same time, and I could scarcely be both in Vitebsk and Moscow. As long as I was director of the Academy, I had little spare time to paint. At all times, I was busy raising funds to meet our expenses, scaring up supplies of every kind, or visiting the military authorities to obtain deferments for teachers or pupils. So I came and went, inspected all schools in the province where art-classes were taught, and was constantly being called to Moscow for conferences with the central authorities there. While I was away from Vitebsk, Impressionists and Cubists, Cézannians and Suprematists, whether on the faculty or among the students, used to engage in a kind of free-for-all behind my back. One day, when I returned to Vitebsk from Moscow, I found, across the facade of the school building, a huge sign: Suprematist Academy. Malevich and his henchmen had simply fired all the other members of the faculty and taken over the whole Academy. I was furious, handed in my resignation at once and set out again for Moscow, in a cattle-car, as the railroads had no other rolling-stock available at that time even for travellers on official business."

"But surely your friends in Moscow refused to accept your resignation?"

"On the contrary, when I called at the Ministry of the Commissar for Education, I was told I had already been fired. A whole file of denunciations and affidavits was produced, and I was told that some of the Suprematists had accused me of being authoritarian, uncooperative, and a whole lot of other things. Reports of all this reached Vitebsk, and the students staged a protest as a result of which I was reinstated, though not for very long. My Suprematist colleagues continued to intrigue against me and I then arranged to move to Moscow, where I began to free-lance, working mainly for the Jewish Theatre until I returned to Berlin and Paris in 1922. Not only did I then have more time to paint, but I even managed in

Issachar Ryback (1897–1935), born in the Ukraine, is generally considered an important contributor to the Jewish art movement in Russia.

Alexander Granovsky, founder of the Kamerny, the forerunner of Moscow's Jewish Theater.

COLORPLATES 24–31

55

Moscow to write my book *Ma Vie,* which was subsequently published in Paris. I had chosen to live in France because I have always felt that France is my real home, because only in France, and especially in Paris, do I feel truly free as a painter of light, and of colour. I have already stated to you that Russian painters, in my opinion, have but rarely managed to develop a real sense of colour in their own country.". . .

"On your return to Paris you surely found it difficult, at first, to integrate yourself again in the Paris art-world?"

"Perhaps. . . . But I did not come directly from Moscow to Paris. Instead, I stopped for a while in Berlin, where I found myself, in those difficult years of inflation and of the birth-pangs of the Weimar Republic, in an atmosphere that was not unlike that of the early years of the Russian Revolution. Besides, I met in Berlin a number of Russian friends, from Leningrad, Moscow, and even Vitebsk, who had likewise emigrated, if only for a while. Berlin had become, right after the First World War, a kind of clearing-house of ideas where one met all those who came and went from Moscow to Paris and back. Later, I found for a short while a similar atmosphere on the Paris Left Bank, in Montparnasse, then again in New York during the Second World War. But in 1922, Berlin was like a weird dream, sometimes like a nightmare. Everybody seemed to be busy buying or selling something, and even when a loaf of bread cost several million marks, one found patrons to buy pictures for several thousand million marks which one had to spend again the same day, in case they might become valueless overnight. In apartments around the Bayrischer Platz, one could find as many theosophical or Tolstoian Russian countesses talking and smoking all night around a samovar as there had ever been in Moscow, and in the basements of some restaurants in the Motzstrasse there were as many Russian generals and colonels, all cooking or washing dishes, as in a fair-sized Tsarist garrison-town. Never in my life have I met as many miraculous Hassidic Rabbis as in inflationary Berlin, or such crowds of Constructivists as at the Romanische Kaffee.

"When I was a refugee in New York during the Second World War, I often thought of all those whom I had known in Vitebsk, in Saint Petersburg, in Moscow, in Paris, and in Berlin, all those who had been less fortunate than I and who had not escaped from the horrors of persecution and of war."

* * *

At this point, Madame Chagall interrupted our conversation, reminding the master that he had an appointment with the dentist. With the agility and speed of an acrobat, he leapt from the couch and prepared to leave. When Madame Chagall asked him, as he slipped into his jacket, whether he had enough money on him to pay his cab-fares, he suddenly became a clown, felt all his pockets and replied: "Yes, yes, but where are my teeth?" Then feeling his jaw, he added: "Oh, they are still there!" In a twinkling he was gone.

Two days later, I returned, to submit to Chagall the first draft of my manuscript and check with him the many dates and details that I had hurriedly noted as he spoke. When he had approved the whole interview, he concluded: "The poet Mayakowsky used to say to me in Moscow: 'My dear Chagall, you're a good fellow, but you talk too much.' I see that I have not improved with age. . . ."

BELLA CHAGALL

From *First Encounter*

1939

Bella Rosenfeld in 1910.
Collection Ida Chagall, Paris.

A shadow darkened the chink in the doorway. My laughter froze on my lips. Who was it? What was Thea hiding from me?

The door opened wider, without a sound. I felt hot with apprehension. I dared not move, dared not look around. I felt as if something were scorching me. Light spread over the walls, and against them appeared the face of a boy, as white as the walls.

Where had he come from? I'd never seen him before. He was not like my brothers' friends, or like anyone else I knew. He stood as if afraid to hold himself upright. Had he only just woken up? He lifted one hand and forgot to lower it again. It just hung there in midair.

What did it mean? Was he trying to say hello to me, or about to box my ears? Was it I who'd awakened him? Why was he sleeping here anyway, and in almost broad daylight? His hair was tousled. It grew in little curls all over his head, clustering over his brow and hanging down over his eyes.

When you did catch a glimpse of his eyes, they were as blue as if they'd fallen straight out of the sky. They were strange eyes, not like other people's—long, almond-shaped. They were wide apart, and each seemed to sail along by itself, like a little boat. I'd never seen such eyes before. Or perhaps I had, in pictures of animals in books. His wide mouth was open, with the corners stretching up almost to his ears.

I couldn't tell whether he was going to talk to me or bite me with those sharp white teeth. Then he coiled himself up, an animal about to spring. It was as if, in preparation for stretching out his arms and legs, he only bent them all the more. And all this time he was laughing. Was he still laughing in his sleep? Or was he laughing at me?

I was always sure everyone was laughing at me. And this boy was obviously delighted to meet a girl who was afraid of him. How could Thea play such a trick on me? Why hadn't she told me right away that there was a visitor?

I was angry. When I thought of the stupid things I'd been saying! He'd heard them all, and now he was laughing in my face.

Now I knew why Thea hadn't said anything, and had let me do all the talking. She was embarrassed because he was there. Or was she embarrassed because of me? Who was he?

I didn't know what to do with myself. I stood rooted to the spot. I'd have liked to run away from my altered friend and her odd visitor. He was still laughing at me with that mouthful of teeth, as if he'd like to grind me to pieces. What was he thinking? He seemed to be pondering something. His brow furrowed, as if to make a path for his crowding thoughts. He came closer. I looked at the floor. No one said anything. We could hear one another's heartbeats.

I couldn't stand it any longer.

"Thea, I must go home!" I could scarcely move my parched lips. My head was burning, and my whole body felt as if I were being scourged.

Then the boy said, "Why? What's the hurry? You have such a lovely voice. I heard you laughing."

He was speaking! And to me! *He* wasn't overawed by the silence. But his words were killing me.

I didn't understand. He didn't even know me. What did he want? What was that he'd said about my voice?

I looked at Thea.

Bella Chagall, the artist's first wife, was for many years the inspiration for many of Chagall's paintings. First Encounter, *published in 1945, a year after her death, is a memoir produced by Chagall and their daughter Ida from Bella's many notebooks.*

"This is the artist," she said, coming to life at last. "I told you about him."

I blushed to the roots of my hair, as if I'd been caught stealing. Thea was speaking hastily, defensively. A flood of syllables poured over me.

"Oh? Really?"

I didn't know what to say. Her words trapped me like a spider's web, winding around my arms and neck and skin as if to throttle me. I grabbed my hat and cape, and ran out of the room, out of the house, out into the street.

"Phew!" I felt cooler out in the breeze. My head was back on my shoulders. My feet were no longer like lead, and ran along of their own accord. But the boy's face ran along beside me like a shadow, blowing on my cheeks and whistling in my ears. If I chased it away, it came back from another direction.

MARC CHAGALL

From *My Life*

Bella

1922

I am at Thea's, lying on the sofa in the consulting room of her father, a physician. I liked to stretch out that way near the window on that sofa covered with a black horsehair cloth, worn, with holes in several places.

The same sofa, undoubtedly, on which the doctor examined pregnant women and sick people suffering from stomach, head or heart trouble.

I lay down on that sofa, arms above my head and, dreaming, looked at the ceiling, the door, the place where Thea usually sat.

I'm waiting for her. She's busy. She's preparing dinner—fish, bread and butter—and her dog, big and heavy, keeps turning around her legs.

I lay down there on purpose so that Thea would come over to me, so she would kiss me. I held out my arms, the arms of salvation.

The bell rings. Who is that?

If it's her father, I'll have to get up from the sofa and go away.

Who is it then?

It's a friend of Thea's. She enters and I hear her voice, babbling away to Thea.

I stay in the consulting room. I don't leave. Yes, I did go out, but the friend, whose back was towards me, didn't see me.

I feel . . . what do I feel?

On the one hand, I'm annoyed at having my rest interfered with, my hope that Thea would perhaps come and sit beside me.

On the other, that young girl's visit and her voice, like that of a bird from some other world, trouble me.

Who is she? I'm afraid. No, I want to speak to her, to be near her.

But she's already saying good-bye to Thea. She scarcely glances at me and goes away.

Thea and I go out for a walk. On the bridge we meet her again. She is alone, all alone.

Suddenly I feel that I shouldn't be with Thea, I should be with her.

Her silence is mine. Her eyes, mine. I feel she has known me always, my childhood, my present life, my future; as if she were watching over me, divining

In 1908 Chagall was studying at the Svanseva School in St. Petersburg, but he returned to Vitebsk often to visit family and friends. Through his friend Victor Mekler he met Thea Brachman, the intelligent and expressive daughter of a prosperous physician. It was Thea who opened up a whole new world for Chagall, engaging him in provocative conversation and introducing him to the intellectuals of the middle class. In 1909 Chagall met Thea's best friend, Bella Rosenfeld, and his life was transformed.

my innermost being, though this is the first time I have seen her.

I know this is she, my wife.

Her pale coloring, her eyes. How big and round and black they are! They are my eyes, my soul.

I knew that Thea was nothing to me, a stranger.

I have entered a new house and I cannot be parted from it.

* * *

Vitebsk is a place like no other; a strange town, an unhappy town, a boring town.

A town full of young girls who, whether from lack of time or inclination, I did not even approach. Dozens, hundreds of synagogues, butcher shops, people in

The Fruitseller. 1909–10. Watercolor on paper. 7 $\frac{1}{2}$ x 5 $\frac{1}{2}$ in. (19 x 14 cm). Collection Marcus Diener, Basel.

Bella Writing. 1915. Watercolor and ink on paper. 8 x 12 in. (20.3 x 30.5 cm). Musée National d'Art Moderne, Centre Georges Pompidou, Paris.

the streets.

Is that Russia?

It's only my town, mine, which I have rediscovered.

I come back to it with emotion.

In that period I painted my series of Vitebsk of 1914. I painted everything I saw. I painted at my window. I never went out on the street with my box of paints.

I was satisfied with a hedge, a signpost, a floor, a chair.

Imagine yourself seated at the table, in front the samovar, a humble old man leans back in his chair.

I look questioningly at him: "Who are you?"

"What! You don't know me? You've never heard of the preacher of Slouzk?"

"Then listen; in that case, please come to my house. I'll make. . ." What shall I say?. . . How explain to him? I'm afraid he'll get up and go away.

He came, sat down on a chair and promptly fell asleep.

Have you seen the old man in green that I painted? That's the one.

Another old man passes by our house. Gray hair, sullen expression. A sack on his back . . .

I wonder: Is it possible for him to open his mouth, even to beg for charity?

Indeed, he says nothing. He enters and stays discreetly near the door. There he stands for a long time. And if you give him anything, he goes out, as he came in, without a word.

"Listen," I say to him, "don't you want to rest a while. Sit down. Like this. You don't mind, do you? You'll have a rest. I'll give you twenty kopeks. Just put on my father's prayer clothes and sit down."

You've seen my painting of that old man at prayer? That's the one.

It was good to be able to work in peace. Sometimes a man posed for me who had a face so tragic and old, but at the same time angelic. But I couldn't hold out more than half an hour . . . He stank too much.

"That's all, sir, you may go."

You've seen my old man reading? That's the one.

I painted, I painted and finally, though I protested a bit, I found myself, one rainy night, standing under a wedding crown, of the most authentic sort, just as in my pictures. I was blessed according to the ritual, as was proper.

But a long comedy preceded that ceremony. Here it is.

The parents and all the numerous family of my . . . yes . . . yes . . . of my wife, were not pleased with my origin.

Why not? My father, a simple clerk. My grandfather . . .

And they? Just imagine, they owned three jewelry stores in our town. In their showcases, multicolored fires glittered and sparkled from rings, pins and bracelets. On every side clocks and alarm clocks rang the hour. Accustomed as I was to other interiors, this one seemed to me fabulous.

At their house, three times a week, they prepared enormous cakes, apple, cheese, poppy-seed, at the sight of which I would have fainted. And at breakfast, they served mounds of those cakes which everybody fell upon furiously, in a frenzy of gluttony. And at home, at our house, a simple meal like a still life à la Chardin.

Their father fed on grapes as mine did on onions; and fowl which, at our house, was sacrificed only once a year on the eve of The Atonement, was never absent from their table.

Her grandfather, a white-haired old man with a long beard, wanders about the apartment, hunts for Russian books, Russian passports, and whatever he finds he throws into the stove, burns it. He cannot stand having his grandsons attend Russian schools.

Useless, useless.

They must all go to the cheder, become rabbis!

He himself does nothing but pray all day long. And on the Day of Atonement, he is completely out of his head.

But he's already too old to fast.

The great rabbi himself has authorized him to take several drops of milk during the day of fasting.

My wife holds the spoon for him.

He is bathed in tears, his tears fall on his beard, in the milk.

He is in despair. The spoon, shaking, scarcely wets his lips on the day of fasting.

I have no strength left to talk about it. My head is in a whirl.

My fiancée's mother said to her daughter:

"It looks to me as though he even puts rouge on his cheeks. What sort of a husband will he make, that boy as pink-cheeked as a girl? He'll never know how to earn his living."

But what can they do if that's the way she likes him.

Impossible to convince her.

"You'll starve with him, my daughter; you'll starve for nothing."

"And besides, he's an artist. What does that mean?"

"And what will everybody say . . ."

Thus my fiancée's family argued about me and, morning and night, she brought to my studio sweet cakes from her house, broiled fish, boiled milk, all sorts of decorative materials, even some boards which I used for an easel.

I had only to open my bedroom window, and blue air, love and flowers entered with her.

Dressed all in white or all in black, she seemed to float over my canvases for a long time, guiding my art.

I never finish a picture or an engraving without asking for her "yes" or "no."

So what did I care about her parents, her brothers! May God protect them!

My poor father.

"Come, Papa," I say to him, "come to my wedding." He, like me, would rather have gone to bed.

Was it worth while to make friends with such high-class people?

I arrived very late at my fiancée's house to find a whole synhedrion already gathered there.

Too bad I'm not Veronese.

Around the long table, the great rabbi, a wise old man, a trifle crafty, a few big, imposing-looking bourgeois, a whole Pleiad of humble Jews, whose insides crisped as they waited for my arrival and . . . for the marriage feast. For without me there would have been no marriage feast. I knew it and I was amused at their agitation.

That this is the most important night in my life, that soon, without music, without stars and without sky, against the yellow background of the wall, under a

The Raised Blouse. 1911. Ink on paper.
11 1/2 x 8 1/2 in. (29 x 21.5 cm).
Collection Marcus Diener, Basel.

red baldaquin, I shall be married—what do those gluttons care!

And I, as that solemn hour draws near, turn pale in the midst of the crowd.

Seated, standing, parents, friends, acquaintances, servants, came and went.

For them tears, smiles, confetti were already ripening. All that is proper to lavish on the fiancée.

They waited for me and, as they waited, they gossiped.

They were embarrassed to acknowledge that "he" was an artist.

Besides, it seems he's already famous . . . And he even gets money for his pictures. Did you know that?

"Nevertheless, that's no way to earn a living," sighs another.

"What are you saying? What about the fame and the honor?"

"But, after all, who is his father?" a third man wants to know.

"Ah! I know." They fall silent.

It seemed to me if they had put me in a coffin, my features would have been more supple, less rigid, than that mask that sat beside my future wife.

How I regretted that stupid timidity which prevented me from enjoying the mountain of grapes and fruits, the innumerable savory dishes that decorated the vast marriage table.

After half an hour (what am I saying? much before that) the synhedrion was in a hurry, blessings, wine, or perhaps curses rained down on our heads framed in the red baldaquin.

I thought I was going to faint. Everything whirled around me.

Deeply moved, I squeezed my wife's slender, bony hands. I wanted to run off with her to the country, to take her in my arms, to burst out laughing.

But after the nuptial benediction, my brothers-in-law led me to my house, while their sister, my wife, remained in her parents' home.

That was the height of ritual perfection.

At last, we are alone in the country.

Woods, pines, solitude. The moon behind the forest. The pig in the stable, the horse outside the window, in the fields. The sky lilac.

It was not only a honeymoon, but even more a milkmoon.

Not far from us a herd of cows belonging to the army was pastured. Every morning, soldiers sold pails-full of milk for a few kopeks. My wife, who had been brought up chiefly on cakes, gave me the milk to drink. With the result that, by autumn, I could scarcely button my coats.

As noon approached, our bedroom looked like one of those inspired panels in the great salons of Paris.

I was the winner. I chased a mouse that leapt triumphantly up my easel. At that my wife thought: So he really is capable of killing something.

But the war rumbled over us. And Europe was closed to me.

MARINA BESSONOVA

"The Master from Vitebsk"

1987

Marina Bessonova, art historian and chief curator of the State Pushkin Museum of Fine Arts in Moscow.

Marc Chagall was the last of the renowned "old" masters of the 20th century. He lived so long that it seemed as if he himself would open the exhibition commemorating his centenary. We can only turn to Picasso for comparison when considering the powerful artistic impulse that for eighty years poured out such a variety of works: paintings, engravings, stage sets and finally, during Chagall's last years, stained glass and mosaics. He established himself as a painter at a time of bold Cubist experiments, at the very birth of the 20th-century's new pictorial culture. When he died there was no one like him, a master and a wizard still conjuring with paint in our own days, which are far less conducive to profound meditations before the easel.

* * *

Talented young artists from different countries flocked to Paris, drawn like fearless moths to the bright and purifying flame lit by Apollinaire and Picasso. Many were fated to be consumed by this fire. Modigliani spread his wings and burst into flame; Otokar Kubín's works ceased to stand out among the universally high quality of the Expressionists and Cubists; the skilled stylists Kisling and Fudjita took their place in the history of art, but only as representatives of the Paris School. Yet when Chagall was declared to be the head of that same school in the early 1930s this was already an honour for the school and not for Chagall.

He was immediately able to rise above national particularity and colourful exoticism although his cows, donkies, old women with milkpails and Orthodox church cupolas were irresistibly attractive to his viewers.

Mature Cubism teaches us to look at the world not only with binocular but also a certain "rotational" vision; we delve into the very essence of the way shapes are formed. This discovery was also far from the cold and calculated rationalism that some modern researchers are inclined to attribute to French Cubism. But in the paintings he made in the early 1910s Chagall blew apart these pasted collages of forms as if he had detonated a powerful shell. His bodies had not yet lost their dense weightiness although they had become transparent, and they flew in all directions as if borne on a strong explosive wave. Léger and Apollinaire were soon to see these nightmarish scenes in real life in the trenches of the First World War. Evidently Apollinaire sensed a certain powerful prophetic force emanating from the canvases of the young artist from Vitebsk: Chagall would not allow the "blazing flame" (of which Apollinaire had written in the first manifesto of the new art in history) to be extinguished. . . .

Chagall's ability to transform everyday activities into miraculous happenings also did not escape the sharpened perceptions of Europe's *avantgarde* painters. This was one of Chagall's main artistic qualities and had already found expression in his early years. In Paris the scenes he had witnessed during childhood in Vitebsk and Lyozno passed before his eyes. In *Birth* everything glorifies the miraculous appearance of a new life. The composition shows the new mother in the foreground, facing away from the infant as in icons of the Nativity, and the colour scheme relies on sharp geometrical contrasts between light and shade. The midwife, partially concealed by the edge of the canvas, holds the glowing kerosene lamp high above her head like a torch: the bright light cuts through the gloom of the cellar with its menacing semi-circular window beyond which reigns darkness. The father bearing the dazzling infant in his arms hovers at the foot of the bed in the depths of the picture; and his small figure helps define the particular "miraculous" space that transforms the interior of this cramped and tiny room.

The First World War interrupted Chagall's Parisian discoveries. He returned to his native town where he became involved in the tense pre-revolutionary life of Russia. On his travels between Vitebsk, Petrograd and Moscow he observed scenes from soldiers' lives away from the front and the first disfiguring scars of war: refugees from the villages of Byelorussia, and wounded soldiers marching alongside the new conscripts. Together with the trench sketches of Léger and Zadkine, the verse written at the front by Apollinaire, the engravings of Goncharova, and Barbusse's *Under Fire*, Chagall's drawings and watercolours were an indictment of that senseless and inhuman war. . . .

All researchers have noticed a sharp increase in the everyday themes illustrated in Chagall's art in the years of war before the [Russian] Revolution. For this there may be many explanations. The artist was once again involved in a familiar environment with its own colourful and lively daily existence: after the dreams of Paris, his heart was stirred by the joy of recognition. Then, confronted by an advancing and alarming reality, he temporarily abandoned his visionary approach. Finally, a major event had occurred in Chagall's private life. Marriage

The Russian Couple. 1910. Ink on paper. 8 5/8 x 7 in. (22 x 18 cm). Collection Marcus Diener, Basel.

Fernand Léger (1881–1955), a Cubist painter formally trained as an architect. His works typically presented geometric shapes of machinery, and he later depicted the everyday working man.

63

to Bella and the birth of Ida had brought with them the simple human desire to depict his loved ones again and again, recording the hours and days of their happy existence together. This was how his landscapes and his interiors with portraits of Bella and the diminutive Ida came into being: they sit at the *dacha* round a table laid with plates of ripe wild strawberries, or in front of a window that opens onto a clearing in the woods or reveals the overgrown garden. These were the views of the Russian landscape that were so dear to him, and which he would miss with acute nostalgia abroad. In the late 1920s and early 1930s he became fully aware that he would never return to his native haunts; he missed them deeply and began to visit Switzerland where the snow-covered distant mountains and the majestic fir-trees somehow reminded him of his lost homeland. . . .

In Chagall's early Paris canvases Vitebsk flew in dismembered fragments across the sky but in 1914 it descended to the earth, once again whole. In the *Newspaper Vendor,* one of Chagall's masterpieces, the mournful figure appears like a vision before us while behind him there stands an old Russian town with its main street and square framed by small wooden houses and dominated by the vast Church of the Prophet Elijah.

COLORPLATE 10

Yet alongside these scenes of daily life at the dacha and in Vitebsk there run a parallel series of symbolic portraits. Chagall depicted "red" and "green" Jews, many-coloured rabbis praying or meditating over the Scriptures and, duplicating their ritual solemnity, there also appeared a series of heads belonging to "blue" and "green" lovers. It is as though colour has ceased to be simply a means of emotional expression for the artist and, while still sealed in its tubes, has escaped his control and is already dictating the subject of his next painting. It is in these pre-revolutionary paintings that we should look for the sources of the colourful visionary approach that shaped all Chagall's subsequent work.

COLORPLATE 9

COLORPLATE 32

It was then he painted *The Birthday* which became a model for all his following works. A pair of lovers have become weightless and rise in a swirling ecstatic movement within the space defined by the room. The interior is filled with many petty domestic objects and recalls paintings by the Dutch Old Masters where a real everyday setting is reproduced in detail but each item also has a hidden meaning. An urban room is thus transformed before our eyes into a place where miracles can happen.

COLORPLATE 13

Chagall's marriage gave his art a new theme, the possibility of uniting earthly and heavenly love. And in his post-revolutionary paintings the first to embody that "cosmic" upheaval were a pair of lovers. In the vast canvas, *Over the Town,* they soar over Vitebsk supporting one another, as if "restraining" their thrusting flight into infinity. They are constrained to the earth's surface with difficulty: in the universally famous *Promenade* Bella spins around the artist's arm like a satellite, just about to leave this world. Bold lovers alone are permitted everything and Chagall, seated on his wife's shoulders, reaches into the heavens to share a toast with the angels flying by (*Double Portrait with Wineglass*, 1917).

COLORPLATE 15

COLORPLATE 16

COLORPLATE 20

IRINA ANTONOVA

Fantastic Chagall

1987

Irina Antonova, art historian and director of the Tret'iakov Gallery in Moscow.

Mark Chagall belongs to the glorious group of rebels and dreamers whose work in the early decades of the 20th century marked the beginning of a new era in the arts. Russia's artists, writers and musicians made a very significant contribution

COLORPLATE 16. *The Promenade*. 1917. Oil on canvas. 67 x 64 ³/8 in. (170 x 163.5 cm).
The National Russian Museum, St. Petersburg. Photograph: Agence Novosti.

COLORPLATE 17. *Rider Blowing on a Trumpet*. 1918. Aquatint, crayon, and gouache on paper.
9 x 11 ⁷/₈ in. (23 x 30 cm). Collection Ida Chagall, Paris.

COLORPLATE 18. *The Cemetery Gates*. 1917. Oil on canvas. 34 1/4 x 27 in. (87 x 68. 5 cm).
Musée National d'Art Moderne, Centre Georges Pompidou, Paris.

COLORPLATE 19. *Bella with a White Collar.* 1917. Oil on canvas with varnish.
58 5/8 x 28 3/8 in. (149 x 72 cm).
Musée National d'Art Moderne, Centre Georges Pompidou, Paris.

COLORPLATE 20. *Double Portrait with Wineglass.* 1917–18. Oil on canvas.
91 ³/4 x 53 ¹/2 in. (233 x 136 cm). Musée National d'Art Moderne,
Centre Georges Pompidou, Paris. Photograph: Art Resource, New York.

COLORPLATE 21. *The Apparition.* 1917–18. Oil on canvas. 58 1/4 x 50 3/4 in. (148 x 129 cm). Private collection.

COLORPLATE 22. *Cubist Landscape*. 1918. Oil on canvas. 39 ³/₈ x 23 ¹/₄ in. (100 x 59 cm).
Musée National d'Art Moderne, Centre Georges Pompidou, Paris.

COLORPLATE 23. *The Wedding*. 1918. Oil on canvas. 39 3/8 x 46 7/8 in. (100 x 119 cm).
Tret'iakov Gallery, Moscow. Photograph: Agence Novosti.

to this universal process, and were themselves innovators in many fields. This was hardly surprising since the country was on the brink of a great social revolution.

As it turned out, Chagall spent most of his life in France. However, like Rakhmaninov, Chaliapin and Bunin, he remained a distinctively Russian artistic phenomenon. In a century of "total" influences, Chagall imitated no one and no one, incidentally, attempted to follow him. His artistic conceptions were enigmatic, the means he used to get to the heart of things was highly original, and his dialectical approach unpredictable. All this made his art inimitable. He remained unshakably faithful to his own principles and origins and this accounts for the unique character of his work. He drew his strength and inspiration from the simple rituals of everyday life in his native Vitebsk, the natural surroundings of his childhood, and the unadulterated sources of folk art.

For almost eight decades the artist created his own mythical world in which Biblical tradition, images from popular folklore, figures from the circus and the fairy tale, and everyday items blended to form a fantastical alloy. Chagall belongs to a class of artist that has always been a rarity throughout history. Such magicians and fantasists move us and stir our awareness by displacing the familiar and expected and, combining all in a "magical chaos," immerse us in a world of illusions and visions. The driving force in their art is the unbounded fertility of the imagination. "It is possible that there is a mysterious fourth or fifth dimension," wrote Chagall, "and we don't just see it: intuitively, it gives birth to an equilibrium of plastic contrasts that astonishes the viewer's eye with its new and unusual relations."

Among Chagall's artistic predecessors could be mentioned the disconcerting works of Bosch and the sarcastic vision of Goya; among writers, we may recall the sinisterly ironical Hoffman, the mysterious Edgar Allan Poe and, of course, Chagall's own great countryman Gogol. The Russian writers and artists Bulgakov, Chekrygin and Platonov were also gifted with fourth-dimensional vision . . . Louis Aragon once compared Chagall's contradictory vision of the world to that expressed in Shakespeare's *Midsummer Night's Dream*. For all the differences dividing these great artists and writers they all share an element of irony that is an essential part of their work. Yet as Nabokov wittily remarked, "a single hissing consonant divides the comic aspect of things from their cosmic aspect." The art of such painters, wrote the same author, is directed "towards those mysterious depths of the human soul where the shadows of other worlds pass by like the shades of nameless and soundless vessels."

Chagall is a master of the decorative metaphor. This is what gives meaning to his poetics. However, there are no allusions, allegories or rebuses in his art. It is filled with genuinely poetic symbols and does not require speculative intellectual exercises from the viewer but a responsive mind and soul.

The artist retained a tender affection for the country of his birth. Among his idols he named Rublyov, Vrubel, Gogol, Blok and Tchaikovsky. He always joyfully received countless Soviet guests at his house in the south of France, and in the 1960s he executed a series of lithographs devoted to Mayakovsky which he gave as a gift to the Pushkin Museum in Moscow. . . .

He was a great painter, an ironic and good-hearted storyteller—a merry person with sad blue eyes who helped us to keep smiling and recall our childhood . . .

Study for La Promenade. 1916–17. Wash drawing. 8 5/8 x 7 1/2 in. (22 x 19 cm). Musée National d'Art Moderne, Centre Georges Pompidou, Paris.

Sergei Rakhmaninov (1873–1973), Russian composer, pianist, and conductor; Fyodor Chaliapin (1873–1938), Russian basso; Ivan Bunin (1870–1953), Russian poet and novelist.

Hieronymus Bosch (1450–1516), Dutch painter; Francisco José de Goya (1746–1828), Spanish painter.

Nikolay Vasilevich Gogol (1809–1852), Russian poet.

Vladimir Nabokov (1899–1977), Russian novelist and poet.

Vladimir Mayakovsky (1893–1930), one of Russia's most compelling poets of the twentieth century.

CHAGALL IN PARIS

MARC CHAGALL

"Why Did I Go to Paris?"

1979

A page in Chagall's handwriting recounting his arrival in Paris, dated 1910–1911 in the upper right corner.

I was not the only one in those days who took the road to Paris, the capital of Art. So why did I go to Paris, what did I find there, and what sort of art was I dreaming of—though it was no a suitable time for dreaming. Painters were absorbed in purely technical experiments. You did not talk aloud about your dreams of art, unless it was merely a question of ephemeral theories, which followed each other in rapid succession. In these best periods of technical discoveries, painters seemed to hold their tongues. Was the soul silent out of modesty? Or for some other reason? I don't know. Even the one who combined in himself the painter and the inventor maintained a delicate and stubborn silence throughout, while provoking noisy outbursts in others. So I arrived in Paris as though driven by fate. Words coming from my heart flowed to my mouth. They almost choked me. I kept stammering. The words crowded outward, anxious to be illuminated by this Paris light, to adorn themselves with it. I arrived with the thoughts, the dreams, that one can only have at the age of twenty, but perhaps these dreams had been bottled up in me for a long time. It can usually be said that one does not go to Paris with fully packed bags. One goes there without ballast, to study, and then leaves again with baggage—sometimes. I would certainly have been able to express myself in my native town, in the circle of my friends. But I aspired to see with my own eyes what I had heard of from so far away: this revolution of the eye, this rotation of colors, which spontaneously and astutely merge with one another in a flow of conceived lines, as willed by Cézanne, or freely dominant as demonstrated by Matisse. That could not be seen in my town. The sun of Art then shone only on Paris, and it seemed to me, and seems to me still, that there is no greater revolution of the eye than the one I encountered in 1910 on my arrival in Paris. The landscapes, the figures of Cézanne, Manet, Monet, Seurat, Renoir, Van Gogh, the Fauvism of Matisse, and so many others astounded me! They attracted me like a phenomenon of nature. Far from my native country, its fences stood out in my imagination against the background of houses. I saw there none of the colors of Renoir. Two or three dark spots. And one would have had to live a life alongside them with no hope of finding this liberated artistic language that should breathe by itself, as a man breathes.

In Paris I frequented neither schools nor teachers. I found them in the city itself, at every step, everywhere. There were the tradesmen in the market, the café waiters, the concierges, the peasants, the workers. Around them hovered this astonishing "freedom-light," which I have never seen elsewhere. And this light passed easily onto the canvases of the great French masters and was reborn in art. I couldn't help thinking: only this "freedom-light," more luminous than all the sources of artificial light, can give birth to such shining canvases, in which revolutions in technique are as natural as the language, the gestures, the work of the passersby in the street.

I was then in my twenties, and my feelings were confused because I had seen nothing similar in the other countries through which I had passed. I perhaps did not see it with the eyes of reason, but with the eyes of the soul. And it was as though this soul had been newly and differently broken up for cultivation in these

In 1910 Chagall left Russia for the first time and arrived in Paris, thanks to a grant given to him by his patron Max Vinaver. Vinaver's stipend allowed Chagall to remain in Paris for almost four years.

The Impressionist and Post-Impressionist masters.

Fauvism, the term (meaning "wild beasts") first coined in 1905 by French writer and art critic Louis Vauxcelles (pseudonym of Louis Mayer) to describe the style of painting in which colors are the all-important theme of the work. Henri Matisse (1869–1954) was the principal artist of the Fauve group. Fauvism eventually gave way to Cubism.

academies that were the markets and streets of Paris. There I saw still lifes that were richer, newer, and more pictorial than the still lifes of Snyders; they were just like the still lifes of Chardin and Cézanne. There I saw landscapes on the outskirts of Paris that were not heavy museum landscapes like those of Hobbema or Ruysdael, but tangible, throbbing with the spirit of these times, like the landscapes of Van Gogh, Monet, and Seurat; and all the chance passersby were alive and whole, as in Cézanne, Renoir, and the others. Things, nature, people, illuminated by this "freedom-light," were immersed, one would have said, in a bath of color. Never before had I seen such pictures. And it was the crowning of a unique period in the art of that time in this unique country of the world.

From the street, from the square, from the fields, you enter the French rooms of the Louvre, where this pictorial revolution sought its sources so as later to surpass them. A comrade with whom I had arrived in Paris said to me one day, "Poor us, what can we do, what can we achieve here? Everything has been said and said again. Better to buy a ticket and go home." But I remained, and I remained myself. I replied, to myself as well as to my comrade, "Why take something from others, and in everyone's view? They make me enthusiastic, and my enthusiasm having, so to speak, gone around the world, comes back to its starting point." Having witnessed this unique technical revolution of art in France, in thought, in the soul if you like, I went back to my country and lived as though turned inside out.

The doubts, the dreams that had already tormented me when I was still a young boy in my native town now gave me no respite. Exactly what painter would I have liked to be? I do not say, would I have been able to be? Young as I was, I did not conceive of Art as a profession, not as a trade: paintings did not seem to me destined exclusively for decorative, domestic purposes. I said to myself: Art is in some way a mission, and one needn't be afraid of such an old word. And whatever the revolution in realistic technique may be, it has touched only the surface. It is neither the so-called real color, nor the conventional color, that truly colors the object. It is not what is called perspective that adds depth. It is neither the shadow nor the light that illuminates the subject, and the third dimension of the Cubists still does not allow you to see the subject from all sides. Did I perhaps speak of a certain "vision of the world," of a conception that would lie outside the subject and the eye? But to think like that, during that technical, realistic period of art, laid you open to the accusation of falling into "literature." I confess that when I heard this word uttered by young avant-garde painters and poets, I went a little pale. I went pale, not from shame, not from fear for myself, but rather from fear for the others, for the ones who said it, through foreseeing some of the consequences. I saw myself as in a mirror, different and strange; it seemed to me that each word uttered, not to mention its effect at the time, sooner or later has its consequences.

While I was under the spell of the eye of French painters, of their sense of measure, I couldn't help thinking: perhaps another eye, another view, exists, an eye of another kind and otherwise placed, not there where one is accustomed to find it. For example, the trees painted by Monet are good for Monet. Perhaps they are waiting, these trees, to be shown once again. Perhaps, it seemed to me, other dimensions exist—a fourth, a fifth dimension that would not simply be that of the eye, and which, I insist, did not seem to me to have anything at all to do with "literature," with "symbolism," or with what is called poetry in art. Perhaps it was something more abstract, liberated—abstract not in the sense of not recalling the real, but rather something ornamental, decorative, and always partial. Perhaps it was something that intuitively gave rise to a range of plastic as well as psychical contrasts, infusing the picture and the eye of the spectator with new and unaccustomed elements and conceptions. There, in brief, is the feeling that took possession of me in Paris in 1910.

As for literature and symbolism in art, did I not flee them myself? Literature, as I saw it, was not confined exclusively to the large compositions of the old "Romantics," but was to be seen just as well in the simple still lifes of the Impressionists and Cubists, since "literature" in painting is everything that can be

Jean Baptist Chardin (1699–1779).

Meindert Hobbema (1638–1709) and John Michael Ruysdael (1694–1770), both Dutch landscape painters.

Probably Chagall's friend Victor Mekler, also an art student from Vitebsk. He left Paris a year later.

explained and told from beginning to end. And it seemed to me that it was only by, so to speak, "killing" a still life or a landscape—and not simply by breaking them up and distorting them in their forms and surface—that it was possible to bring this same still life or landscape back to life. Thus a kind of dualism took shape in me. On the one hand, I became enthusiastic over these splendid examples of formal art: sometimes Delacroix, sometimes Ingres or Chardin. On the other, the soul was sinking in spite of everything into a certain sadness and was thirsting for a way out.

Eugène Delacroix (1798–1863); Jean-Auguste-Dominique Ingres (1780–1867).

MARC CHAGALL

From *My Life*

1922

IN PARIS

In 1910, after he had selected two pictures, Vinaver guaranteed me a monthly subsidy that would permit me to live in Paris.

I set out.

Four days later, I arrived in Paris.

Only the great distance that separates Paris from my native town prevented me from returning to it immediately or at least after a week, or a month.

I even wanted to invent some sort of holiday as an excuse to go home.

The Louvre put an end to all those hesitations.

When I made the tour of the Veronese room and the rooms in which Manet, Delacroix, Courbet are hung, I wanted nothing more. . . .

In Paris I thought I had found everything, in particular the art of my craft.

Everywhere I saw convincing proof of it in the museums and in the Salons.

Perhaps the East had lost its way in my soul; or the memory of that dog-bite re-echoed in my mind.

But it was not only in my profession that I sought the meaning of art.

It was as though the gods stood before me.

I didn't want to think any more about the neoclassicism of David, of Ingres, the romanticism of Delacroix and the reconstruction of early drawings of the followers of Cézanne and of Cubism.

Pierre Jean David (1788–1856), French sculptor.

I felt we were still playing around on the surface, that we are afraid of plunging into chaos, of shattering, of turning upside down the familiar ground under our feet.

The day after my arrival, I went to the Salon des Indépendants.

The friend who went with me had warned me it would be impossible to cover the entire Salon in a single day. He, for example, came out exhausted every time he visited it. Pitying him from the bottom of my heart but following my own method, I rushed through all the first rooms as if I were racing ahead of a torrent and I dashed towards the middle rooms.

That's the way I conserved my strength.

I went straight to the heart of French painting of 1910.

And there I clung.

No academy could have given me all I discovered by gorging myself on the exhibitions of Paris, on its picture shop windows, its museums.

Beginning with the Markets where, for lack of money, I bought only a piece of a long cucumber, the working-man in his blue overalls, the most zealous followers of Cubism, everything showed a definite feeling for order, clarity, an accurate sense of form, of a more painterly type of painting even in the works of lesser artists.

I don't know whether anyone has been able to form a clearer idea than I of the almost insurmountable difference which, up to 1914, separated French painting from the painting of other lands. It seems to me they had very little notion of it abroad.

As for me, I've never stopped thinking about that.

It is not a question of the natural aptitudes, more or less great, of an individual, or of a people.

Other forces come into play, organic or psycho-physical on the whole, that predispose one either to music, painting, literature, or sleep.

After living for some time in a studio at the Impasse du Maine, I moved into another studio more in keeping with my means, "La Ruche" (The Beehive).

That was the name given to a hundred or so studios surrounded by a little garden and very close to the Vaugirard slaughterhouses. In those studios lived the artistic Bohemia of every land.

While in the Russian ateliers an offended model sobbed; from the Italians' came the sound of songs and the twanging of a guitar, and from the Jews debates and arguments, I sat alone in my studio before my kerosene lamp. A studio jammed with pictures, with canvases which, moreover, were not really canvases but my table napkins, my bed sheets, my nightshirts torn into pieces.

Two or three o'clock in the morning. The sky is blue. Dawn is breaking. Down below and a little way off, they are slaughtering cattle, the cows low and I paint them.

I used to stay up all night long. It's now a week since the studio has been cleaned. Frames, eggshells, empty soup cans lie around helter-skelter.

My lamp burned, and I with it.

It burned until its glare hardened in the blue of morning.

Not until then did I climb up into my garret. I should have gone down into the street and bought some hot croissants on tick, but I went to bed. Later the cleaning woman came; I wasn't sure whether she came to set the studio to rights (is that absolutely necessary? At least, don't touch my table!) or whether she wanted to come up and be with me.

On the shelves, reproductions of El Greco, of Cézanne, lay side by side with the remnants of a herring I had cut in two, the head for the first day, the tail for the next and, thank God, a few crusts of bread.

But perhaps Cendrars will come and take me out to lunch.

Before my friends entered the studio, they always had to wait. That was to give me time to tidy up, to put on my clothes, for I worked in the nude. In general, I can't stand clothes, I'd rather not wear them and I have no taste in dressing.

No one buys my pictures.

I didn't think that was possible.

Once only, M. Malpel offered me twenty-five francs for a picture I was showing in the Salon—in case I shouldn't sell it.

"But, by all means, why wait!"

I don't know now what happened; twenty years later the pictures are selling. They even say that a real Frenchman, Gustave Coquiot, collects my pictures.

I should go to see him and thank him.

And I, on the eve of war, scattered haphazard nearly four hundred of my canvases in Germany, Holland, Paris, a bit everywhere.

No matter. At least, since they cost them nothing, the people who have them will take the trouble to hang them on their walls. . . .

In those days, one-man exhibits were rare: Matisse and Bonnard were almost the only ones to have them. The idea never so much as entered our heads.

I frequented the ateliers and the academies of Montparnasse and at the same time I was eagerly preparing for the Salons.

But how could I carry such conspicuous canvases through "La Ruche" and across Paris?

COLORPLATE 6

El Greco ("The Greek," 1541–1614), Spanish painter born in Greece.

Pierre Bonnard (1867–1947) became a painter after selling a poster to a champagne maker in 1889. He shared studios in Paris with Édouard Vuillard and Maurice Denis. His studio was a meeting place for the Nabi movement, which disbanded in 1899.

Temptation (Adam and Eve). 1912. Oil on
canvas. 63 ³/₁₆ x 44 ⁷/₈ in. (160.5 x 113.9 cm).
The Saint Louis Art Museum. Gift of Morton
D. May.

A good-hearted refugee agreed to take care of it, more for laughs than for anything else.

On the way my handcart met other handcarts also carrying pictures to the Salon. All of them were heading towards the wooden booths near the Place de l'Alma.

There I was shortly to see what distinguished my work from traditional French painting.

At last, the pictures are hung. In an hour the vernissage. But the censor walks over to my canvases and orders one of them removed: *The Ass and the Woman.*

My friend and I try to persuade him:

"But, sir, it's not at all what you think. No pornography is intended."

It's settled.

He agrees. The picture is hung again.

When I complained of being persecuted even in the Salon, the wife of a doctor whom I sometimes visited for conversation and consolation, told me:

"Well, all the better. That's what you deserve. Then don't paint that kind of picture."

I was only twenty, but I was already beginning to fear people.

But then the poet Rubiner came, Cendrars came and the light in his eyes was enough to console me. Many a time he gave me advice, for he was anxious about me, but I never listened to him, though he was right.

He persuaded me that I could work peacefully side by side with proud cubists for whom I was perhaps a nobody.

They did not bother me. I looked at them out of the corner of my eye and I thought:

"Let them eat their fill of their square pears on their triangular tables!"

Undoubtedly my early trends were a little strange to the French. And I looked at them with so much love! It was painful.

But my art, I thought, is perhaps a wild art, a blazing quicksilver, a blue soul flashing on my canvases.

And I thought: Down with naturalism, impressionism and realistic cubism!

They make me sad and they cramp me.

All questions—volume, perspective, Cézanne, African sculpture—are brought on the carpet.

Where are we going? What is this era that sings hymns to technical art, that makes a god of formalism?

May our folly be welcomed!

An expiatory bath. A revolution of fundamentals, not only of the surface.

Don't call me temperamental! On the contrary, I'm a realist. I love the earth.

THE POETS

With you I spring into the depths of Montjoie. As if dazzling lights flashed around you. As if a flight of white seagulls, or flakes of snowy spots, in single file, rose towards the sky.

There, another flame, light and clear-toned, Blaise, my friend Cendrars.

A chrome smock, socks each of a different color. Waves of sunshine, poverty and rhymes.

Threads of colors. Of liquid, flaming art.

Enthusiasm for pictures scarcely conceived. Heads, disjointed limbs, flying cows.

I remember all that, and you, Cendrars?

He was the first to come to see me at "La Ruche."

He read me his poems, looking out of the open window and into my eyes; he smiled at my canvases and both of us roared with laughter.

There was André Salmon. But where is he?

André Salmon (1881–1969), French poet, writer, and art critic who was a close friend to Apollinaire and Max Jacob.

Half Past Three (The Poet). 1911. Oil on canvas. 77 ⅛ x 57 in. (196 x 145 cm). The Philadelphia Museum of Art. The Louise and Walter Arensberg Collection.

I hear his name spoken. His pale face glows. I have just shaken hands with him.

Here is Max Jacob. He looks like a Jew.

That's the way he looked to me alongside Apollinaire.

One day we went together to lunch not far from "La Ruche."

I wasn't sure whether he had even forty sous in his pocket. And he, did he think I had enough to pay for the meal?

We lunched on salad, sauce, salt, everything that begins with an "s."

Afterwards, we climbed slowly up to his place in Montmartre. He had much free time and I had even more.

At last, his apartment house, his courtyard, his dark little hole, the entrance door at the side—a regular Vitebsk courtyard. Little pictures are hung in the entrance, just beyond the threshold.

What did we talk about? In what language?

I understood very little. To tell the truth, I was alarmed.

His eyes glistened and rolled constantly. He stretched his body, moved about restlessly. Suddenly, he was quiet. Moving his half-opened mouth, he whistled. Then he laughed and his eyes, his chin, his arms, called to me, captivated me.

I said to myself: "If I follow him, he will devour me whole and throw my bones out of the window."

Max Jacob (1876–1944), French poet and artist.

Here is the garret of Apollinaire, that gentle Zeus.

In verses, in numbers, in flowing syllables, he blazed a trail for all of us.

He came out of his corner bedroom and a smile spread slowly over his broad face. His nose was sharply pointed and his gentle, mysterious eyes sang of voluptuousness. He carried his stomach as if it were a collection of complete works and his legs gesticulated like arms.

In his garret there were always many discussions.

In one corner sits a nondescript little man.

Apollinaire goes over to him and wakes him:

"Do you know what we must do, Monsieur Walden? We must arrange an exhibit of this young man's works. You don't know him? . . . Monsieur Chagall . . ."

One day Apollinaire and I went out together to dine at Baty's in Montparnasse.

On the way, he suddenly stopped:

"Look, there's Degas. He's crossing the street. He's blind."

Alone, frowning, looking surly, Degas was striding along, leaning on his cane.

While we were eating, I asked Apollinaire why he didn't introduce me to Picasso.

"Picasso? Do you want to commit suicide? That's the way all his friends end," replied Apollinaire, smiling as always.

What a whale of an appetite, I thought, as I watched him eat.

Perhaps he has to eat so much to feed his mind.

Maybe you can eat talent. Eat, and above all, drink, and perhaps the rest will come of itself.

Wine rang in his glass, meat clattered between his teeth. And all the while he was greeting people right and left. Acquaintances on every side!

Oh! Oh! Oh! Ah! Ah! Ah!

And at the slightest pause, he emptied his glass, resplendent in his huge napkin.

Lunch over, swaying and licking our lips, we walked back to "La Ruche."

"You've never been here?"

"That's where Bohemians, Italians and Jews live; there are some young girls, too. Perhaps we'll find Cendrars in the corner café, Passage de Dantzig."

"We'll surprise him. He'll open his mouth as wide as two eggs, and quickly tuck in his pockets some verses he's just written."

I dare not show Apollinaire my canvases.

"I know, you're the standard bearer of Cubism. But I should like something else."

What else? I'm embarrassed.

We go down the dark corridor where water drips ceaselessly, where piles of garbage are heaped up.

A round landing; a dozen or so doors with numbers on them.

I open mine.

Apollinaire enters cautiously, as if he were afraid the whole building might suddenly collapse and drag him down in the ruins.

Personally I do not think a scientific bent is a good thing for art.

Impressionism and Cubism are foreign to me.

Art seems to me to be above all a state of soul.

All souls are sacred, the soul of all the bipeds in every quarter of the globe.

Only the upright heart that has its own logic and its own reason is free.

The soul that has reached by itself that level which men call literature, the illogic, is the purest.

I am not speaking of the old realism, nor of the symbolism-romanticism that has contributed very little; nor of mythology either, nor of any sort of fantasy, but of what, my God?

You will say, those schools are merely formal trappings.

Primitive art already possessed the technical perfection towards which pre-

Man Carrying Street. 1916. Ink on paper. 12 ⁵/₈ x 8 ⁵/₈ in. (32 x 21.8 cm). Musée National d'Art Moderne, Centre Georges Pompidou, Paris.

Study for The Drinker. 1911. Gouache on paper. 8 x 10 in. (20. 3 x 25.4 cm). Musée National d'Art Moderne, Centre Georges Pompidou, Paris.

sent generations strive, juggling and even falling into stylization.

I compared these formal trappings with the Pope of Rome, sumptuously garbed, compared to the naked Christ, or the ornate church, to prayer in the open fields.

Apollinaire sat down. He blushed, swelled out his chest, smiled and murmured: "Supernatural! . . ."

The next day I received a letter, a poem dedicated to me: "Rotsoge."

Like beating rain, the meaning of your words strikes us.

Surely you are dreaming today of aquarelles, of the new surface of painting, of poets of ravaged destiny, of us all of whom in times past you spoke.

Has he gone, has he faded away or is he still with us, with his brilliant smile on his mortal face?

And I am dragging out my days on the Place de la Concorde or near the Luxembourg Gardens.

I look at Danton and Watteau, I pull off leaves.

Oh! If astride the stone chimera of Notre Dame I could manage with my arms and my legs to trace my way in the sky!

There it is! Paris, you are my second Vitebsk!

GUILLAUME APOLLINAIRE

From *Chroniques d'Art*

1914

The Jewish race has not yet made its mark in the plastic arts. Among the moderns, for example, Pissarro is virtually the only important Jewish pioneer of Impressionism.

Berlin's Sturm Gallery has brought to Germany the works of a number of young French painters, in particular Delaunay and Fernand Léger. Currently exhibited at the gallery are works by a young Russian Jewish painter, Marc Chagall. I will add that paintings of his may be seen in Paris at the Malpel Gallery, on rue Montaigne.

Chagall is a colorist whose imagination at times derives from the fancies of Slavic folk imagery, yet always transcends it.

He is an extremely supple artist, capable of monumental paintings, and unconstrained by any single school.

For Apollinaire. 1911. Pencil on paper.
13 x 10 ¼ in. (33 x 26 cm). Musée National
d'Art Moderne, Centre Georges Pompidou,
Paris.

JEAN-JACQUES LÉVÊQUE

"Chagall and the Poets"

1982

Guillaume Apollinaire (pseudonym of Wilhelm Apollinaris de Kostrowitsky, 1880–1918), poet and critic, was an early supporter of Chagall who, upon seeing Chagall's work for the first time, described it as "supernatural."

Jean-Jacques Lévêque, French author and art critic.

He is asleep / He is awake / Suddenly he paints / He takes a church and paints a church / He takes a cow and paints with a cow / With a sardine / With heads, hands, knives / He paints with a bull's sinew / He paints with all the dirty passions of a small Jewish town.

Most of us are acquainted with this poem by Blaise Cendrars, one of several that he dedicated to painting, to Chagall—for that lover of life, of myths, and who had employed some rather ignominious epithets concerning art critics, was able in his poems of rare daring (especially at that time) to find the most striking counterpoints with plastic forms to accompany them. However, Chagall, undoubtedly because of the subjects he treats and because of his style, has found his best commentators among the poets.

* * *

When Chagall arrived in Paris in 1910 it was during the effervescent period of Montparnasse. The painter first lived with his compatriot Ehrenbourg, Impasse du Maine, but he was attracted by "La Ruche," that high place of living art. La Ruche's title to glory is not only to have been the refuge of Léger and Soutine, but it was also where Cendrars, thanks to Chagall, discovered painting. It was also a time of friendship. Chagall made several sincere and valuable ones that accompanied his work in a time of complete evolution: Canudo, publisher of the review "Montjoie," Guillaume Apollinaire, of course, who was to write admirably about the painter, Léger, everyone's friend and also interested in poetry, Max Jacob who, like Chagall, inherited a rich folklore that was never dissociated from life, André Salmon, Roger de la Fresnaye, Robert Delaunay, Modigliani, André Lhote, Albert Gleizes, Maurice Raynal, Roger Allard, Dunoyer de Segonzac....

Remembrance. 1914. Mixed media on paper.
12 1/2 x 8 5/8 in. (31.7 x 22.3 cm). The
Solomon R. Guggenheim Museum, New York.
Gift, Solomon R. Guggenheim, 1941. Photo-
graph by Robert E. Mates, © the Solomon R.
Guggenheim Foundation, New York.

*Paul Eluard (1895–1952), French poet and
friend of the Surrealist painters in Paris.*

*Max Ernst (1891–1976) organized, with André
Breton, the Dada group.*

Thus, the first interlude ended, outside of Russia that he was later to refind at
war and, soon after, in revolution. However, the letter from Blaise Cendrars,
"Come back, you are famous and Vollard is waiting for you," was enough to bring
him back to Paris to a studio where Lenin had lived, Avenue d'Orléans. In 1923,
the surrealists rehabilitated the art of the unconscious mind, the virtues of madness, of desire, of the dream, of the irrational and a new quest for the Grail.
Eluard, Ernst and Breton asked him to join them and, thus, Chagall became with
others, and in spite of himself, and in virtue of a logic peculiar to surrealists, an
artist worthy of appearing on the list of a movement which was taking an increasingly definite form and winning the interest of a larger public. However, the quality of this language that re-establishes the simple life, the magic of everyday living and distills a sort of wiseness, came to full bloom in the illustrations of the
Fables of La Fontaine, commissioned by Ambroise Vollard in 1925. Soon after,
he worked on *The Circus.* Chagall's themes are always involved with the magical
aspects of life. During this period he wrote *My Life.* Chagall walks straight into
his legendary world; his relationship with poetry is suddenly blended with his
relationship with life. Has he been done justice? André Breton in his penetrating
studies on painting situates Chagall very precisely: "For a long time there existed

a large gap in the origins of Dadaism and Surrealism—which were to bring about the fusion of poetry and the plastic arts—in that Chagall was not given enough credit. The poets themselves owe much to him—Apollinaire himself was inspired by Chagall in writing perhaps the "freest" poem of this century, "Across Europe," the Blaise Cendrars of "Trans-Siberian Prose"—right up to Maiakowsky and Essenine who speak of him in their most paroxysmal accents. . . ."

This fundamental understanding between the painter and the poets is centered in a well-defined domain that corresponds to the revelation of a marvelous realism in which painters, poets and even musicians cooperated at the beginning of the century. Each painter creates a geography according to certain unconscious impulses, the motors of the soul undoubtedly, and if one painter goes directly towards immediate reality, if another goes towards the cosmos, a last one will plunge into the crowd with the delight of a Peeping Tom. Chagall, true to himself, has decided to go towards the most natural and intemporal poetry. It is his element, his leaven. The blue and red rivers he makes flow through forests of heads, his animals endowed with wings that decuple space, his faces marked by the sign of recognition, his houses capsized like shipwrecks—in short, that universe both healthy but outmoded, supercharged by the power of dreams—are poetic space. The attraction this work has for poets is not the least proof that it can only be understood through poetry. . . .

A prophet, the poet in this case, like the painter, speaks of the multiple aspects of the world, of its instants, of its problems. It is a place of grief, of tears and joy of which, since the beginning of expression, art is made, whether by word or by image. Thus, Chagall has attained, not simply the secret of beings and things but the most total reality, the most general: the reality of legends.

BLAISE CENDRARS

"La Ruche"

c. 1915

Stairways doors stairways
And his door opens like a newspaper
Covered with visiting cards
And then it closes again.
Disorder, this is the land of disorder
There are photographs of Léger, photographs of Tobeen that you really
    don't see
And behind your back
Behind your back
Frenetic works
Sketches designs frenetic works
And oil paintings . . .
*"We guarantee the absolute purity of our
Catsup"*
Says a label
The window is an almanac
When the giant steamshovels of the lightning raucously unload the barges
    of the
sky and empty the rumbling dumpcarts of thunder
The heavens fall
Pellmell

Dadaism (1916–1922), nihilistic precursor of Surrealism, started in Zurich during World War I. Dadaism was an anti-art movement intended to be outrageous and scandalous.

Surrealism, the brainchild of André Breton, followed the demise of Dadaism in 1922. Breton gathered up the remnants of the Dada group and assigned the word "surrealiste" to their work, defined by Apollinaire as "pure psychic automatism." Surrealists intended to express verbally, visually, or in writing the time process of thought.

Blaise Cendrars (1887–1961), French poet, novelist, and adventurer, was one of Chagall's first friends and admirers. Before leaving Paris for Russia in 1914, Chagall left his paintings with Cendrars. Years later, thinking Chagall was dead, Cendrars sold most of the paintings. On his return to Paris in 1922 Chagall broke his relationship with Cendrars.

Cossacks the Christ a rotting sun
Roofs
Sleepwalkers a few goats
A werewolf
Petrus Borel
Insanity winter
A genii split like a peach
Lautréamont
Chagall
Poor child beside my wife
Morose enjoyment
His shoes are down at the heels
There's an old stewpan full of chocolate
You see the lamp double
And my drunkenness when I go to see him
Empty bottles
Bottles
Zina
(We talked of her)
Chagall
Chagall
Astride ladders of light

GUILLAUME APOLLINAIRE

"Rotsoge"

c. 1915

To the painter Chagall

Your scarlet face your biplane convertible into hydroplane
Your round house where a smoked herring swims
I must have a key to eyelids
It's a good thing we have seen Mr. Panado
And we are easy on that score
What do you want my öld pal M.D.
90 or 324 a man in the air a calf who gazes out of the belly of its mother
I looked a long while along the roads
So many eyes are closed at the roadside
The wind sets the willow groves weeping
Open open open open open
Look but look now
The old man is bathing his feet in the basin
Una volta ho inteso say Ach du lieber Gott
And I began to cry reminiscing over our childhoods
And you show me a dreadful purple
This little painting where there is a cart which reminded me of the day
A day made out of pieces of mauves yellows blues greens and reds
When I left for the country with a charming chimney holding its bitch in leash
I had a reed pipe which I would not have traded for a French Marshal's baton
There aren't any more of them I haven't my little reed pipe any more
The chimney smokes far away from me Russian cigarettes
Its bitch barks against the lilacs

Portrait of Apollinaire. 1911–12. Ink and colored pencil on paper. 10 ⁵/₈ x 8 ⁵/₈ in. (27 x 22 cm). Musée National d'Art Moderne, Centre Georges Pompidou, Paris.

And the vigil lamp is burned out
On the dress petals have fallen
Two gold rings near some sandals
Kindle in the sun
While your hair is like the trolley cable
Across Europe arrayed in little many-colored fires.

PIERRE SCHNEIDER

From *The Louvre Dialogues*

1967

Pierre Schneider, an American writer and art critic living in Paris. He is the art critic of the French magazine L'Express.

Marc Chagall took the walk we are about to begin fifty-seven years ago for the first time. It was the day after he arrived in Paris in 1910.

"I hurried at once to the Salon des Indépendants (the Salon d'Automne was for successful artists). I went quickly to the moderns, at the far end. There were the Cubists: Delaunay, Gleizes, Léger. . . . And then, I raced to the Louvre. A magic name . . ."

"Why to the Louvre?"

"I felt that the truth was there. The moderns hadn't passed the test yet. There, it was serious."

"The test of time?"

"No, not time. Something else . . ."

Fifty-seven years ago, but the memory is still clear:

"Way up, in the Grande Galerie, I discovered Bassano's big painting. A mixture of people and animals. I sensed that it was very important."

Robert Delaunay (1885–1941), inventor of "Orphic Cubism," which was mainly concerned with the emotional effects of pure color.

Albert Gleizes (1881–1953), one of the first of the flat-pattern Cubists and abstract artists.

Bassano, of the family of four Venetian painters working in Bassano in the sixteenth century.

Beyond a doubt, the Louvre had shown him, as a welcome, a kind of Chagall. The dream of the self-educated adolescent from Vitebsk, then, did have an equivalent in the pictorial tradition of the Latin West. The undertaking became possible. The museum as a school? It does not seem so:

"I go to the Louvre to fortify myself, control myself. One hopes to learn something, but it is no use. Nothing helps us. There are no assurances, no certitudes. Learn?" He laughs. *"Nothing! One does not learn how to paint. I am against the well-drawn, the well-painted. Cézanne had no draftsmanship, nothing."*

Is not that precisely what the Louvre is? Here, time and place no longer exist; there are no more fathers, sons, or brothers; no more causes, or effects. He says:

"It is the cemetery for genius."

But what he means by that is that the work, behind the frontier marked by the museum, is snatched from history, released.

"Death helps one to see a great deal."

Thus the adventure would be very simple. A dream, so intimate that it occurs in the margin of history, encouraged by the encounter with a work that owes nothing more to time, materializes. A symbol of such a conjuncture: at this very moment, Chagall is being exhibited at the Louvre.

In fact, he seems to have foiled the ravages of time, like a refugee who has eluded a hundred police round-ups. This man of eighty years and more is possessed of a stupefying physical vigor and mental vivacity. His eyes are now mocking, now tender, his smile ready, his step and speech rapid. There are people who polish themselves little by little until they become their own myth. What makes of Chagall a legendary being—passers-by recognize him and ask for his autograph—on the contrary, is that he simply has not changed. An uninterrupted childhood, because nourished exclusively by his dreams. All attention to his interior monologue, as Harpo Marx, whom Chagall resembles a little, is silent in his films. Angels do not age.

Simple, too simple. Chagall's eyes are wide open.

"I see things. I am a terrible, a formidable critic. Ever since 1910, I have rarely been wrong. Except about Rouault: he bored me."

Georges Rouault (1871–1958), French painter of religious subjects and the circus. A pupil of Gustave Moreau.

I admit that I was skeptical, at first: criticism must be able to bite. But as we wended our way along the quays, our conversation convinced me: the angel has teeth.

"Bonnard? A beefsteak that has been handled too much. 'Finger painting.' A little bourgeois. A man who does not look you straight in the eye. Matisse, yes! That rousing anarchy, that dash!"

"You have never been wrong, you say?"

"Yes, of course. I believed in Gleizes too much. I saw in him a sort of Courbet of Cubism. Today, I have a higher opinion of Delaunay at the time when he was modest than later, when he was pushing himself. He used to reproach me: 'Chagall, you don't know the tricks of the trade.' But he knew them. And yet, today, I notice, his work is falling apart. On the other hand, I used to think: La Fresnaye, he is a nice artist; now, he has gained scope."

Roger de la Fresnaye (1885–1925).

This is because then Chagall was immersed in history, which is always unjust:

COLORPLATE 24. *Introduction to the Jewish Theater*. 1920. Tempera and gouache on canvas.
111 $^7/_8$ x 308 $^3/_4$ in. (284.2 x 784.2 cm). Tret'iakov Gallery, Moscow.

COLORPLATE 25. *Introduction to the Jewish Theater* (detail). 1920.

COLORPLATE 26. *Introduction to the Jewish Theater* (detail). 1920.

COLORPLATE 27. *Music*. 1920. Tempera and gouache on canvas.
83 7/8 x 41 in. (213 x 104 cm). Tret'iakov Gallery, Moscow.

COLORPLATE 28. *Dance.* 1920. Tempera and gouache on canvas.
84 1/4 x 42 1/2 in. (214 x 108.5 cm). Tret'iakov Gallery, Moscow.

COLORPLATE 29. *Drama.* 1920. Tempera and gouache on canvas.
83 1/2 x 42 1/8 in. (212 x 107 cm). Tret'iakov Gallery, Moscow.

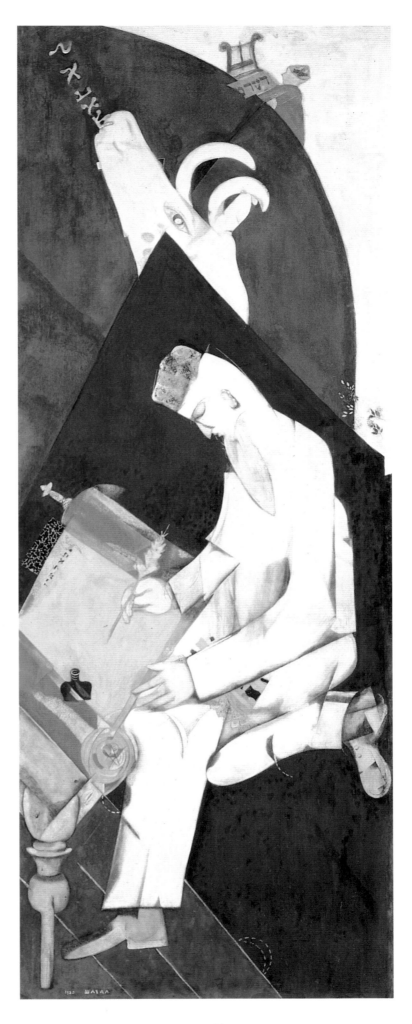

COLORPLATE 30. *Literature*. 1920.
Tempera and gouache on canvas. 85 x 32 in. (216 x 81.3 cm).
Tret'iakov Gallery, Moscow.

COLORPLATE 31. *Love on the Stage*. 1920. Tempera and gouache on canvas.
111 $^{7}/_{8}$ x 98 $^{1}/_{4}$ in. (284 x 249.6 cm). Tret'iakov Gallery, Moscow.

To My Betrothed. 1911. Gouache, oil, and watercolor over graphite on paper. 24 x 17 ½ in. (61 x 44.5 cm). The Philadelphia Museum of Art. Gift of Fiske and Marie Kimball.

Francis Picabia (1879–1953), French painter who claimed to have painted the first abstract painting before Kandinsky.

Camille Corot (1796–1875).

Kurt Schwitters (1887–1948).

Françoise Jean-Baptiste Pater (1695–1736).

"I saw the chemical difference between Picabia and Léger very clearly, but it didn't matter much. The closer you get to your times, the less close you feel. Even Corot seemed too realistic to me during that period. Monet, I did not want to look at him. I discovered him after the war, on the boat that brought me back from America. There, on the ocean, I asked myself the question: whose color really pours forth naturally? And I answered: Monet. Today, for me, Monet is the Michelangelo of our times, from the chemical point of view."

History's attenuation liberates clearsightedness, as one can only see that a lamp is lighted after sundown. On the condition, naturally, that it is burning.

"I can tell if you were born with a voice or not. There is no professionalism. The technique employed means nothing. Dadaism is not so great, but Schwitters made some marvelous works."

Chagall has a name for that lighted lamp, that critical mind:

"In our own times, the eye does not work very well. We do not see the differences. We do not see the chemistry. But later, we see it automatically. Because it alone exists. Watteau endured for us not because of his figures, but because of chemistry. Pater has the same figures, but he has not endured. Today, for me, there is chemistry. All the rest—realism or anti-realism, figuration or non-figuration—no longer matters."

Well, then, why can we not see clearly right off, why not turn on in art that second lighting which extinguishes everything that is not what Chagall calls "chemistry"? Because it is not possible.

"To arrive at that, at the Louvre, I told myself that we had to overthrow what was before us, which was the realisms."

The road to lucidity necessarily passes through its opposite. A god is only omnipotent in relation to man, and the untemporal is born of time. The lamp of second sight can only light itself at the blinding fire of history. Despite his personal, historical, geographical and cultural distance from the Parisian milieu which greeted him in 1910, Chagall at once and instinctively understood this: before going to the Louvre, he ran to the Salon des Indépendants. A simple phrase, spoken in passing, says more on this subject than lengthy explanations:

"I am the same age as Juan Gris."

At five minutes to ten, outside the great Denon Door, which is the main entrance, the crowd is already forming.

Juan Gris (1887–1927), Spanish artist who arrived in Paris in 1906. His paintings were a form of analytical Cubism.

"The Louvre, what a magic word! Going to the Louvre is like opening the Bible or Shakespeare. Of course, there are some boring things. Guido Reni is a pompier *but a* pompier *of great class."*

"Is there a spirit of the place?"

"Without any doubt. Transport the Louvre to the Trocadéro and it would lose everything. The Louvre is a magical thing. It has to do with the proportions, the architecture of the galleries. Even its shadows are propitious. The walls are extraordinary. At the Metropolitan Museum, at the National Gallery in Washington, you won't find this magic. At the Hermitage, yes. A large part of the fascination that the Louvre has for artists comes from this."

"There are those, however, who dream of burning it down."

"What for? Those who are inside it are just people like us. They had the good luck, or the bad luck, to get into the Louvre; that's all. Anyhow, half of them might have to get out again. The risk of destruction is not there."

"Where, then?"

"In the 'museographic' hanging, which smacks of vandalism. I don't like the way the Louvre has been reorganized very much. It is no longer recognizable. I loved those paintings that used to climb in serried ranks up to the moldings. Everything was on a par. It was intimate. Now the tendency is to put a single painting on one wall. They impose what should be seen, they emphasize. The isolated painting, set apart, says: respect me. I like to look, to find."

And Chagall informs me that while he has never stopped going to the Louvre, ever since 1910, it has always been by chance—or at least seemingly so. The other day, when I suggested that the two of us make this visit, he answered:

"Yes, but I don't want to go on purpose."

I was a little annoyed, I admit: the demand seemed to me not only impossible to satisfy but also gratuitous. But was it? In the form of a game, Chagall was presenting me with the problem that had been his own: how does one cultivate ingenuousness? The paradox was a parabole. And indeed the solution did exist since, at that very moment, we were entering the doors of the Louvre.

Chagall pulls me up the staircase opposite the one dominated by the *Winged Victory* and along toward the enormous suite of rooms on the second floor that harbors the juggernauts of French painting. Surprise: without the slightest hesitation his gaze travels to the canvases of a painter I imagined would be at opposite poles from his own nature, Courbet:

"He is an artist I am passionate about. Of the same breed as Masaccio, as Titian."

Masaccio (a.k.a. Tommuso di Giovanni, 1401–1428?); Titian (c. 1487–1576).

His eye wanders around the immense hall, stopping for an instant on *The Raft of the Medusa*:

"Yes, even Stags Fighting, *which is a little academic, touches me more than Géricault and his technique. Of course, it is eloquent; and Gros, too, with his* Battle of Eylau, *is quite something. But I don't feel like endorsing him, all the same. In the whole room, Courbet is the one who stands up."*

Theodore Géricault (1791–1824); Antoine-Jean Gros (1771–1835).

The Soldier Drinks. 1911–12. Oil on canvas. 43 x 37 ¹/₄ in. (109.1 x 94.5 cm). The Solomon R. Guggenheim Museum, New York. Photograph by Robert E. Mates, © The Solomon R. Guggenheim Foundation, New York.

"Why?"

"I don't know. He moves me. To tears, almost. He is the artist of life."

He is standing before *The Studio*:

"Somewhere, there, is the tragedy of death."

Against their background, a fog of variable density, are light or dark groups, like pulsations:

"Time, which comes, which goes, like a wave. We are shadowy. That is our sickness."

Now Chagall is before *The Burial at Ornans*. Chagall? I have trouble recognizing him. The voice is neutral, the speech precise, the eye active. He speaks, falls silent, steps back, moves closer, says something more, as an artist returns to his easel to place another brushstroke on his canvas:

"That sickliness, that execution, those flattering yet solid forms . . . I think of Braque: he could not do a bird properly, he would add some white, but that white! . . . Courbet's whites; the dog, the hats are vivid spots. And the blue of the man's stockings in the foreground: it is apart, not linked to the rest. It is very modern. . . . The enormous poetry of our times . . . Courbet is a naturalist, and yet he is a great poet. . . . The idea of death is everywhere in Courbet: it is not in Delacroix and Géricault, although they treated the theme of death."

After a fairly long silence, during which, at Chagall's suggestion, I think about the strange marriage of energy and decay in Courbet, he says:

"Perfection is close to death. Watteau, Mozart . . ."

And then, as we are heading for the transitional rooms where the paintings from the Beistegui Collection are hung, Chagall adds:

"Courbet was right when he turned toward reality. As for myself, I do not understand myself. I only know one thing: my paintbrush is guided from my belly."

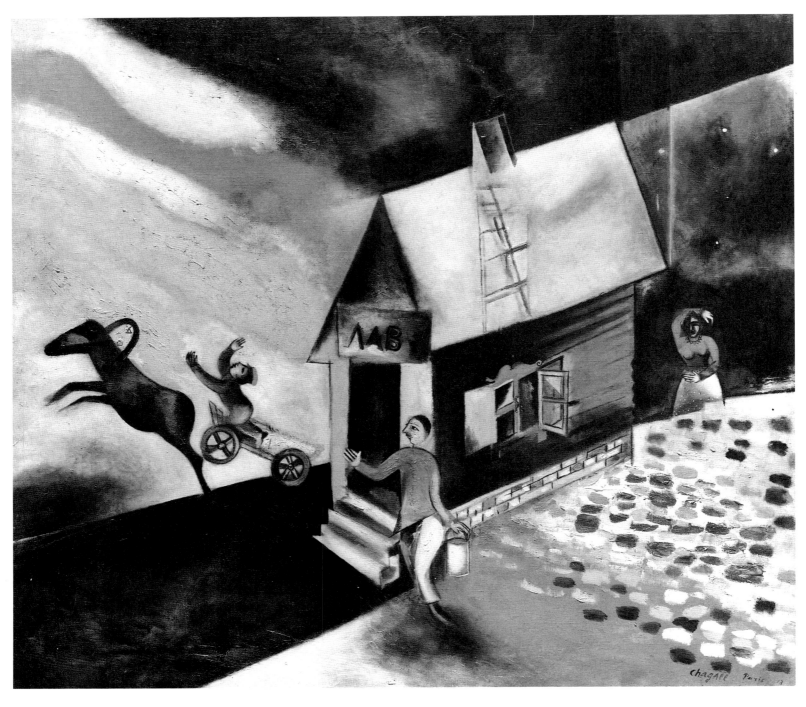

It is the guiding of the paintbrush that counts."

Now we are before *Lucretia* by Rubens, another in the family of vigorous, exuberant artists:

"He is a pig, but he is a great artist."

He does not linger at all. David, on the other hand, attracts him. Here is the unfinished *Napoleon*:

"I like it when paintings are left empty. . . . David has a delightful touch." His gaze shifts to the Ingres portraits, very close by. *"It is better than Ingres. A nobility. It is not dry, like Ingres."* He indicates the *Portrait of Madame de Verninac: "A delightful gray. What softness in the background!"*

We come to the thick-set *Madame Panckouke* by Ingres:

"He is more secretive, antinatural, abnormal. David is normal. Ingres disturbs me. There is something overstuffed about him. There is a sort of impotence in his portraits. They seem overworked, chiaroscuro. One thinks of Magritte." A pause. *"If one has an academic soul, one has had it since birth."*

In front of Delacroix's *Portrait of Chopin*:

"A great work. The great Delacroix is there. It is almost a Soutine."

The Flying Carriage. 1913. Oil on canvas. 42 x 47 ¹/4 in. (106.7 x 120 cm). The Solomon R. Guggenheim Museum, New York. Photograph by Robert E. Mates, © The Solomon R. Guggenheim Foundation, New York.

René Magritte (1898–1967).

And at Delacroix's *Self-Portrait*:

"One really senses that Manet will come. What intelligence!"

A glance at the Chassériau that happens to be there on a temporary basis (they have removed several paintings by Ingres to send them to the Centennial Exhibition):

Theodore Chassériau (1819–1856).

"A sort of La Fresnaye. He began with tricks."

He hastens over to Géricault's *Mad Woman*, which also replaces an Ingres portrait:

"There, this is the great Géricault. When Géricault painted reality, he was a great madman. When he made The Raft of the Medusa, *he was carrying out a plan. . . . One has to have a great deal of strength to sit down before a head and make a study of it."*

Farther on, the halls leading to the Grande Galerie occupied by the foreign collections. Chagall does not want to go there. He seems to prefer the French school today. I lead him, almost by force, to Goya's *La Marquesa de la Solana*, framed by the Davids and Ingres:

"It is like a Watteau—but no: it is not from our country. Like Velásquez. One can weep before Courbet and Watteau, but not before Velásquez or Goya. They are gods, but foreign gods. Zurbarán perhaps—such freshness! And Greco—but he was Greek. There is always that bullfight quality: this Goya succeeds like a moment of truth."

He turns away immediately to look at *Madame de Verninac* again:

"That yellowish liquid, what nobility! It is the café crème *one dreams about in foreign countries. I like that gray better than Goya's superb gray. That is what I left Russia for."*

This preference for French painting, since the beginning of our tour, is full of significance. Transposed in time and space, it re-enacts the young twenty-year-old's choice in leaving Vitebsk for Paris.

"My training has been French. I detest the Russian or Central European color. Their color is like their shoes. Soutine, myself—we all left because of the color. I was very dark when I arrived in Paris. I was the color of a potato, like Van Gogh. Paris is light." . . .

We retrace our steps through the French galleries, this time all the way to the Staircase of Honor. David's self-portrait:

"It is beautiful like Cézanne. It kills all of Ingres."

Delacroix, *The Women of Algiers in Their Apartment*:

"Magnificent, like his self-portrait. It moves me. His Raphaelesque folds are better than Courbet's. Courbet thought about death too much; he was an invalid."

Now we have come to the great neoclassical hall.

"Aie! Aie! Aie!" But he breathes freely again looking at *The Rape of the Sabines* and *The Coronation of Napoleon*:

"No matter what he does, David is never academic. One is born academic. Neither Delacroix, nor Courbet, nor Géricault is—but Ingres."

Chagall's gaze wanders among the David canvases.

"Madame Récamier, *marvelous. There is some Manet in it. But in* Leonidas, *there is Poussin. What softness, wrapped over everything! Never any dryness."* He points toward *The Oath of the Horaces*.

No chemistry without acid:

"Perhaps I might not feel so tenderly toward David if people weren't talking about Ingres so much these days."

The Cimabue in the staircase. The tone changes, as if we were passing from history to truth:

"Cimabue! My love, my god! When I arrived in Paris, it was a great shock." Silence. *"It transcends everything. That devoutness . . . No, I am not talking about the subject matter, but about the touch. Cimabue is more penetrating than Giotto. . . . You have to go to Watteau to find the equivalent. Rembrandt, Monet, Caravaggio, Masaccio, Cimabue, Watteau, these are my gods!"*

We descend the staircase. Passing before *Winged Victory*, Chagall whispers to me:

Menageries (Study for The Cattle Dealer).
1912. Gouache and ink with pencil on paper.
6 x 12 1/4 in. (15.2 x 31 cm). Private collection.

"It moves me more than Brancusi."

We pass a fresco, brought back from Ostia, *Hero Armed With a Sword*:

"This was done by a simple artisan. Art is like a good child: it should not go to school. One must not try to draw well, *paint* well. *School is harmful. When I came to France, there was no professionalism in me. I had no mission. For me, that has not changed."*

A window, through which we glimpse the delicate gray of Paris. Chagall goes over to it:

Constantin Brancusi (1876–1957).

"There is why we left Vitebsk. It is all of Le Nain, it is Watteau. The French are not always great, far from it, but there is this gray, this landscape in them. Fauvism can be as violent as it likes, it remains—in a Dufy, for example—French. Van Dongen has much more talent, but he vomits it."

Chagall is determined not to leave the French domain. Despite his age, despite the kilometers we have already covered, he drags me to the other end of the Louvre, way up high, where the new rooms for the eighteenth and nineteenth centuries are located, and again it is a David, *Madame Trudaine*, that greets us:

"The touch, marvelous! He is perhaps the first to have used such a light touch. The execution, it's everything; it is like the blood—the chemistry."

So saying, he goes over to the *Seated Nude, Mademoiselle Rose* by Delacroix:

"What nobility! Things like this, after all, are greater than Courbet."

There are Corots all around us. Chagall comes to a halt before *La Trinità dei Monti*:

"Ah! What an artist! There, that is France. It leaves one speechless. There is a god. He transcends everything. It looks like nothing. . . . That blondness, that gray, that is France. . . . What were the Impressionists trying to do, after him? He already did everything. A real painter. He has the chemistry. He is a prince. He can do anything. He is a Mozart." . . .

"The great chemistry is the same, always and everywhere," Chagall says before a Fayum portrait. *"This Fayum portrait and a Corot are the same thing."*

The "great chemistry" is that by which we rejoin the community of nature, the "little chemistry" being that by which we rejoin the human community:

Fayum portraits of the Fayum region of Upper Egypt dating from the first century B.C. to the third century A.D.

"The only pleasure I have: when the chemistry I produce in my canvases approaches the chemistry of nature. Like Monet, or the old Titian. . . . But one must live through one's times to reach that point."

For Chagall also, chemistry today is, above all, a matter of color. It is color that digs a tunnel to the untemporal in the canvas. Color depth: *"The color must be penetrating, as when one walks on a thick carpet,"* he wrote some time ago.

MARC CHAGALL

On Exhibiting His Paintings

November 14, 1911

Dear Sir,

Permit me to write you that which I omitted to say in my letter to Monsieur Dobuzhinsky. In sending three pieces to the *World of Art* Exhibition, I should like to exercise my rights as an exhibitor and show two works without approval by the commission: *Interior (The Birth)* and *The Room*.

Respectfully yours,
M. Chagall
Paris. Impasse du Maine 18

[Inscriptions]
[To the right of the upper drawing:]
No. 1 [*Birth* 1911]
Yellow frame
Plain ochre

[To the right of the middle drawing:]
No. 2 [*Interior II* 1911]
Very black frame of plain, unmoulded wood

[To the right of the lower drawing:]
No. 3 [*Dead Man* 1908]
Very yellow frame, *sky-coloured*
As far as possible:
In view of the possible objections of the Russian censorship, to keep my works on show as far as you can.

Hanging:
Not in a small room nor in shadow: not opposite a window with direct light. Hang leaning forwards: it would be good if they were to one side of a window.

Frames:
Should be simple, no. 2 could be recessed (in silvery-yellow ochre), 2 (very black), 3 (a lemon yellow)
Let me thank you in anticipation for everything
Chagall.
[The third page of this letter carries two drawings: part of the right-hand side has been cut away so that some of the righthand drawing and its inscription have been lost.]

The Painter in Front of His Easel. 1914. Watercolor and drawing on paper. 10 x 8 in. (25.4 x 20.3 cm). Musée National d'Art Moderne, Centre Georges Pompidou, Paris.

COLORPLATE I

103

[Above left-hand painting:]
A trace of the previous frame has been left on this painting (no. 3) and must be covered by the new yellow frame.
[Below the painting:]
simple, smooth frame of *sky colour*

[Inscription below right-hand painting:]
No. 1 *Interior*, not to go before commission, simple wooden frame *thickly* painted.

[Colour samples provided below:]
No. 1 ochre No. 2 black No. 3 yellow
lemon yellow

The Sacrifice of Abraham. 1912. Gouache on paper. 8 x 6 ³/4 in. (20.3 x 17 cm). Private collection.

RETURN TO RUSSIA

MARC CHAGALL

On the Art School in Vitebsk

April 2, 1920

Vitebsk

My dear Pavel Davidovich,
Thank you very much for your letters: I heartily beg you to forgive me for not replying straight-away. The only reason is that I am, on the one hand, incredibly absentminded and, on the other, I'm also busy. But the main thing is something else that doesn't allow me to put pen to paper. It's also probably because I'm finding it very difficult . . . to get down to painting. Such are the times we live in and the position of the modern artist. I'm very glad that you have written to me: you will find that I shall send you much more by way of an answer—I just need to sit down and do it. You ask, first of all, if I have some materials about the art college and artistic life here, in the town and outside it. I don't think it would be of much interest to collect everything that's published in the local press for you. However, as head of the college and, by force of circumstance, of the province's local artistic activities, I will give you some specific information about the arts here. I had the idea of organizing the art college after I returned from abroad and was working on my Vitebsk series of studies. There were then still a great many lamp-posts, pigs and fences in Vitebsk, and its artistic talents lay dormant. Tearing myself away from my palette, I rushed off to Peter [sburg] and to Moscow and at the end of 1918 the college was founded. It accommodates 500 boys and girls of various ages, with varying abilities, and already of [text indecipherable] trends. Early on, the professorial and administrative staff included (apart from myself) Dobuzhinsky, Puni, Boguslavskaya, Lyubavina, Lissitzky, Kozlinskaya, and Tilberg. Now there are Malevich, Ermolaeva, Kogan, Lissitzky, Pen, Yakerson (a sculptor) and me (apart from the special instructors). The groupings of "trends" has now reached a critical point. They are (1) the young people around Malevich, and (2) the young people around me. We are both equally striving towards the left wing of art; however, we hold different views about such art's means and ends. To talk about this question now, of course, would take a long time. It's better to talk about it when we meet or to write a letter on the subject. I'll take the liberty, perhaps, of sending you my thoughts about this [modern Russian art] separately. I'll tell you one thing: I was born in Russia (and in the [Jewish] Pale of Settlement, moreover) and—though I trained abroad—I have a particularly sharp appreciation of all that's going on here in the arts (especially the fine arts). I remember all too painfully the brilliance of the original. To continue: the college has an art library (not very large, it is true); a joiners' workshop, studios of graphics, printing, decorative arts, and a moulding workshop, apart from the ordinary painting and sculptural studios; its own store of materials and its own . . . bath-house. A college museum is being organized from the award-winning works at the students' shows and from their demonstration sketches. There is a student group and theatrical club at the college which recently, by the way, staged Kruchenykh's [Futurist opera] *Victory over the Sun* in the town, acting and painting the sets themselves. Now they're working on *Hung on the Cross*. A book about the college is being prepared. However, there's rather a problem

Pavel Ettinger (1866–1948), an art specialist and collector, corresponded with Chagall for more than thirty years. Twenty-five of his letters are preserved in the archives of the State Pushkin Museum of Fine Arts in Moscow.

Bella and Ida in 1917. Collection Ida Chagall, Paris.

Members of the Summer 1919 School
Committee. El Lissitzky seated first from left,
Chagall seated third from left, Pen seated third
from right. Collection Ida Chagall, Paris.

with paper. That's roughly what is happening at the Vitebsk People's College of
Art. Outside the college the Studio of Fine Arts is getting ready to erect the second monuments in Vitebsk, to Karl Liebknecht and Karl Marx (in time for May
1st); preparations are being made to decorate the town on May 1st, a district area
school is being organized and a "show-window of the arts" is being opened. The
10th of May Studio is beginning to acquire works by local artists with which to
fill the museum of modern art.

They began to organize a City Museum last year but so far, unfortunately, it
still mostly contains archaeological artistic materials rather than paintings; in this
respect I have already asked both the Museums and Fine Arts Departments of
Narkompros [People's Commissariat of Education] to send us pictures. Art
schools have opened in the surrounding district towns of Nevel, Velizh and Lepel.
There is also a State Studio of Decorative Art (for carrying out all commissions,
which combines all painters and artists). Lectures on art are not a strong point.
Lecturers do not come here from the capitals [i.e. Moscow and Petrograd] and
there is no staff lecturer on art in the college. Help us: perhaps you will find such
a person—let us know and send him to us. So far we've only organized a few
public meetings about art by ourselves.

The town, in short, has now fallen "under the sway" of artists. They fren-
ziedly argue about art and I'm worn out and longing to be "abroad" . . . When
all's said and done, there is no more honourable place for an artist (at least for
me) than behind his easel, and I'm dreaming of when I can do nothing but paint.
Of course, I do a little drawing but it's not the same. As far as your request for
various prints is concerned, I shall try myself to bring you some of them when
possible. As concerns my own drawing for you, I feel very awkward about sending it and do not know if it will do. We should meet sometime and then it would
be possible for you to choose. I hope to come to Moscow (and Petrograd). They
did ask me to organize an exhibition of my works but what's the point of organizing an exhibition of old works dating from before 1918 (and many of those have
been sold and scattered)?

As you can understand: I also want to come on college business and other
matters, and bring some works from Peter [sburg] to sell to the department as
they requested. This is a vast letter. I've written enough. I'm waiting for your
reply. I don't see Lissitzky, unfortunately, and cannot pass on your greetings—
and anyway I couldn't . . . Abram Markovich [Efros: Soviet art and theatrical spe-
cialist] will explain the situation to you. Did you by any chance hear what happened to my paintings at der Sturm [Der Sturm Gallery] in Berlin? Ber [Bir] went

there, after all, and according to Lunacharsky's article, some information came back. By the way, Ber took a letter from the International Bureau to Walden (the editor and owner of der Sturm).

You can write to me either at the college or at 9 Zadurovsky St.

Greetings and best wishes,
Marc Chagall

ANATOLY LUNACHARSKY

"Young Russian in Paris: Marc Chagall"

March 14, 1914

Anatoly Lunacharsky, Moscow's first Commissar of Art, appointed Chagall to head the Art School in Vitebsk.

He is already famous in Paris. His mad, childlike, fantastic canvases are terrible and yet funny at the same time, they irresistibly draw the eyes of visitors to the Salon . . .

Chagall is twenty-four years old; his large, strange eyes stare at me across the silly curls which fall on his forehead. He presents me with paintings and drawings. He has an amazing number of them. He adds that there are other works exhibited in St. Petersburg, Berlin and at the Salon des Indépendants. He clearly works extremely hard . . . *Our Family, Our Dining Room* and *Our Street* are titles which often recur in his work. His inspiration is drawn from the ordinary people of Lithuania. A hard, sad life. But, as if he were running away from the grip of boring people, Chagall mixes everything together. It is funnier, he says. And sometimes it is frightening. Black windows, half-drawn curtains, distorted faces, strange lamps, rickety clocks, heavy poses; reality blends with nightmare. Compositions which are chaotic to the point of satire . . . His childish drawing, simplistic and yet complex, full of expression, reveals an acute observation. And this psychological perspicacity strikes us like the wisdom of the ancients on the lips of a child . . .

IAKOV TUGENDHOLD

"A New Talent"

March 29, 1915

The exhibition "1915" includes the works of a young painter almost unknown in Moscow but already famous abroad, Marc Chagall. Drowning amongst pictorial bric-a-brac, lost in the Rayonnist works, they seem intimate and humble, almost retrograde. But that is a characteristic of all true art, of art which does not obey the demands of fashion but responds to the intrinsic needs of inspiration. Chagall is no stranger to the reality of our age; on the contrary, he was born in Vitebsk but was able, in Paris, to absorb what was to his taste. And his work, which blends

Parisian formalism with the almost childish naivety of the provinces, is full of emotion, depth and spirituality. We find there both the "sacred simplicity" of a true primitive and the cruelty of the descendants of Dostoevsky.

This premature complexity is even found in vastly different works, entirely dissimilar in their style, sometimes carefully faithful to nature, sometimes irrational and capricious. But irrationality and the absurd in Chagall's work are not signs of affectation. Moving beyond Kustodiev and Dobuzhinsky Chagall captures the barely perceptible yet awe-inspiring mystic essence of Russian life. . . . From this sleepy, drab life Chagall creates a marvellous legend . . . His palette, restrained or brilliant, responds to the demands of the image. His drawing can be lyrical and fantastic or realistic, as in the study entitled *At the Barber* . . .

But Chagall is not only aware of provincial life; his work also echos up-to-date European life. His *Soldiers with Bread* is sketched with a surprising mastery. And the nurse with red lips, wearing a dress which accentuates her femininity, is like the symbol of that healthy, life-giving force which every woman bears in times of war . . . Chagall's works which deal with war may be displeasing; but where other painters glory in wood or iron Chagall evokes men. Nowadays, when the mechanical culture is challenging the whole world and when the Futurist demon penetrates every pictorial work, art which expresses love for man and the world, which is full of lyricism, is particularly important.

The Clock is a much more abstract work . . . None the less it is not an illustration to some Symbolist story but a work which stands totally apart: it is the "insomnia" of the painter who, from his distant province, can see "universal" dreams. And it is perhaps in this backward province that new forces will be born; perhaps it is there that a new path will open in Russian art. In any case, Chagall is one of the great hopes of Russian Art.

MARC CHAGALL

On the Jewish Theater in Moscow

1921

"There you are," said Efros, "you've got walls. Do what you want with them."

This was in a building that looked as though it had been flattened after its inhabitants had fled.

"Look, here there will be benches for spectators, and the stage will be over there."

I exclaimed: "Away with the old theatre which stinks of garlic and sweat. Long live . . ."

And I began to paint.

My canvases and sketches were scattered on the floor and the actors had to jump over them, to walk in rooms and corridors that were under repair, amongst woodshavings, paint and sketches.

Bread ration cards and safe conducts littered the floor, reminders of the Civil War. I also lay on the floor. Sometimes that was unpleasant for me. For they lay dead people on the floor thus and people stand by their heads and cry. But in the end I got used to it and lay on the floor whispering my prayers.

I remembered my great-grandfather who had painted frescoes in a synagogue and I wished that I had been his apprentice a hundred years before. Inspire me, grandfather, you who now lie in the ground at Mogilev. Tell me what mysterious force guided your brush at Lezhne. Instill in me, oh bearded grandfather, several drops of Jewish truth.

In order to clear my brain I sent Yefrem, the janitor, for bread and milk. Milk that was not milk and bread that was not bread. Milk mixed with water and thickened with starch; bread of a mixture of oats and tobacco-coloured straw. But perhaps that was real milk, fresh milk from a real revolutionary cow. Perhaps it was Yefrem who added the water? Perhaps that rotter . . .

I ate and drank and felt better. Yefrem inspired me. He was a representative of the working classes or peasant class. What would I have done if he had not been there? His nose, his ugliness, his stupidity, his appearance annoyed and yet fascinated me. He stood by me and smiled beatifically. He did not know what he should look at—me or my work. Yefrem, where are you? Do you remember me? You were perhaps only a simple janitor but sometimes you stood by the entrance and checked the tickets. I have often thought that you could have acted on stage; they put Katz the concierge's wife on stage. She looked like a block of damp wood in the yard, covered in snow; take this block of wood up to the fourth floor and into the room and water runs out of it . . . She howled and declaimed at the rehearsals like a pregnant old nag. And I would not have wished it on my worst enemy to see her breasts. A nightmare! . . .

Granovsky's office was right behind the door. Since the theatre was not fully restored he did not have a lot of work. He lay on the divan, ill.

"How are you, Aleksey Mikhaylovich?"

He smiled at me, or scowled, or even swore. He often looked at me with an air of reproach. I do not know if Granovsky smiles nowadays but, like the ugly Yefrem, his free jokes reassured me. I sometimes wanted to tease him, but I never dared to ask him "Do you love me?"

Over Vitebsk. 1915–20. Oil on canvas. 26 3/8 x 36 1/2 in. (67 x 92.7 cm). The Museum of Modern Art, New York. Acquired through the Lillie P. Bliss Bequest. Photograph © The Museum of Modern Art, New York.

Chagall (rear left) and Bella (front right) with actors from the Jewish Theater, c. 1928. Collection Ida Chagall, Paris.

I had wanted to work in the theatre for a long time. As early as 1911 Tugendhold wrote in one of his articles that in my canvases objects had the air of being alive. He told me that I could paint psychological sets. That made me think. And in 1914 Tugendhold recommended me to Tairov, the director of the Kamerny Theatre in Moscow; Tairov invited me to paint the sets for Shakespeare's *Merry Wives of Windsor.* We met and parted on good terms.

I was full of strength and energy. I had been Commissar of Arts in Vitebsk; I had made art a part of life in the district and had increased the number of my enemies. I was pleased with Efros and Tugendhold's suggestion that I work for the Jewish Theatre. Should I describe Efros? He was all legs. Neither too nervous nor too calm; always everywhere, to left, to right, up, down, here and there. You could see his beard and his twinkling glasses everywhere. We became friends and we see each other once in five years. As for Granovsky, I heard of him for the first time during the war; a worthy follower of Reinhardt, from time to time he mounted mass productions. This had been in fashion in Russia since Reinhardt staged Oedipus. At the same time Granovsky staged productions with a company formed of Jews of various professions. It was they who were later to create the Studio of Jewish Theatre.

I had seen some of these productions, produced in the realist style of Stanislavsky. I had come to Moscow in a state of extreme agitation. I felt that, at least at the beginning, I could have nothing to do with Granovsky. I was unsure of everything while he, he was sure of everything and always spoke ironically. And above all he was not Chagall. He proposed that I should decorate the walls of the theatre. This is a good chance, I thought, to overturn the old Jewish theatre with its realism, its naturalism, its psychology and false beards. So I set to work, hoping that some of the actors of the Jewish Theatre or the Habima Theatre would be influenced by the new ideas and abandon their old, accepted ways. I did a sketch. On one of the walls I wished to show a panorama of the new Jewish theatre; on the other walls and on the ceiling there were to be musicians, a clown, dancers and a pair of lovers flying over the stage, as well as fruits, bread rolls and tables laid for a feast. The work was difficult but I gradually began to make contact.

At this time Granovsky was moving from Reinhardt to Stanislavsky. He had the air of being elsewhere. I sometimes had the impression that I annoyed him. I do not know why but he did not have any confidence in me. I never tried to have a serious conversation with him. It was Mikhoels who broke the wall of silence. He was hungry, like me. He often came up to me, full of dignity, with his huge eyes, his hair sticking up all over the place, his upturned nose and his thick lips.

He looked at my sketch and with a gesture that used his hand and his whole body he attempted to seize it. It is difficult to forget Mikhoels. He asked me to bring my sketches to his home for him to take them in and get used to them. Some time later he joyously announced to me:

"You know, I have studied your sketches. I have understood them. I have totally transformed my role. Now everyone looks at me and no one understands what has happened."

He smiled. I smiled. Little by little the other actors came up to my canvases to get a good look at them and try to understand what they meant and to find out if they themselves could change.

There were few costumes or sets. The day before the opening of the theatre someone brought me a whole pile of old, shabby costumes. In the pockets I found cigarette butts and bits of old, dry bread. I hastily began to paint the costumes. I could not leave my studio, even on the night of the premiere. I was covered in paint. Several minutes before the curtain went up I was still running across the stage to retouch the costumes here and there. I could not cope with this "realism." That was when the quarrel broke. Granovsky placed on stage a simple napkin, a realist napkin. Sighing, I cried:

"Why an ordinary napkin?"

"Who's the director, you or me?"

My poor heart. Oh! My forefathers!

It was suggested that I should stage *Dibbuk* at the Habima Theatre. I did not know what to do. The two theatres were at war. However, I could not go to the Habima Theatre. The actors there did not act; they praised the theatre of Stanislavsky and performed plays like a religious rite.

If things had not gone too well between Granovsky and me, well, Vakhtangov was totally alien to me. At that time he was producing *Cricket on the Hearth*. I thought, "We'll have real difficulty finding a common language."

When someone shows me love I always respond with love. When they hesitate or are doubtful I draw back. In 1922 I was invited to Stanislavsky's Studio Theatre to work on designs for *The Playboy of the Western World* by J. M. Synge. I was very keen on the project but the company rejected my design: "It's incomprehensible," they said. Another designer was called in and the play was ruined.

At the first run through of the Habima Theatre's *Dibbuk* in the presence of Vakhtangov, I said to myself "He is Russian, Georgian. We are meeting for the first time." We looked into each other's eyes, a little embarrassed. "Perhaps he sees chaos or the whirlwinds of the East in my eyes. They are an impetuous people; their art is alien to me. Why am I thus excited? Why do I blush? I am going to give him a drop of poison; he will remember it later. After me will come others who know better how to express my words and make my sighs understood."

Finally I asked Vakhtangov what he thought of the production of *Dibbuk*. He replied gently that there was only one voice in the theatre, that of Stanislavsky. "Not for the Jewish theatre," I told him. "We are following a different path." And I added, "In any case, even without me you would stage the play as I wish for there is no other way." And I left.

Returning to Malakhovka I recalled my last meeting with An-Sky in 1915, at a party at the Kalashnikov Exchange. Embracing me, he had said to me, "I have just written a play, *Der Dibbuk*. Only you can do the sets." Baal-Makhshoves was standing by me and he agreed. What should I do? What should I do?

As I was told a year later, Vakhtangov prepared to stage *Dibbuk* and studied my sketches for hours on end. Tsemak told me that they had sought a designer to produce sketches "à la Chagall." They also "Chagallized" in Granovsky's theatre on more than one occasion.

ALAIN JOUFFROY

"Theater and Revolution"

1982

Alain Jouffroy, French writer, art critic, and at one time the French cultural attaché to the French embassy in Japan.

Chagall detested the "psychological realism" of Stanislavsky, preferring the novel ideas and explorations of Taìroff and Meyerhold. But his hostility to Stanislavsky's realism led him into difficulties after the Revolution. Wachtangoff, a well-known student of Stanislavsky and director of another Jewish theater, the "Habima," invited Chagall to collaborate on the set designs for Anski's *Dibbuk.* Chagall was particularly happy about this since Anski, like himself, was from Vitebsk; but when he presented his project, Wachtangoff opposed it: "All your acrobatics and tricks are nothing," he told him, "there's only one path and that's Stanislavsky's." Chagall, who, as we have seen, wouldn't accept any kind of dictatorship, pounded on the table and cried, "You'll end up copying me anyway," and then left. Wachtangoff later tried, in effect, more or less openly to imitate Chagall, whose work and cult were preserved in Russia for a few years after his departure, until the Kamerny Jewish Theater was shut down during the darkest years of Stalinism. But we can see that Chagall's enemy between 1917 and 1922 was less the bureaucratic and authoritarian spirit of the politicians than the sectarianism of the avant-garde artists themselves.

Apollinaire—who had pronounced the word "supernatural" in 1913, in Chagall's studio in Paris, who would later invent the word "surrealism," and to whom Chagall rendered one of his biggest and most beautiful homages, a picture he had begun to paint in 1911—evaluated Chagall correctly when he wrote in the *Intransigent* (April 1913) that "Chagall reveals a curious and tormented spirit" and specified in 1914: "He is an extremely varied artist, capable of monumental paintings, and he isn't troubled by any system." It could not be better put, if we recall that it is precisely systems that Chagall has fought most violently his whole life; and nothing sheds more light on his behaviour during the years of the Russian Revolution, both at the Vitebsk Academy and among the theatrical world of Moscow: he fought Malevich who had joined forces with Lissitzky, as well as Wachtangoff and the partisans of Stanislavsky.

It was Alexis Granovsky, Director of the Kamerny Jewish Theater, who accorded Chagall the freedom he needed to fulfill his potential. We must compare the large-scale pictures he did for this theater with the *Revolution* sketches of 1937 if we wish to understand the analogies Chagall perceives between the social upheaval of a festival and that of a revolution. An attentive comparison of the actors in the *Introduction to the Jewish Theater* with that picture which Chagall destroyed in the United States after Bella's death during one of the crises of doubt that have occurred rather frequently in his life, reveals at once the most glaring fact: Lenin, standing on one hand on the corner of a table, plays the equilibrist just as do the actors of the Kamerny Theater who are portrayed not far from the musicians. This posture of Lenin, contrary to all the iconography that has accumulated around the leader of the Russian Revolution, in a way makes the history of the world dance, literally turns its meaning upside down: people dream on the earth, or play the violin around a sun that has fallen to the earth, while a donkey sits patiently on a chair. The armed masses, gathered under the red flags, look at the spectacle of Lenin the equilibrist as if he were a great actor, I was about to say the actor Michoels, the most fervent Chagall enthusiast at the Kamerny Theater. In the two compositions, the oblique space is the same and the figures are placed as though in a parade or anniversary celebration in the street. Chagall perhaps remembered the one he organized himself in 1918 in Vitebsk.

COLORPLATE 46

COLORPLATES 24, 25, 26

COLORPLATE 32. *Lovers in Green*. 1916–17. Oil on canvas. 27 5/8 x 19 5/8 in. (70 x 50 cm).
Musée National d'Art Moderne, Centre Georges Pompidou, Paris.

COLORPLATE 33. *The Old Man with Spectacles.* 1920. Gouache on paper.
8 7/8 x 9 1/2 in. (22.5 x 24 cm). Collection Marcus Diener, Basel.

COLORPLATE 34. *Holy Day (Rabbi with an Etrog)*. 1924. Oil on canvas.
41 x 33 in. (104 x 84 cm). Collection Mr. Himan Brown, New York.

COLORPLATE 35. *The Cattle Dealer*. 1922–23. Oil on canvas. 39 ⅛ x 70 ⅞ in. (99.5 x 180 cm).
Musée National d'Art Moderne, Centre Georges Pompidou, Paris.

COLORPLATE 36. *Two Bouquets*. 1925. Oil on canvas. 32 x 39 ¹/4 in. (81.2 x 99.8 cm). Private collection.

COLORPLATE 37. *The Blue House*. 1917. Oil on canvas. 26 x 38 ¹/₄ in. (66 x 97 cm).
Musée des Beaux-Arts, Liege. Photograph: Giraudon/Art Resource, New York.

COLORPLATE 38. *The Violinist*. 1926. Gouache on paper. 19 ¹/4 x 19 ¹/4 in. (49 x 49 cm). Collection Marcus Diener, Basel.

In spite of his success at the Kamerny Theater, Chagall was unable, among the sets and costumes he designed for the theater before leaving Russia, to do those for the *Players,* Gogol's *Marriage,* Synge's *Playboy of the Western World,* and Anski's *Dibbuk,* which Wachtangoff had turned down in '21. Only the sets and costumes for Gogol's *Revizor,* which Razoummy, the director of the "Satirical and Revolutionary Theater," had gone to Vitebsk to ask him about, were completed; Chagall says somewhere that they were very "amusing." A few of his designs have survived however; in particular, the set for *The Playboy of the Western World* in which a silver Christ, hanging upside down from a thread above an immobile golden calf, was to have revolved continuously throughout the play. But this Christ, after fifty years, turns in the same darkness, the same emptiness in 1972, as it did in Moscow in 1920 and '21, exactly as if it had never existed for anyone except historians and Chagall connoisseurs.

Chagall also painted sets for several one-act plays by the famous Yiddish playwright and humorist Shalom Aleichem, including Mazel Tov, The Agents, *and* The Lie.

The *Introduction to the Jewish Theater* is still the Chagallian archetype of the allegorical representation of the life and role of the creator, artist and poet in society. As one of his exegetists says on this subject: "The circus and art lead to nothing but are everything." Thus *The Big Circus* of 1936 picks up the themes of the picture of 1920–1921 in which the strolling acrobats extended an invitation to the festival by standing the world on its head. In the *Introduction,* it is the head of the central violinist that flies away; in *Absinthe* (1913) it is that of the poet; and in *The Big Circus,* it is that of the orchestra conductor. As to the figure walking on his hands at the right of the *Introduction,* he can be seen as following the acrobatic troop of the Jewish Theater; it is as if Lenin, in the *Revolution* of 1937, were only one of the travestied acrobats from the Jewish Theater or the circus, a reinventor of the world, a clown of history. The world, for Chagall as for Jarry, is nothing but its own parody, its mask, its double, but at the same time this double, this travesty, unveils its truth. The game creates the beauty, and if the game should stop, death alone would triumph.

The continuity we can decipher in the *Introduction to the Jewish Theater, The Big Circus* and the *Revolution,* defines the omnipotence of the Chagallian dream, which refuses to barricade the frontiers between domains that everyone separates: love, reality, society, poetry, revolution, the circus. In any case, painting enables him to unify, to reconcile what daily life everywhere fragments and opposes. Painting saved Chagall from misery and the unhappiness of living, but above all it permitted him, as at the time of the first anniversary of the Revolution when he dreamed "of transforming ordinary houses into museums and the vulgar inhabitant into a creator," to connect painting to the history of the world rather than to the history of forms. Certainly, the circus, the theater, revolution "are not life," but precisely what makes it possible to act out, illumine and change life. For Chagall, painting was only the instrument of this transformation: treating one or the other subject, he recaptured all his dreams. That is why the *monumental paintings* that Apollinaire felt Chagall "capable of" in 1914 principally deal with the major, constant theme of this identification of painting with mental revolution and theatrical play, and of this play with life. The pictures of the Kamerny Theater make it possible to establish historically this general interpretation of Chagall's entire work. Their remoteness is therefore all the more meaningful.

Perhaps we should take the fact that most of the sets Chagall designed in Russia are still buried in boxes or cellars, if they have not simply disappeared, as a sign. The picture of the *Revolution,* which Chagall exhibited at Zervo's, then at the Pierre Matisse Gallery in New York before tearing it up into three pieces, also indicates, by its symptomatic presence/absence, the drama that binds, releases and then connects Chagall anew to the history of this country and the revolution he began by applauding. Like his works, the private storms of his life coincide with those that have for the longest time shaken artists and poets throughout the world. The work and life of Chagall can be thought of as a parabolic mirror of the intellectual history of the twentieth century whose principal events he has lived through, endured and surmounted. With this mirror, he has erected one of the most enigmatic monuments to freedom and the imagination.

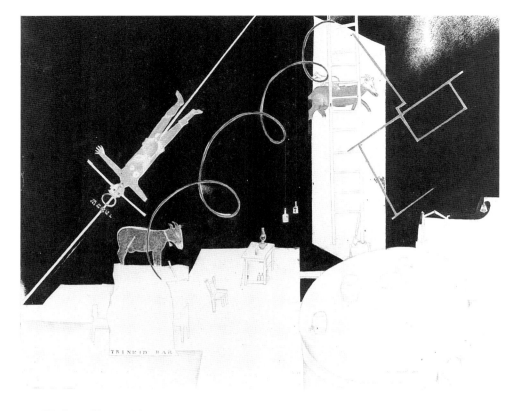

Maquette of set design for Synge's *Playboy of the Western World*. 1921. Gouache and pencil on paper. 16 1/8 x 20 1/8 in. (41 x 51 cm). Musée National d'Art Moderne, Centre Georges Pompidou, Paris.

Today, Chagall is as old as Juan Gris would have been. In one breath, so it seems, he has responded to Mayakovsky's wish that he keep on "chagalling like Chagall"; he has stridden across the twentieth century.

The point of all this is simply that the theater represented for Chagall the most direct intermediary between himself, the world and history. His painting inaugurated a revolution that encountered and intersected the start of a social revolution but that could never identify itself with the State the revolution gave birth to. And yet power fascinates Chagall insofar as it is related to the secret disturbance of his work. Painting allows him to see the world as *a stage* on which, as in the circus, the collective forces are travestied. In the center of this whirlwind he sees himself as the poet *who has lost his head.* There is no authority in the world capable of convincing him that he could not lose it, as the exuberant fantasies of his pictures prove.

OSIP MANDELSHTAM

Review: The Actor Mikhoels

August 10, 1926

Osip Mandelshtam, renowned Russian writer, critic, and essayist.

On the wooden walkways of an unsightly Byelorussian shtetl—a big village with a brick factory, a beer hall, front yards, and cranes—shuffled a strange figure with long hems, made of an entirely different dough from the whole landscape. Through the window of a train, I watched that solitary pedestrian move like a black cockroach between the little houses, among the splashing mud, with splayed arms; and golden yellow glimmered the black hems of his coat. In his movements, there was such an estrangement from the whole situation and, at the

Chagall with the actor Solomon (Schlomoe) Michoels in a Chagall-designed costume for his role as Rabbi Alter for the Shalom Aleichem Evening, January 1921. Collection Ida Chagall, Paris

same time, such knowledge of the road, as if he had to run to and fro, like a wind-up toy.

Sure, big deal, never seen: a Jew with long hems on a village street. However, I remember well the figure of the running Rebbe because, without him, that whole modest landscape lacked justification. The coincidence which that very moment pushed into the street this crazy, charmingly absurd, endlessly refined, porcelain pedestrian helped me understand the impression of the State Jewish Theater, which I recently saw for the first time.

Yes, a short while before that, on a Kiev street, I was ready to approach a similar respectable bearded man and ask him, "Didn't Al'tman do your costume?" I would have asked just like that, with no mockery, quite sincerely: in my head, the realism grew confused. . . .

How fortunate is Granovskii! It's enough for him to assemble two or three synagogue beadles with a cantor, summon a matchmaker-Shadkhan, catch in the street an elderly salesman, and a spectacle is ready and, in essence, even Al'tman is superfluous.

This paradoxical theater, which, according to some critics as profound as Dobrolubov, declared war on the Jewish petite bourgeoisie, and which exists only to eradicate prejudices and superstitions, loses its head, gets drunk like a woman when it sees a Jew, and immediately pulls him into its workshop, to the porcelain factory, scalds and tempers him into a marvelous biscuit, a painted statuette, a green *shadkhan*-grasshopper, brown musicians of Rabichev's Jewish wedding, bankers with shaved layered pates, dancing like virtuous girls, holding hands, in a circle.

The plastic fame and force of the Jews consist of having worked out and borne through the centuries a sense of form and movement, which has all the traits of a fashion immutable for millennia. I am speaking not of the cut of their clothes, which changes, and which we need not value (it doesn't even occur to me to justify the ghetto or the shtetl style aesthetically); I'm talking of the internal plasticity of the ghetto, of that immense artistic force which outlives its destruction, and will finally flourish only when the ghetto is destroyed.

Violins accompany the wedding dance. Mikhoels approaches the footlights and, stealthily, with the careful movements of a fawn, listens to the music in a minor key. This is a fawn who has found himself at a Jewish wedding, hesitant, not yet drunk, but already stimulated by the cat-music of a Jewish minuet. This moment of hesitation is perhaps more expressive than the whole subsequent dance. Tapping on the spot, intoxication comes, a light intoxication from two or three drinks of grape wine, but this is enough to turn the head of a Jew: the Jewish Dionysius is undemanding and immediately produces joy.

During the dance, Mikhoel's face assumes an expression of wise weariness and sad exaltation, as if the mask of the Jewish people, approaching antiquity, is almost identical with it.

Here the dancing Jew is like the leader of an ancient chorus. The whole force of Judaism, the rhythm of the abstract, dancing thought, the whole dignity of the dance, whose only impetus is ultimately empathy with the earth—all this is absorbed in the trembling hands, the vibrating of his thinking fingers, inspired like articulated speech.

Mikhoels is the epitome of national Jewish dandyism—the dancing Mikhoels, the tailor Soroker, a forty-year-old child, a blessed *shlimazel,* a wise and gentle tailor. And yesterday, on the same stage, Anglicized jockey ragamuffins, on tall girl-dancers, patriarchs drinking tea in the clouds, like elders on a porch in Homel.

Violinist in the Snow. 1914. Oil on canvas. 40 x 30 in. (101.6 x 76.2 cm). Los Angeles County Museum of Art. Gift of Mary Day McLane.

AVRAM KAMPF

On The Jewish Theaters of Moscow

1987

Avram Kampf is professor of fine arts at Montclair State College, New Jersey. He is also visiting professor of art history at the Hebrew University in Jerusalem, Israel, and was an advisor to The Jewish Museum in New York.

During the 1920s two Jewish theatres from Moscow, the Jewish State Chamber Theatre and the Hebrew-speaking Habimah, stunned Jewish, Russian, and European audiences with their performances. Both groups were born within the Russian Revolution, when hopes for the blooming of a national art ran high, and both achieved extraordinary artistic standards within a span of a few years. Both theatrical groups were heirs to the Jewish historical tradition, although they made different use of this tradition and ultimately had different goals. Their acting style, their blending of reality and fantasy, their lively national temperament, and the intensity and vigor of their exaggerated gestures and their painted, masklike faces earned them a reputation far beyond the borders of Russia. The rapidity of their movement, their sharp humor and deep sorrow, the unity of word, gesture, music, light and dance were born from the rhythm of Jewish crowds in the marketplace, and from the wondrous, naive Hasidic folktales. Their plays, which were acted before imaginatively designed stage sets, granted them a rare distinction.

The particular style of the actors and the specific energies of the individual and the ensemble derived largely from Marc Chagall's work for the Yiddish theatre. This assumption is shared by Meyer, Erben, and Lubomirsky. The latter stated:

> His influence was visible not only in the stage sets, costumes and make-up techniques, but even in the gestures of the actors. . . . The actors found in the grotesque stylization of European gestures and the exaggeration of the Jewish, as well as in folklore, what they needed to express their idea of the Jewish character. In many cases they came close to the conception expressed in Chagall's forms. Their efforts, together with the trend started by Chagall, gave rise to what was later considered the national form of that theatre.

The St. Petersburg of Chagall's student years was ablaze with artistic, musical, and theatrical activity comparable to any of the West European capitals.

All of Chagall's teachers were leading members of the Mir iskusstva (World of Art), the early modern art movement in Russia, and all of them exhibited a strong bent for stage design, book illustration, and graphic art. They were men of exceptionally wide horizons and accomplishments, who gave their students access to living modern art. Like the Art Nouveau movement in general, Mir iskusstva celebrated the concept of total art, and stage design was seen as the creation of a microcosm of the total art concept (*Gesammstkunstwerk*), which Richard Wagner had pioneered and which Gordon Craig, Appia, Max Reinhardt, and Stanislavsky further developed.

Among Chagall's teachers was Nicholas Roerich, director of the school of the Society for the Protection of the Arts. Roerich was, among other things, a painter, poet, and anthropologist with a keen knowledge of primitive art, who participated in several expeditions to Siberia. He worked with Igor Stravinsky and Sergei Diaghilev as stage designer for their ballet, *The Rite of Spring*. Mstislav Dobujinsky and Leon Bakst, with whom the young Chagall studied at the Zvantseva school of art, then the most modern art school in Russia, were also leading stage designers. Dobujinsky worked for Diaghilev, Stanislavsky, Vesevold Meyerhold, and Evreinov designing the stages of theatres, cabarets, and night-clubs. Bakst was one of the founders of Mir iskusstva, and his sensuous and colorful stage designs and wide knowledge of esoteric and oriental art doubtless contributed greatly to Diaghilev's success. For Bakst the lively, imaginative interplay of colors, their texture and the harmonizing of their tensions were the essence of composition and far more important than fidelity to nature or reproduction of reality. Here his views about the nature of art paralleled those of the stage director Nikolai Evreinov, for whom Chagall did stage designs after his return from Paris, but who already had extensively elaborated his theories about the nature of the theatre in 1908, theories in which many of the seeds of Chagall's artistic orientation can be found. . . .

With the coming of the Revolution in 1917 all latent tendencies reinforced each other and were accelerated. Meyerhold, who had fervently embraced the political goals of the Revolution, found fertile ground for experimentation and innovation. He abolished front curtains, backdrops, and stage sets altogether, playing against the bare brick walls of his theatre. Seeing in Constructivism the most meaningful contemporary expression of the Revolution's impulses and goals, he summoned the artists Popova and Stepanova to fill the empty stage with abstract structures. In the course of his experimentation, he introduced on the stage stairs, arches, escalators, lifts, monorails, cables, ropes, cranes, lifting devices, and rotating walls. He filled the stage with moving lights, projections, and musical instruments. The stage became a "factory," a motorized universe moving in perpetual rhythm. These innovations were complemented by the biomechanical system, in which actors expressed a state of mind or emotional

Chagall, Solomon (Schlomoe) Michoels, and other actors from the Jewish Theater, c. 1928. Collection Ida Chagall, Paris.

experience through precise control of their movements. They turned individual emotions into a social and normative emotion suitable for theatre aimed at a mass audience. This new audience was not versed in Chekhov or Shakespeare; it consisted of soldiers and peasants who wanted to be entertained. Theatre therefore moved toward the circus, which could be enjoyed by everyone.

The Revolution gave rise to street theatres, pageants, processions, and carnivals in which thousands participated. These evolved their own techniques and devices, which influenced the avant-garde theatres in the major cities. The street theatre blurred the separation between stage and audience as well as between the various arts. In addition to acting there was dance, pantomime, music, painting, acrobatics, and clowning.

In the street theatre the stage director usually worked from an elevated podium, and assumed even greater authority. So did the stage designer. While the stage director knew the dramatic art and even literature and music, his knowledge of modern painting was usually minimal. A prime aspect of street theatre was assigned to the general composition and to improvisation of an idea rather than a precisely predetermined text. Psychological determination of individual characters gave way to forms of expression that could be absorbed from a distance.

From the vortex of these turbulent political, social, and artistic developments, the two major Jewish theatres emerged. The Hebrew-speaking theatre Habimah was committed to the renewal of Jewish national life and moved in the orbit of

Peasant Life. 1917. Oil on board.
8 1/4 x 8 1/2 in. (21 x 21.6 cm). Private
collection.

the cultural aspirations of Zionism. The Jewish Chamber Theatre (the Kamerny)
was supported for different reasons by the Yevsektsia and by intellectuals of the
Jewish Theatre Society, and was encouraged to develop a Yiddish national theatre, as were other national theatres. From the beginning, the Jewish Chamber
Theatre aspired to be a world theatre performing in Yiddish.

Alexander Granovsky, Nahum Zemach, Yevgeny Vachtangov, Chagall,
Nathan Altman, Isaac Rabinovich, Robert Falk and many other painters, musicians, and actors participated in the creation of significant innovations of modern
Russian art and theatre, and adapted their innovations and practices to the goals
of the Jewish theatres and their audiences.

Granovsky, the founder of the Kamerny, was an experienced professional
director, an assimilated Jew ignorant of Yiddish literature and culture, and
unspoiled by any knowledge of the pre-revolutionary Yiddish theatre. He had
studied at the University of Munich, was a pupil and assistant of Reinhardt, and
had wide experience as a lighting designer, technician, and theatrical and cine-
matic director, in addition to possessing extraordinary organizational skills.

At the beginning of 1919 he assembled in Petrograd a group of thirty young
students who had no experience in the theatre and trained them for the stage by
exposing them to the most distinguished instructors in acting, voice, music, dic-
tion, movement, dance, and acrobatics, as well as intensive courses in Jewish literature, culture, and folklore, thus molding them into an artistically unified
ensemble. Granovsky aimed to remove himself completely from the old Jewish
ghetto theatre and establish a theatre in the Yiddish language fully equal in its
standards to other Soviet avant-garde theatres. For the first performances of his
group in Petrograd he used stage designers like Alexander Benois and Chagall's
former teacher, Dobujinsky.

When Granovsky's group moved to Moscow, at the end of 1920, the theatre
critic Abram Efros recommended Chagall as stage designer, and as decorator for
the long drawing room of the half-destroyed luxury villa on Chernyshevsky
Street, which was to be turned into the auditorium of a small theatre seating
ninety. As Chagall recalls in his autobiography:

Ah, I saw it, here is an opportunity to do away with the old Jewish theatre, its psychological naturalism, its false beards. There, on these walls I shall at least be able to do as I please and be free to show everything I consider indispensable to the rebirth of the national theatre.

Here was Chagall's chance to make a significant statement about the theatre in general and the new Jewish theatre in particular. The very idea of a national Jewish art was appealing and brought him close to other Jewish painters who lionized him and saw in his work the realization of their goal. For several years they had been theorizing about the possibility of creating a modern Jewish art that would be utterly avant-garde. They had explored the various manifestations of Jewish folk art, and investigated the art and architecture of wooden synagogues, Hebrew illuminated manuscripts, gravestones, the structure of the Hebrew letter, and the various ritual objects used for home or synagogue. On the basis of folk art they hoped to create the structure of a modern Jewish art. Issachar Ryback, El Lissitzky, Boris Aronson, Joseph Tchaikov, and Isaac Rabinovich had done significant work in this area, and in 1920 the political atmosphere still seemed promising for such endeavor. Had not the Revolution promised the liberation of all nationalities of Russia and the development of their specific cultures?

Chagall himself had deep roots in the Jewish tradition and was firmly planted in the ideas and practices of contemporary art. His preoccupation with Jewish portraits, holidays, and folkways and his illustrations of Jewish books after his return to Russia in 1914 made him the logical choice. Defying the cold and famine of the Moscow winter of 1920, he worked on the mural and the sets for the theatre, while Granovsky and his group rehearsed for the forthcoming Shalom Aleichem evening. . . .

The murals, painted on canvas, filled the small auditorium and stunned the spectators. The introduction to the new national theatre, a 12 x 36-foot oil painting, was like a "Manifesto," as Meyer observed.

The compositions of the murals were firmly constructed, as Chagall then also employed Constructivist geometrical elements in his paintings. Yet into this formal design of planes were integrated shafts of bright color and wide bands and circles, lively, moving performers—musicians, actors, acrobats, clowns. The long-legged critic Efros carries the painter with his palette like a gift toward the director. In addition the painter introduced giants and dwarfs, goats and cows, umbrellas, heads and limbs. The informal air of the commedia dell'arte and its closest Jewish manifestation, the Purim jesters, dominate the canvas with their perpetual, frenzied movement, their exaggerated gestures, their mocking, farcical postures, and their jazz rhythm and abandoned dancing. The theatre became a circus. The actors wore pointed hats and round caps, crazy-quilt, diamond-shaped patches on their ill-fitting trousers decorated with Hebrew script, and dotted, wide, rectangular signs. These patterns also appear in the sketches for the costumes he designed for the forthcoming play. The scene of the mural evokes the quintessential spirit of the new Yiddish theatre. The movement must never stop. One could apply to the mural the words of the review that a critic gave the Yiddish theatre when it performed in Berlin:

In every theatre there are moments when one may relax. Not here. Cubistic liveliness . . . they talk not only with their hands but almost with their hair, calves, soles, and toes.

At the opposite end of the hall, Chagall designed for the stage curtain a sketch of circular and angular motifs combined with two goat heads turning away from each other when the curtain opens. Apparently this sketch was not used. Moshe Litvakov mentions a black curtain with the design of a white goat turned upside down.

The murals and the sketch for the curtain are two-dimensional abstract forms that combine playful, figurative elements in a firmly unified composition. They form a stylistic unity that dissolved the walls of the small auditorium into a mass of color and movement. Erben writes:

> The effect of Chagall's pictures was extraordinary. The people who poured into the theatre were dismayed, bewildered, amused. They stood in front of them and discussed them, and more and more people came. The theatre itself had become a side issue. When anyone appeared on the stage to talk about the aims of the Jewish theatre he was forced by the audience to explain the pictures on the walls.

We also find Constructivist and folkloristic elements in the sets Chagall painted for *Mazeltov, The Agents,* and *The Lie,* the three one-act plays that composed the Shalom Aleichem evening of the opening night of the theatre. Reacting against the crude, farce-like presentation of the traditional Yiddish stage, in his sets and costumes Chagall expressed the lyrical humor of Shalom Aleichem, the strain between dream and reality that the artist felt were in accord with the author's conception. Clearly, the artist was on home ground.

The Wedding Table mural (1920) as installed at the Fondation Pierre Gianadda, Martigny, Switzerland. Tempera and gouache on canvas. 25 1/8 x 314 1/2 in. (64 x 799 cm). Collection Tret'iakov Gallery, Moscow. Photograph: Heinz Preisig. Courtesy Christina Burrus.

COLORPLATES 24, 25, 26

Chagall's murals for the Jewish Theater in Moscow are among the greatest masterpieces of his career. After being neglected and improperly stored for decades, the murals were restored in 1991 to be shown in a worldwide touring exhibition.

Russian Village Street. 1914. Gouache, watercolor, and pencil on paper. 17 3/4 x 22 1/8 in. (45 x 56 cm). Private collection.

THE ART OF
MARC CHAGALL

ALEXANDRE BENOIS

"On the Exhibition of 'Jewish Art' "

April 22, 1916

Alexandre N. Benois (1870–1960), painter, art historian, and critic who was co-founder of the publication Mir Iskousstva *("The World of Art"). Later he became the chief curator of painting at The Hermitage Museum in St. Petersburg.*

I shall take advantage of this to give you my impressions of the works of Chagall. He is a real Jew. Which does not mean that his work has no value except that it is authentically Jewish. No. But despite a long period abroad the young artist has been able to retain all his freshness; he has kept the candour, fantasy and sensitivity of his childhood. And what is charming in his work is not his exotic character but this capacity for capturing the soul of anything, of revealing the "smile of God" in the most trivial everyday scene. That is characteristic of all real artists . . . That this "Jewish hole," dirty and smelly, with its winding streets, its blind houses and its ugly people, bowed down by poverty, can be thus attired in charm, beauty and poetry in the eyes of the painter—this is what enchants us and surprises us at the same time . . .

Chagall is always true and sincere, even when his work is symbolic. He does not seek to transform reality or make it more cheerful. He simply loves what he sees. And this love changes everything. Without losing its sadness the saddest of spectacles charms and moves us. I do not know the miserable world which

Purim. 1916–18. Oil on canvas. 18 ⁷/₈ x 25 ¹/₂ in. (47.8 x 64.7 cm). The Philadelphia Museum of Art. The Louis E. Stern Collection.

Chagall paints. I would certainly die of boredom if I had to walk along its fences or talk to its people. And yet, through the magic of his art, Chagall brings them close to me.

Chagall is still very young; we can therefore forgive him several errors. Sometimes he is garrulous, often even superficial. But he is a true painter, a painter right through to his fingertips, able, in his *moments d'élection,* to allow himself to be carried away by his inspiration, while submitting to the rules of his craft.

Five years ago Chagall arrived in Paris. He was then still an inexperienced provincial. But far from allowing himself to be influenced by passing fashion, far from losing his first freshness, there he deepened his mastery of line and colour. Chagall's colour is restrained. His pictures are often monochrome; rejecting violent effects they present a subtle harmony which forms the charm of the painter.

ABRAM EFROS and IAKOV TUGENDHOLD

From *The Art of Marc Chagall*

1918

Critics Abram Efros and Iakov Tugendhold wrote the first monograph on Chagall, published in Moscow in 1918. The complete book has been translated from the Russian by Benjamin and Barbara Harshav and published in Marc Chagall and the Jewish Theater *(see Bibliographical Index).*

"THE EMPEROR'S CLOTHES," BY ABRAM EFROS

Here is a book about an artist—young but already famous—perhaps the most brilliant of our *hommes d'aujourd'hui,* but one who has experienced a hard lot: to be recognized without being understood. Marc Chagall fell under the wheel of one of those quiet artistic revolutions that seem to occur unnoticed and coincidentally, but whose victims include the most unusual talents.

What happened? What happened is the deepest rupture, still unnoticed and unaccounted for, of the most solid relationships between traditional antagonists—the artist and the masses. Oh, the roles have changed in an amazing way! The imperially conservative masses—Her Highness the Masses, the masses, slandered and adored, whom all revolutionaries of art have cursed and yet tried to captivate; the masses surrounding the artist like guards around Saint Sebastian, the masses marching over the corpses of innovators, the implacable, stubborn, pursuing, stinging, branding masses—what has happened to her in our time?

We see before us those strange idyllic years when the masses began, obsequiously, to accept everything the creative caprice of the artist offered her. She became his searching slave. She agreed to everything. She blessed everything with her thousand-mouth blessing: nothing appalled her—and nothing surprised her! The grief of many young artists who wished, in vain, to have their own period of rejection is understandable and legitimate: the masses really violated the good canons of rejection, established by the experience of so many heralds of new values in art.

Poor Chagall! He too experienced the meaning of this popular complacency, the worrying smile of devotion, and the frowning brows of attention. He too knew that if they hail a recognized writer so as not to read him, they hail a recognized artist so as not to look. Shuffling through an exhibition, one figure throws to another, hurrying to sneak by Chagall: "Ach, Chagall . . . He is very talented . . ."—"Yes-yes . . . Very-very . . .,"—and, relieved, they vanish into the next gallery, where they regain human language and, with a profusion of words, they burst into excitement before the *comme il faut* canvases of some Excellency.

The Emperor's clothes . . . Andersen's tale . . . till the first fool screams: "The Emperor is naked. . . ." Well, this is so understandable! Art blinds like Lady Godiva with her nakedness. That's why experienced viewers and true appreciators, art historians and art critics—all wear glasses and increase their size every year. But the masses can glue her eyes to the forbidden crack without fear: she won't go blind because she doesn't see anything anyway.

Art criticism is often an act of grace in relation to the profane, and an act of justice in relation to the artist; it teaches the former to see and gives the latter an opportunity to be understood. Must it linger at the deaf lawsuit between Chagall and his viewers? It seems that the time has come to stand up between them, especially since the artist is right and, this time, the viewers are not so guilty—for Marc Chagall put before them truly the most difficult problem: about the boundaries of what is permitted in art.

Cover of the first monograph on Chagall by Abram Efros and Iakov Tugendhold, published in Moscow in 1918. Collection Jacob Baal-Teshuva.

"The Nature of His Art," by Abram Efros

He enters the room the way practical people walk in, with confidence and precision, overcoming space, striding forcefully, testifying to a consciousness that the earth is earth and only earth. But look: at a certain step, his body totters and snaps drolly; like Pierrot collapsing in half in a puppet theater, fatally stung by betrayal and bending slightly sideways, cracked, with an expression apologizing for some guilt unknown to us, Chagall approaches, shakes hands—and sits down obliquely, as if falling into the chair. Chagall has the beaming face of a young fawn; but in conversation, the kindly softness sometimes evaporates like a mask, and then we think that the corners of his lips are too sharp, like arrows, and he bares his teeth tenaciously, like an animal, and the gray-blue kindness of his eyes too often shines with the fury of strange explosions, perspicacious and blind at the same time, making his interlocutor think he is probably reflected in some fantastic manner in the mirrors of Chagall's eyes, and perhaps will later recognize himself in one of those green, blue, red, flying, dishevelled, folded-over, twisted people— in Chagall's future paintings. And when hours pass in conversation, talking about the dear mundane world, work, his wife, his child, Chagall suddenly boils over with some prophetic phrase like: "We talk only as if before God, our way is faultless because it is God's way . . ."—we are no longer amazed; we even understand Chagall, we can see what strong but rational-intangible threads link Chagall's phantasmagoric expressions with his stories about dear daily life, illuminating it and permeating it with light, and opening, behind the first plane of his words, a second, third, fourth, and more planes—the planes of his soul. They are as inevitable in Chagall and as essential to his flesh and blood as those unexpected gray strands cutting through the bright curling hair of the not-yet-thirty-year-old artist. . . .

It is hard to get close to Chagall because you have to overcome his contradictions, to be able to synthesize them. Behind the elements of his art thrusting out in all directions, you have to find one axis and a general guiding force dominating the multitude of colorful parts.

Chagall—a master of mundane life, but also Chagall—a visionary; Chagall—a storyteller, but also Chagall—a philosopher; a Russian Jew, a Hasid—but also a pupil of French Modernism; but also, in general, a cosmopolitan fantasist, soaring like a witch on a broomstick above the globe and in his swooping flight carrying behind him a multitude of various particles from a multitude of various lives that descend in a swarm on his canvases when times of meditation and creativity emerge, and the flowing and roiling elemental force of Chagall's visions is graphically transformed into images and colors.

Were Chagall only a visionary, it would not be difficult to accept him, as it was not difficult to accept the visions of Curlanis. It would be even easier were Chagall a pure depicter of mundane life, even if he were the most left and radical among the artists creating forms of new realist painting today: we are already experienced enough with various "deformations" not to be scared of them, and perhaps even to find some charm in them. Finally, it would not be difficult to be tempted by the possibility of deciphering a convoluted and complex allegory if Chagall's headless and green people were only allegories that could be changed into a simple and easily understood parable, like the monsters, scarecrows, and cripples in Goya's etchings.

But Chagall is neither this nor that nor the other. His visions live entirely in the confines of the simplest mundane life, while his mundane life is entirely visionary. The people and objects of daily life are permeated with the nature of specters, but these Chagallian specters are by no means shadows with no mass or circumference or hue, and whom chopping or stabbing is as senseless as chopping or stabbing the air. Chagall's spectral daily life has all the palpability and weight of normal objects and bodies. And if, nevertheless, he is governed by some law that tears him apart and brushes people, animals, and objects around the air, confounds all logic and sense of earthly proportions and interrelations, the poor law of allegory or the low law of a crossword puzzle is least guilty in it; we face here not a logical game, but an authentic, unconditional seeing of an immense internal saturation. . . .

In the development of Chagall's art so far, three periods clearly emerge. External boundaries determine the first as a preparatory, provincial-Petersburg period, when Chagall came from his Vitebsk Province to St. Petersburg to study painting, attended Bakst's school, and worked on his first independent paintings. The second period—abroad; Chagall left for Paris, where he became "Chagall," impressing the turbulent Bohemia of La Ruche with his unusual canvases, which promoted him to the ranks of the most interesting "masters of tomorrow," and which were taken triumphantly to exhibitions of the new art in Berlin and Amsterdam. In this period such chimerical canvases were created as *Paris Through the Window, The Carter, The Calf Seller, The Brides,* and so on, with their headless bodies, two-faced heads, and flying cows. Finally, the current period—the period of his return to Russia at the outbreak of the Great War, when Chagall created his Vitebsk cycle: *The Barbershop, The Shtetl Lyozno, In the Provinces, On the Outskirts of Vitebsk, The Praying Jew, The Birthday, The Guitarist,* and others.

The internal line of his creative work passed through those chronological boundaries amazingly whole. Chagall had no interruptions, no treading water, no deviations. The originality of Chagall's art was evident from the beginning and it always went its own way; the boundaries of the above-mentioned external periods of development indicated only turning points and the interrelations of the two

Chagall. 1918. Gouache on paper. 18 7/8 x 13 3/8 in. (47.8 x 34 cm). Musée National d'Art Moderne, Centre Georges Pompidou, Paris.

COLORPLATE 11
COLORPLATE 35

COLORPLATE 13

major elements of his work. These elements, inseparably linked to each other from Chagall's first steps, are the genre of mundane life and visionary mysticism. Chagall's earliest paintings created the basic "Chagallian" impression: the unreal countenance of real life. The Chagall of those works is a dreamy child who grew up in a Hasidic family in a Jewish shtetl. But childhood and Hasidism mean a dream multiplied by a dream; this is the source of the boundless ore of Chagall's fantasy. And the mundane life around him is the life of a small Vitebsk town; that is, the very quintessence of everyday life, the very thick of the most pitiful poverty and opaque existence. . . .

Today, Chagall stands in the very heart of his Vitebsk period—what the results will be we can only vaguely guess. There are reasons to think that Chagall's present road leads him to that "grand art" of transformed daily life indicated in several of his recent big works—in the magnificent *The Praying Jew,* in *The Green Old Man,* and such; here the shtetl Jews have grown into enormous national figures, deeply rooted in their mundane typicality and, at the same time, endowed with all the internal significance of a symbol.

However, new traits have recently begun to break through in Chagall's works, traits of an even denser, hotter, hastier, voluntarily obsequious submission to "the tyranny of small things," the rule of dear daily life. I saw a new series by Chagall:

his dacha cycle. A man lives in a dacha with a front yard with green trees, on the balcony hang red dotted curtains, on the table sits a golden samovar, and, in a wicker basket, scarlet and blue berries—here he is, man in Paradise, as if, after a hard earthly road, he now abides "in a place of light, a place of grains, a place of peace...."

Is it a final reconciliation with everydayness that the subdued artist has to go through? But what will then link his "grand art" with the "apology for a dacha"?

How can we know? . . . Except for guesses, what does Chagall leave us? We must admit courageously that there is nothing more hopeless than predicting his future, for among our artists, there is no spirit more free and unexpected in his creative ideas than this God-intoxicated Chagall. . . .

"The Artist Marc Chagall," by Iakov Tugendhold

In French exhibitions of recent years, the works of the young artist from Vitebsk, Marc Chagall, attracted my attention. Fiery-colored like Russian *lubok*, expressive to the point of grotesque, fantastic to the point of irrationality, they stood out not only among the works of Russian painters, but also against the background of the young French painting. I remember the impact they made in the Autumn Salon among the "Cubist" canvases of Le Fauconnier and Delaunay, those Fauvist innovators. While the mind-boggling brick structures of the Frenchmen exuded cold intellectualism and the logic of analytical thought, what was astonishing in Chagall's paintings was some childish inspiration, something subconscious, instinctive, unbridled, and colorful. As if by mistake, next to the adult, too-adult, works, works of some child, truly fresh, "barbaric," and fantastic had landed here. Those multicolored crooked huts with graves in the middle of the street and a fiddler chirping on the roof, that fiery-bloody Golgotha with Judas removing the ladder, could have repelled with their coarse expression, their savagery of theme, the loudness of their colors. But it was impossible not to see them or not to absorb their sharp aroma, because, behind them, you felt the all-conquering force of a great talent, and a foreign talent at that. *"Tiens, il y a quelque chose—c'est très curieux!"*—said the Frenchmen, and indeed, in Chagall, you guessed something inexplicable in European terms, and therefore "curious," as many things in the "barbaric" polychrome music of the Russian ballet seemed curious.

At another exhibition, Chagall showed works refined in their polychromy and ornamentation. Headless flying people, sentimentally inspired animals, houses outside of time and space as in a sweet and wild childish dream, were painted in black and white, gold and silver, scarlet, cerise, and other unusual and subtle shades. Chagall's fantastics and palette seemed overly tense, unhealthy, and delirious, but you couldn't doubt their sincerity—could such phantoms and such outbursts of painterly heat be invented on purpose?

Chagall roused interest; merely condescendingly approved and almost boycotted by the powerful in Russia—he was accepted in the bosom of Paris bohemia, invited to exhibit in Amsterdam, Brussels, Berlin. But the war stopped his rapid rise—Chagall found himself where he came from: in the godforsaken Russian province, in his native Vitebsk. The result of his return to his native and familiar places was a series of studies of mundane life, surprisingly realistic, strong and calm, but quite varied. Chagall is still steeped in searching, in frenetic pluralism, at the junction of many roads—like a child who has before him an infinity of influences, wishes, and opportunities. But even what he has accomplished so far allows us to talk about him as an artistic phenomenon, as something authentic and original, which has already come to light and begun glittering fantastically.

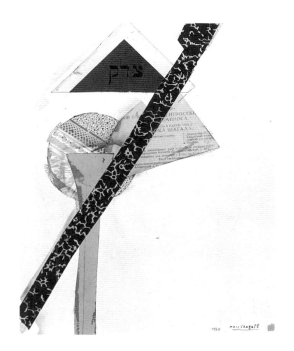

Collage. 1920. Pencil, pen, ink, and collage on paper. 15 3/8 x 11 in. (34.2 x 27.9 cm). Musée National d'Art Moderne, Centre Georges Pompidou, Paris.

E. TÉRIADE

"Chagall and Romantic Painting"

1926

*E. Tériade (pseudonym of Efstratios
Eleftheriades), Greek-born writer and
publisher of many works including Chagall's
105 etchings illustrating the Bible.*

As for Chagall, he is a painter who was born a Romantic. But a painter first and foremost, for he brings everything back to painting, and that's what matters. His Romanticism, which has been gradually disappearing as he increasingly seeks balance and paints in beautiful colors, takes its predestined place only in the spirit of his work, and not in its plastic unity, which remains essential and pure. And it is thereby that Chagall rejoins the tradition of Romantic painting.

To see the world through bouquets! Huge, monstrous bouquets in ringing profusion, haunting brilliance. Were we to see him only through these abundances gathered at random from gardens, harmonized who knows how, and naturally balanced, we could wish for no more precious joy!

These are well-bred flowers, who have discovered connections and made slow and daring friendships.

We will look at the world through this lavish plant life, to the forgotten, undistinguished childhood, the village ennobled by heartfelt memories, the tender details that reward fully the slow discovery of things. Why would we refuse to see life through the vivid joy of these bouquets? Why do we always want to see it straight on, or from too close, and try to justify false realities? Let us take a position: Everything is memory. And dreams express things best, and embellish them until they recreate them. Dreams grow our ideas to the limits of our desires.

Chagall places in front of himself a heavy bouquet, nourished by clear saps and he captures its abundance. He allows himself to be invaded. In its near and constant presence, he eventually dozes. He dreams.

Figures travel across Chagall's paintings on the rhythm of a weightless imagination. We let ourselves follow his soul's commands. And when we depart toward long unknowns, by high-speed means of communication, it is not only our spirits that venture forth, but we somehow feel that even our bodies have followed his direction . . . Chagall has captured us at the exact instant when we were passing through friendly landscapes. He stopped himself in midflight, in order to capture himself.

He explores unusual balances, and nothing keeps him from hanging himself as he tries to keep his balance in the void that he would fill with his own kind of cries, or to take on his fragile shoulders the weight of the people he loves.

He is a magician, who pulls unforgettable things out of his hat, from Russian landscapes with gray wooden boards, to odd dancing women, to embracing couples and cows grazing in green pastures. Except that he cannot get them back in, cannot make them disappear into the bottom of his hat. What has come out begins to live, and he goes on.

His figures bathe in favorable atmospheres, created to envelop them. They are no longer people from life. They are disguised as plastic personages. And as such, they receive a ticker-tape parade, dusted with shadows and color that endow them with an enviable place in the domain of painting.

In Chagall, abstraction is constant, but rather than reducing things to geometric elements, abstracting them first, in order to then construct the unity of his plastic world, he prefers to leave them as they are. As if through a dream pursued that spontaneously connects things on the plane of the imagination, he arranges his memories of beings and objects according to an order dictated by his soul, and with the feeling of establishing a reality that is truly his own.

COLORPLATE 39. *The Rooster.* 1928. Oil on canvas. 31 $^{7}/_{8}$ x 25 $^{1}/_{2}$ in. (81 x 65 cm).
Thyssen-Bornemisza Museum, Lugano. Photograph: SCALA/Art Resource, New York

COLORPLATE 40. *Loneliness*. 1933. Oil on canvas. 40 1/8 x 66 1/2 in. (102 x 169 cm).
The Tel Aviv Museum of Art. Gift of the Artist.

COLORPLATE 41. *The Western Wall (The Wailing Wall)*. 1932. Oil on canvas. 28 ³/4 x 36 ¹/4 in. (73 x 92 cm). The Tel Aviv Museum of Art. Gift of the Artist.

COLORPLATE 42. *The Lovers*. 1929. Oil on canvas. 21 ⅝ x 15 in. (55 x 38 cm).
The Tel Aviv Museum of Art. Gift of Oscar Fisher.

COLORPLATE 43. *The Bridal Couple*. 1927–33–35. Oil on canvas. 58 ¹/₄ x 31 ⁷/₈ in. (148 x 80.8 cm).
Private collection. Photograph: Giraudon/Art Resource, New York.

COLORPLATE 44. *Russian Village*. 1929. Oil on canvas. 28 ³/4 x 36 ¹/4 in. (73 x 92 cm). Private collection.

COLORPLATE 45. *White Crucifixion*. 1938. Oil on canvas. 60 3/4 x 55 in. (154.3 x 139.7 cm). The Art Institute of Chicago. Gift of Alfred S. Alschuler. Photograph © The Art Institute of Chicago. All Rights Reserved.

COLORPLATE 46. *Sketch for The Revolution*. 1937. Oil on canvas. 19 ¹/₂ x 39 ¹/₂ in. (49.7 x 100.2 cm).
Photograph © Philippe Migeat. Musée National d'Art Moderne, Centre Georges Pompidou, Paris.

Chagall's oeuvre is a continuing drama of plastic interrelationships, an uninterrupted search for perilous unities. To connect, to unite these two so essentially different materials, these delicate scumblings, their tones muted by distance, with the jostling brilliance of these oily pastes, to place in contact decorated planes, pious care, and the primitive harshness of the roughed-out surfaces, to arrange the free flow of his arabesques over the deviations of his planes, these are all tasks at which only a painter can succeed.

As mad about blue, today, as he has been about violets and yellows or whites and blacks, he has become, since his return to France, the commentator of its clear transparencies. With this color, he has rediscovered the purity that exists only in this country's air, the azure into which the most beautiful dreams disappeared, as they took on defined forms. But here, too, he achieves the miracle of blurring limits and placing his intoxicated soul in them. The feeling for spectacle, which every good Russian has, continues to diminish in his work, which no longer takes in more than those elements necessary for plastic expression, and the pure values that organize it. Chagall takes life with its appearances, and breathes into it the intimate logic of its creation. He has a powerful breath, sustained by a generous soul. No sooner does a work emerge from him, than it takes on its own existence, with its personal organism, beside beings and the things of life. Chagall is so pleased with it that he thinks he'll make another one.

Self-Portrait with Grimace. 1924–25. Etching and aquatint. 14 1/2 x 10 7/8 in. (37 x 27.5 cm). Collection Jacob Baal-Teshuva.

RAISSA MARITAIN

On Chagall's Surrealism

1958

Raissa Maritain and her husband, Catholic philosopher Jacques Maritain, were close friends of Chagall during his American years and the years he spent with Virginia Haggard.

Chagall detests realistic art in all its forms. Any brute representation of things distresses him. He does not shun natural forms, however; on the contrary, he makes them his through the love he bears them; but by the same token he transforms and transfigures them; he brings out, he draws from them their own surreality, finding there the symbols of joy and life in their fullest spiritual vitality.

Impressionism, fauvism, cubism, "all these conceptions seemed too terrestrial to me," Chagall said, speaking of his first impressions when he arrived in Paris in 1910 (he was twenty). "It was necessary to change nature, not only materially and from without, but also from within. . . ."

From the very first his attention had been captivated by the Louvre, where Manet, Delacroix, and Courbet were revealed to him. "It was as if the gods stood in front of me." But in spite of the gods he had still remained obstinately true to the deep tendencies of his own art, "a mad art perhaps, flaming quicksilver, blue soul shooting forth onto my canvases. . . ."

Each of Chagall's canvases—in its serenity, pictorial solidity, and infallible science of color—lives on the stir of poetry, I mean that poetry which is the soul of each and every work of art, and which calls for an assent, a response of our whole being, as every great work of art does. Poetry, in this sense, is the manifestation of a mysterious knowledge, an experience full of savor, which is born in the depths of the soul and seeks to fructify into a work, as the strength of the tree rises from the depths of its roots to the sky of its fruit. And it is, no doubt, because of this poetic experience where his work comes to life, that Chagall, who does not profess any dogmatic religion, finds it astonishing that it is possible for

some to conceive of an art deprived of mysticism. "My heart calmed"—we read in the artist's invaluable confidences which make the fine book that Jacques Lassaigne wrote on him still finer—"my heart calmed when I looked at the icons by Rublev, our Cimabue. With him I was born to mysticism and religiosity."

Chagall will always love icons, but henceforth these icons will be the images of Christ which he himself will paint. There are quite a few of them in his work. The first one was, I believe, the *Crucifixion* of 1938. Sometimes Christ crucified is the central subject of the canvas, sometimes he appears in the most unexpected environment—now with the Virgin Mary, now with the painter himself. What the heart and the hand of Chagall are looking for is, I suppose, at one and the same time the symbol of the suffering of the world and the suffering of the Jewish people, and of the mystery of the Messiah.

COLORPLATE 45

A painting by Chagall is a presence which imposes itself even upon those who are deaf to poetry's voice. But to those who hear are told, through the very power of this art, a thousand dreams and mysteries which are, as it were, the secret network of the arterial tree of the work; they assure life, they express the ineffaceable images of childhood, the wishes of the heart, the joy of the eyes.

Chagall's surrealism is the liberation of his own inner world. The universe created by Chagall is in ignorance of hatred and discord; it utters grace and joy, fraternity and love. The suffering of the world is also present, under the sign of a grave and melancholy contemplation; but the symbols of consolation are always near at hand. The Chagallian world capsizes with pity.

146

The loving, spiritual joy in which Chagall's art is steeped was born with him in Vitebsk, on Russian soil, on Jewish soil. It is, then, imbued with melancholy and tears, run through by the dart of nostalgia and difficult hope. This joy resembles no other; I would say that, while it thrusts its roots deeply into the full reality of life, it draws therefrom, at the same time, the tragic feeling of its own frailty. Look only at the faces of Chagall's musicians, of his beggars, of his rabbis; they are faces eternally true, at once miraculously able to assert the happiness of life and to confront the executioner and death.

"Arriving in France I still had loam on the roots of my shoes. It takes a long time for this loam to dry and drop off. . . . When all the memories of Vitebsk vanished away (and they were real, palpitating signs which had nourished my soul so long) I was obliged to find something else. . ." "the landscapes of France, . . . Paris,"—and those animals of La Fontaine (and of Chagall) in whom so sweet and profound a loving inspiration is alive, in an admirable plastic form. "To sum up," he wrote, "for what I succeeded in doing I am indebted to Paris, to France, whose atmosphere, men, and nature were for me the true school of my life and my art."

JACQUES MARITAIN

Chagall's World

1929

When Saint Francis had wedded Poverty, he began to sing with unbelievable freedom the world's most delicate and newest song. He tamed the wolves, made a convent of birds, and in all unlikelihood and truth, his heart dilated with love, he took the air, afoot or on his mule out on the backs of what the Psalm calls the exultant hills.

Thus it is that Chagall weds painting; in all humility and cheer! His clear eyes see all bodies in a happy light, he delivers them from physical laws, and makes them obey the hidden law of the heart: agile, free, without heaviness, sagacious and eloquent as the ass of Balaam, fraternal, sweetened one toward the other, the pig toward the poet, the cow toward the milkmaid . . . A laughing gaze, sometimes melancholy, rummaging through an innocent and malicious world.

A quite real world, however, like that of childhood. Nothing is firmer, warmer, more dovetailed, than the handclasp of the airplaning couple by which they hold one another up in the open air. Nothing reveals a truer knowledge of the animal world than these astonishing illustrations of the fables of La Fontaine that were to be admired at the gallery of M. Ambroise Vollard, in the fluid brilliance of which the good humor of the Ile-de-France mingles with the revery of Russian forests, La Fontaine with Kriloff and with the tales of Kota Mourliki.

On the visual plane everything looks topsy-turvy. In fact, on the spiritual plane a stroke of magical light has put everything in place. Each composition of Chagall—a real discharge of poetry, a mystery in the sanest clarity—has both an intense realism and spirituality.

Occasionally he opens up his toys to see what is inside; this because he loves them! He knows that in the brain of the cow the little farmer-woman is sitting; he knows that the world is capsizing around the lovers, bucolic and disastrous. He has won the amity of creation, and parades his couples around the sky with the assent of the little villages.

Night at Orgeval. c. 1950. Oil on canvas. 39 5/8 x 25 1/2 in. (106 x 64.8 cm). Private collection.

One asks one's self what knowledge, very sure and almost painful in its perspicacity, permits him to be so faithful to life in such complete freedom. No mistake can be made on the love of things, of beasts, of the whole of reality—love too nostalgic to be pantheistic—that animates such knowledge and keeps it in good wind.

Now and then these reminders of Siennese profiles, of Florentine visitations, make one feel the gravity that constitutes the basis of so much fantasy, and understand the great love for Angelico of this veritable and admirable primitive. Pitiful, melancholic, haunted by the departure of perpetual wandering, singing of poverty and hope, it is the very poetry of the Jewish spirit that moves us so profoundly in these miraculous Rabbis, as in the marvels of aerial mobility and fiery truth that spring from the world of forms and colors invented by him for the Yiddish Theater of Moscow.

At a time when the implacable creative force of a Picasso and the pathetic genius of a Rouault would have sufficed, it seems, to occupy all painting, we are grateful to Chagall for showing us that there are—so different, but not incompatible, for no beauty exhausts the multiple fecundity of art—still other sources of poetry. These hold fast in a singularly close manner to the lyricism of a race. But then, is it not a virtue already almost Christian—this taste for freshness and humility and difficult balances, for seeing the world thus from the angle of a happy catastrophe?

This obsession with miracle and freedom, with the innocence and a fraternal communication among all things reveals to us in Chagall an evangelical sentiment unconscious of itself and as if enchanted, where sometimes a certain grating of the world of the senses reminds us that here and there the devil still furtively shows his horns through the flowery bars of this luminous universe.

Chagall knows what he says; he does not perhaps know the range of what he says. That St. Francis would have taught to him, as to the larks.

KATHARINE KUH

The Pleasure of Chagall's Paintings

1961

Katharine Kuh, art critic and former curator at The Art Institute of Chicago.

Chagall, the artist, is not easy to understand. His strange animals, weary old men, Russian carts juxtaposed over rooftops, though partially explained by the traditional cliché of his Russian background, still remain baffling. That he is a Russian may account for his surprising Byzantine color but scarcely explains his indifference to normal laws of gravity.

Chagall, in discussing his work, says that he is not a product of Russian literature, of folk tales, and Jewish lore. "There is nothing anecdotal in my pictures— no fairy tales—no literature in the sense of folk-legend associations." But he admits at the same time that "every painter is born somewhere. And even though he may later return to the influences of other atmospheres, a certain essence—a certain 'aroma'—of his birthplace clings to his work. . . . The vital mark these early influences leave is, as it were, on the handwriting of the artist."

With Chagall the inner eye must not be discounted but no less the outer eye, that eye concerned with visual dynamics and rhythms. It is not because he is a Russian that he ignores naturalistic perspective and correct gravity; it is solely because he is an artist. Chagall takes all the liberties that his profession allows when he organizes strange unrelated objects into unexpected compositions. For him an animal is not less romantic than a loving couple emerging unexpectedly from a traditional bouquet of flowers. His source material is drawn from his past, not his use of it, and this is important to remember. . . .

To the uninitiated, Chagall's work poses questions not easily answered. To say that his philosophy is animistic does not explain winged fish and donkeys nonchalantly strumming "Uncle Neuch's" violin. Rapturous lovers floating over snowbound villages, and conversely, winged angels solidly moored to flowered landscapes cannot be whistled away because of Chagall's love for his Russian village or for the French Riviera. Neither are these dreams. He uses what he needs and he uses what he knows to build paintings rich in fantasy and suggestive moods. His storehouse of emotional associations has always been the source of his art; witness how the mundane facets of life in Vitebsk, its architecture, domestic animals, and Jewish ritual, are irrationally combined with the artist's later experiences, his happy marriages, his pleasure in the fruits and flowers of the Riviera, his visions of Paris. . . .

Snowing. 1939. Gouache on cardboard.
26 ¹/₂ x 20 ¹/₄ in. (67.3 x 51.4 cm). The Saint
Louis Art Museum.

Chagall's moods change chronologically. His pictures can be tender, sardonic, passionate, witty, or sad, depending chiefly on the timbre of his life at a given time. During the early years of his more than happy marriage with Bella, his paintings, frankly sensuous, reflect the depth of his love. His work after the fall of France is impregnated with suffering. It was at this time that he painted his famous *Crucifixion,* a little earlier *The Martyr.* His color, vivid and wild during the happier Parisian days, becomes appropriately subdued, recalling his earlier work from the more somber environment of Vitebsk.

But it is best to accept Chagall's work without laborious probings. He tells us that his paintings are to be looked at—not interpreted. Once he said in an interview, "For me a picture is a plane surface covered with representations of objects—beasts, birds, or humans—in a certain order in which anecdotal illustrational logic has no importance. The visual effectiveness of the painted composition comes first. Every extrastructural consideration is secondary." He is not illustrating dreams, fantasies, or folk legends; in short, he is not an illustrator, nor is he a mystic or a symbolist, as is so commonly said. For Chagall tells us clearly that his problem is a visual one; his only restrictions those which involve looking and seeing. The Renaissance tradition of rational subject matter and naturalistic perspective is in part responsible for our confusion. He, like many of his contemporaries, has developed a freer form than was possible during the Renaissance when artists were struggling to conquer the previously unsolved problems of chiaroscuro and perspective.

The Martyr. 1940. Oil on canvas. 64 3/4 x 44 7/8 in. (164.5 x 114 cm). Kunsthaus Zurich.

It is possible that Chagall's enigmatic choice of subject matter will always baffle the newcomer, but it is to be remembered that many artists have used their childhood environment as the basis for their work. So also has Chirico called upon his brief early years in Greece, while Picasso refreshes himself periodically with images from his Spanish homeland. What could be more logical than Chagall's use of visual memories, culled from his deeply emotional Jewish childhood in Russia? From these associations he fashions powerful compositions, which, with eerie precision, evoke the moods of his past. To those who accept him, I know of no artist living today who can exceed Chagall in the ability to give enjoyment and pleasure.

MARC CHAGALL

To Benois

March 1935

The Dream. 1939. Gouache and pastel on paper. 20 ¹/2 x 26 ⁷/8 in. (52 x 68.2 cm). The Phillips Collection, Washington, D.C.

Paris

Dear Alexander Nikolaevich,

I am not usually in the habit of writing to art critics. Criticism is "independent" after all. But you are a Russian—and so this question also immediately touches a sore spot. Do not think that I'm complaining about anything, although over the years I have developed the appearance of one who complains. However, do believe me: I perhaps have certain private reasons for this that, as a person of different background, you would not be familiar with. And, it seems, in essence that you and I cannot agree: we are people and artists of two different generations and artistic outlooks. One might say that we have "little to talk about"—were it not that I remember your delightful lines of another time: then all around us and within us was delightful (I lost them in Russia and would gladly read them again one of these days).

But much has happened since then. After all, before that period (1914) you didn't know about me; everything that I did abroad between 1908 and 1914 was left behind there, and then I was "another" person there, whom you would not have "recognized." It's very painful to me, that you may only think that I was, or am, not "in earnest." It's a pity that I do not have with me a copy of my book *Ma Vie*—You would then see if I was born on this earth to not "be serious," to "joke" and to "fool around." Especially when, as a boy, I "chemically" saw our Russian painting from the time of Stasov up to the Revolution and after it. No, we will never, it seems, agree with Russian artists in our artistic language, but nevertheless I was born in Russia, and nevertheless I'm overflowing with ("undivided") love for her, and I was and am, alien to all regimes: the Old Russia, Soviet Russia and the emigration. But I don't want to end this letter on a "plaintive" note. Quite the opposite: I am grateful to you for the many tender words in your article.

And I would like to think that some time in the future the work of certain Russians living abroad will be seriously used to help the mother country and her art.

I remain respectfully yours,
with best wishes,
Marc Chagall

ANDRÉ BRETON

The Importance of Chagall

1945

The Lights of Broadway. 1931. Pen and ink sketch for *Lieder und Poemen* by Lessin-Abraham Walt. Musée National d'Art Moderne, Centre Georges Pompidou, Paris.

For a long time one serious failing at the roots of those movements—Dada, Surrealism—which were to achieve the fusion of poetry and visual arts consisted in underrating the importance of Chagall. Yet the poets themselves were deeply indebted to him—Apollinaire for his "Across Europe," possibly the freest poem of this century, and Cendrars for the "Transiberian"; even Maiakosky and Essenine echo to him in their most convulsive moments. The poet's resistance came later; it was based on the suspicion, no doubt partly justified, that Chagall had turned mystic (and in the twenties and thirties any such suspicion brought an automatic and final condemnation). Today it is possible to situate Chagall's work more fairly. His complete lyrical explosion dates from 1911. It marked the triumphal appearance, through his work and no other, of the metaphor in modern painting. In order to consummate that shuffling of the spacial plane which Rimbaud had prepared us for many years earlier, and, at the same time, free objects from the law of gravity, tear down the barriers of the elements and kingdoms, in Chagall's work the metaphor immediately found a visual support in the hypnogogical image and in the eidetic (or aesthesiac) image, which only later came to be endowed with the characteristics that Chagall had bestowed upon it. No work was ever so resolutely magical: its splendid prismatic colors sweep away and transfigure the torment of today and at the same time preserve the age-old spirit of ingenuity in expressing everything which proclaims the pleasure principal: flowers and expressions of love.

André Breton (1896–1966) trained as a doctor and discovered Freud's theories of the unconscious while working with psychiatric cases in World War I. He developed a theory of art and literature based on psychoanalysis and exerted great influence through the Surrealist manifestoes of 1924, 1930, and 1942. Breton took the word surrealiste *from Guillaume Apollinaire, who had used it in 1917, and defined it as "pure psychic automatism by which it is intended to express verbally, in writing or in any other way, the true process of thought."*

While in Paris Chagall befriended many writers and poets, including Max Jacob, Guillaume Apollinaire, and André Breton. Chagall never considered himself a Surrealist and did not join that or any other artistic movement, although he was invited to do so.

RENÉ BERGER

"Chagall and the Presence of the Myth"

1961

René Berger, French writer and art critic.

It has been too often repeated that Chagall is the painter of the Russian soul. The fact is that a number of his canvases were inspired by his native soil. In almost all of them the log huts of Vitebsk reappear like an insistent refrain. But in listing themes, are we not tempted to confuse art and folklore?

It is also often said that the Jewish soul found its first interpreter in Chagall, and this claim is supported by reference to the rabbis, the torah, the candelabra, the Bible, the many patriarchs and prophets. Is the iconography of a man's work, however, sufficient to decide its meaning?

Much has been said too of his gift for evoking magic. The steppes, Vence, the banks of the Seine, the Old Testament, nature—they are all transformed by the touch of his brush. Like the teller of fables (after all, he illustrated La Fontaine) he makes animals speak, gives them a human face and voice. But Chagall is not a teller of fables, and if by chance the foal appears in the mare's belly, or the clock has flapping wings, it is not magic for all that. The fable implies a connivance with the spectator from which his art is exempt. As for magic, its nature is to disconcert. The art of Chagall astonishes, but does not disconcert.

Fantasy, then. It is to amuse us that the painter perches the ass on a tree, that he ravishes a fiddler to the clouds . . . The spectator soon enters into the game, delighted to find in himself a humour he knew nothing of!

No, I see neither magic nor fantasy in the work of Chagall and I would also dare to maintain that his grace, about which we are all in agreement, but on which we do not agree, is entirely voluntary. By which I do not mean that it is an affair of premeditation. But that is it the fruit of long and careful meditation, of constant vigilance, this appears to me certain. The grace of Chagall deceives us if we persist in seeing it as the product of supernatural gifts. For my part, I believe rather that it results from a precise intention, that of constructing a world in conformity with a fundamental need which is sustained by the artist at the price of the perseverance of his whole being. . . .

Without breaking with the world as we see it, Chagall breaks with the physical enslavement to which our existence is subject. Weight no longer wields power, or rather it relaxes it. So things do not entirely lose their weight; if they give the impression of floating, it is only in appearance. Lightened, their density remains safe. A secret attraction prevents them from becoming the victims of chance. In this Chagall's painting differs fundamentally from a vision or a dream. It is never aberrant, even less does it cause delirium. Beings and things are linked together and through this they remain bound to our condition, without being blended with it. Their cohesion corresponds to our need for coherence. If the fish flies, it is neither subterfuge nor miracle, still less a conjuring trick, and certainly the opposite of fantasy. It flies because, as Chagall paints it, *the possibility of flying is in its nature. . . .*

Freed from his condition, not enfranchised, man escapes from the straitjacket of anatomy. His body expands in moments of joy, opens out towards the light, becomes diffused when clouded with melancholy. Brilliant creatures, firing the sky like a torch, lovers irrigating the earth in the fusion of their joy, *the human figure chooses the form that suits it best.* The beating of the heart finds its echo in nature. No more stereotyped copies or stale old gestures!

Flowers in a Dream. c. 1930. Oil, gouache, crayon, and pastel on paper mounted on board. 27 x 20 ¾ in. (68.6 x 52.7 cm). The Baltimore Museum of Art. Bequest of Sadie A. May.

Mexico. 1942. Gouache on paper. 24 x 17 in.
(61 x 43 cm). The Baltimore Museum of Art.
The Cone Collection, formed by Claribel Cone
and Miss Etta Cone of Baltimore, Maryland.

There is therefore a sharp difference between Chagall and the expressionists
with whom he is sometimes confused. The expressionist pushes his art to burst-
ing-point, but its clangor reechoes in solitude. However powerful his art, it carries
the scar of its wounds, no doubt because it is in the nature of art to reject the
absolute affirmation of the individual. Chagall has always known this and never
forgotten it. He is mindful of the fraternal vocation of art, and even his peculiarities awake in us sympathy, which is agreement in nature.

Nor does Chagall attempt to remake the world. There is no presumption in
his work, which springs from love. But in order to love, there must have been,
from the beginning and before one's own time, something to love. That has been
provided in profusion by the Creator on the earth and in the heavens, and the
artist responds to it by his offering. Not that he is a "religious painter." But it cannot be denied that his art is rooted in faith, that every one of his works is an act of
grace.

His drawing reveals this. Instead of seeking to capture the form, he steals
after it, as if to reserve an ultimate safeguard. Objects are suggested rather than
delineated. His line is less an outline than a voice.

155

At Cock's Crow. 1944. Oil on canvas. 39 x 28 ¹/₈ in. (99 x 71.5 cm). Private collection.

In colour also he shows himself as watchful and attentive. It is diffused through forms, sometimes frosted, sometimes clear, not yielding to the temptation of material opacity, in order to fulfill the Pentecost which painting is for Chagall: tongues of fire divined in the sky, in the leaves, tremulous aureoles surrounding bodies. The Spirit does not dissolve on earth, it breathes its life into our world to raise it to its intelligible vocation.

It may perhaps be objected that such an interpretation does not take into account the fabulous beings which people his canvases: animal musicians, bird-headed minstrels, persons the wrong way up or whose head has been removed from the body when it is not split into two monsters. We should compare him with Goya. The monster attacks the order of things. It deliberately distorts; it intentionally provokes anxiety. It always represents more or less avowed rupture, aggression.

There is nothing of this with Chagall. His most surprising creatures neither offend nor wound. They are bizarre, but with a soothing virtue. As much may be said of their introduction into the theme, which when the first astonishment is over, invites conciliation.

Chagall's art does not violate nature. It unveils one of its aspects, certainly an unusual one, but which, through an unsuspected affinity with it, responds to an expectation, sometimes even to a need, of humanity. It is not demoniac but essentially human. It puts away doubt and strengthens our reason for being. What strange painting, which paradoxically drives away strangeness! Doubtless because though it may be an offering, an act of grace, it is also a welcome, which no one can withstand.

The art of Chagall has been compared to that of the ikons, which is clearly a mistake. There is no likeness in subject or in spirit. This disparaging comparison however throws light on a certain feature. It is that Chagall, even in his most animated compositions, obtains by movement what the ikon obtains by hieraticism: the expansion of time. . . . Like the stars in their courses, the canvases of Chagall induce a sense of eternity remote from the passage of time, becoming reborn in the order which they create and in which they participate.

It would be wrong to overlook the debt of surrealism to Chagall. Even before the term was invented, the doctrine formulated, Chagall had made room for the subconscious, the dream. André Breton acknowledged this, belatedly but with exemplary honesty: "For a long time," he wrote, "it was a serious omission at the origin of the movements—Dada and surrealism—which brought about the fusion of poetry and the plastic arts, that full justice was not done to Chagall . . . His total lyrical explosion dates from 1911. It is from that instant that metaphor, through him alone, marks its triumphal entry into modern painting."

It is easier today to understand why this acknowledgement should have been belated. By limiting itself to certain aspects of man, surrealism has declined. Its myth has taken its place in the succession of other historical myths. To recognise this is not to disparage it. But man is neither body, nor soul, nor mind, nor a subconscious, nor an automatic being, *exclusively*. He is that perpetual possible which history unrolls like a film, and which the art of Chagall persuades us is not yet finished. By the liberty of his genius, Chagall sets to work the very *virtue of myth,* which alone is not metaphor, but presence.

JAMES JOHNSON SWEENEY

Chagall—A Conscious Artist

1946

James Johnson Sweeney, former director of The Solomon R. Guggenheim Museum, the painting department at The Museum of Modern Art in New York, and The Museum of Fine Arts in Houston. In 1946 he organized a major Chagall retrospective at The Museum of Modern Art that later traveled to The Art Institute of Chicago.

"It is the glory and the misery of the artist's lot," as André Lhôte once said, "to transmit a message of which he does not possess the translation." This is particularly applicable to Marc Chagall. . . .

Chagall arrived from the East with a ripe color gift, a fresh, unashamed response to sentiment, a feeling for simple poetry and a sense of humor. He brought with him a notion of painting quite foreign to that esteemed at the time in Paris. His first recognition there came not from painters, but from poets such as Blaise Cendrars and Guillaume Apollinaire. To him the cubists' conception seemed "earthbound." He felt it was "necessary to change nature not only materially and from the outside, but also from within, ideologically, without fear of what is known as 'literature.'" And his approach to a certain degree anticipated that reaction from the materialist, or physical emphasis in painting which was to announce itself two or three years later in the work of Marcel Duchamp and to flower in the surrealist movement of the nineteen-twenties.

Unlike so many of the vanguard artists in Paris at that time, Chagall employed readily recognizable representational forms in his work. Still if you ask Chagall to explain his paintings even today he will reply: "I don't understand them at all. They are not literature. They are only pictorial arrangements of images that obsess me . . . The theories which I would make up to explain myself and those which others elaborate in connection with my work are nonsense . . . My paintings are my reason for existence, my life and that's all."

Yet it was with Marc Chagall in his early Paris work, as André Breton has said, "and with him alone, that the metaphor made its triumphant return into modern painting." This is Chagall's contribution to contemporary art: the reawakening of a poetry of representation, avoiding factual illustration on the one hand, and non-figurative abstractions on the other. . . .

Chagall is a conscious artist. While the selection and combination of his images may appear illogical from a representational viewpoint, they are carefully and rationally chosen elements for the pictorial structure he seeks to build. There is nothing automatic in his work. In fact his much talked of illogicality appears only when his paintings are read detail by detail; taken in the composite they have the same pictorial integrity as the most naturalistic painting, or the most architectural cubist work of the same level of quality. He is an artist with a full color sense. He has a deep regard for technique. He is a subtle craftsman who, rather than dull his hand in virtuosity, affects clumsiness. He is an artist who has been content with a limited repertory of representational forms. But his work of nearly forty years shows a persistent effort to bring out new and richer effects from his consciously limited thematic material by unaccustomed arrangements and by a steady development of a more complex technique. In an age that has fled from sentiment he has drawn constantly on it for his stimulation. And our debt to Chagall is to an artist who has brought poetry back into painting through subject matter, without any sacrifice of his painter's interest in the picture for itself, and entirely aside from any communication that can be put into words.

To Charlie Chaplin. 1929. Pen and ink on paper. 16 7/8 x 11 in. (42.8 x 30 cm). Musée National d'Art, Centre Georges Pompidou, Paris.

GILBERT LASCAULT

"Monumental Paintings"

1982

Gilbert Lascault, author, critic, and art historian based in Paris.

It is important to remember that several of Marc Chagall's canvases are enormous, monumental works: *Homage to Apollinaire* (1911–1912), 82 1/4 x 78"; *Golgotha* (1912), 68 1/2 x 75 1/2"; *The Cattle Dealer* (1912), 38 x 80"; *To My Wife* (1933–1934), 52 x 77 1/2"; *The Red Roofs* (1953–1954), 90 1/2 x 83 7/8"; etc. . . .

There is a critical force in Chagall's large canvases. They do not aim at producing an illusion of reality nor attempt to make us believe in the illimitable nature of our measured, encircled spaces hedged in by political and economic powers. They do not pierce the walls in an illusory way, but initiate, on the level of feeling, a dialectical struggle between the recognition of limits and the desire for the unlimited, between gravity endured and gravity conquered. But their critical force, far from restricting them to a purely negative function, to a reticent analysis of how things are, has its origin in a wild affirmation, in a joy that sweeps everything along with it. . . .

Neither purely negative criticism of constraints nor total obliviousness to limits, the large paintings of Chagall introduce the spectator inside a circus

Golgotha *refers to* Calvary, *colorplate 7.*
COLORPLATE 35
COLORPLATE 80

Photograph of Bella posing for *Double Portrait* as Ida looks on, 1925. Collection Ida Chagall, Paris.

universe, an obvious theatrical set. The sheer size of the canvases, the phenomena of transparency, the disturbance of physical laws, the abolition of gravity and the geometry that makes love with a cow or the moon, all contribute to create the madness of the theater, or the theater of madness. In the *Prose of the Transsiberian* Cendrars exclaims: "Like my friend, Chagall, I could make a series of crazy pictures." There is no reason then to be surprised at the fascination the theater exerted on Chagall after the Revolution. . . . For Chagall, the truth of the theater lies in its unreality. The set is a picture that envelops the characters in order to free them. In a sketch for the set for Gogol's *The Revizor* (1920) everything floats: a ladder, geometrical forms, an enormous carriage pulled by a loco-motive-ant. . . . A new world is produced in which the impossible becomes the rule, where dream and reality, joy and sadness celebrate a marriage festival, as in Sholem Aleichem's stories and plays (for which Chagall designed many sets).

But now we must insist again on the scale of the works and show why the monumentality of certain pictures is lost on us (a fortunate loss). From this point of view, Chagall's large paintings constitute the exact antithesis of the famous lace collar in the portrait by Clouet—that collar painted in *trompe-l'œil* and smaller than life-size which Claude Levi-Strauss refers to in *La pensée sauvage*. In relation to it, Levi-Strauss analyzes the strange charm of small-scale models; the reduction of size leads man to believe, correctly or not, that he dominates the object in its entirety more easily; he thinks he has a more direct, immediate knowledge of it. . . .

Chagall's works never allow us to take possession of them, master and know them in this way. The larger the picture, the more our lack of power becomes evident and the more the mystery of the visible endures. Chagall's world cannot be divided, put into compartments, broken down into components; on the other hand, it cannot be dominated as a coherent whole, weighed and measured. The grandeur, the monumental quality of certain canvases is thus one of the means Chagall uses to flout any attempt at structuring them and to lead us astray, away from any path or ownership and into the chaotic and joyous field of personal freedom. The *Homage to Apollinaire* remains (*partly* because of its enormous size) one of the least comprehensible, and most fascinating and secret pictures of the twentieth century. Even when he does smaller works, Chagall never uses the reduction of scale in order to imprison a world, know and control it.

For that matter, Chagall never has recourse to "objects." . . . Chagall's painting is not abstract; it rejects every kind of "formalism," but it takes no interest in

Homage to Apollinaire. 1911–12. Oil on canvas. 78 3/4 x 74 5/8 in. (200 x 189.5 cm). Stedelijk van Abbemuseum, Eindhoven.

objects, desires no knowledge of nor power over things. A pictorial storyteller, Chagall likes the narrative form; he moves not among things but among stories.

The Hasidic tradition has often been pointed out as one of Chagall's formative influences. In Vitebsk, where Chagall was born, a Hasidic community had existed for a long time and, according to Franz Meyer, the painter's parents were Hasidim. Meyer also mentions that the disciples of Abraham Kalisker (a Hasid) made, in the course of certain preaching activities, "dangerous leaps in the street and on the public squares" and lost themselves in "farces." They were, in a way, clowns and acrobats intoxicated by God, and Meyer relates them to the clowns and acrobats of Chagall.

Hasidism probably had more of a profound and less of an immediately observable influence on Chagall. It taught him to love stories, to see in narration not a simple means of distraction but a way of *waking* people up. The Hasidic tradition is made up of countless anecdotes, short stories and fables, which it prefers to reasoned arguments. As Rabbi Nahman of Bratislava states: "Most people believe that stories are made to put you to sleep; me, I tell them to wake people up." In this universe the narrations have a life that precedes their expression; they are much stronger than the person who tells them. As Rabbi Bounam puts it: "One day there was a story that wanted to be told."

COLORPLATE 47. *Nude Over Vitebsk*. 1933. Oil on canvas. 34 1/4 x 44 1/2 in. (87 x 113 cm). Collection Ida Chagall, Paris.

COLORPLATE 48. *Bridal Couple at the Eiffel Tower.* 1938–39. Oil on canvas. 59 x 53 ³/4 in. (150 x 136.5 cm).
Musée National d'Art Moderne, Centre Georges Pompidou, Paris.

COLORPLATE 49. *The Apparition of the Artist's Family.* 1935–47. Oil on canvas. 48 ¹/₂ x 44 in. (123 x 112 cm).
Musée National d'Art Moderne, Centre Georges Pompidou, Paris.

COLORPLATE 50. *Midsummer Night's Dream.* 1939. Oil on canvas. 46 1/8 x 34 7/8 in. (117 x 88.6 cm).
Musée de Grenoble. Photograph: André Morin.

COLORPLATE 51. *The Flayed Ox*. 1947. Oil on canvas. 39 ³/8 x 31 ⁷/8 in. (100 x 81 cm). Collection Ida Chagall, Paris.

COLORPLATE 52. *Tribute to the Past.* 1944. Oil on canvas. 28 x 29 ³/4 in. (71 x 75.5 cm). Private collection.

COLORPLATE 53. *Wall Clock with a Blue Wing*. 1949. Oil on canvas. 36 1/4 x 28 3/4 in. (92 x 73 cm). Collection Ida Chagall, Paris.

COLORPLATE 54. *Madonna of the Village*. 1938–42. Oil on canvas. 40 ⅛ x 38 ½ in. (102 x 98 cm).
Thyssen-Bornemisza Museum, Lugano. Photograph: SCALA/Art Resource, New York.

The rabbis and the profane storytellers accept the disconnected, broken structure of these stories, the holes, gaps, sudden transitions and omitted explanations. One need only read *The Magic Tailor* by Sholem Aleichem to see how difficult it is to know what the story is talking about, whether it is joyous or sad, and to remain forever in the dark about how the thing reluctantly called a "goat" was bewitched. . . . Without doubt Rabbi Nahman of Bratislava developed the art of uncontrolled narration the furthest. In his stories Elie Wiesel (*Hasidic Celebration*) writes:

> Each fragment contains the whole and threatens it. . . . The human condition, made up of questions, is translated by its very explosion. . . . If Rabbi Nahman tightens the episodic events and lets the narrative float, it is because he prefers the infinitely small to the infinite, a life with leaps and starts to a life without surprises.

Chagall has the same preferences. In particular, the changes in scale and the absence of supporting points on the large canvases disorient us; there is no concern for the habitual rules of composition: figures are massed together in certain areas of the picture, whereas other areas remain empty; we never receive a message, but the existence of an enigma is imposed upon us. Chagall multiplies the signs but provides us with no key. Why, in the *Homage to Apollinaire*, did the painter inscribe his name twice near the upper edge, once in the normal way and the second time without the vowels? Why did he write his first name nearby, half in Roman characters, half in Hebraic letters? How is this repetition of the name, this fragmentation of the first name, related to the bisexual being figured in the work and to the four names inscribed at the bottom of the picture?

CHAGALL ON ART AND LIFE

Chagall on "Jewish Art"

1922

A few words, comrades, on the topic you asked me to write about at length—my opinion on Jewish art.

Just recently in Jewish artists' circles a hot debate went on about the so-called Jewish art.

In the noise and fever, a group of Jewish artists emerged. Among them was Marc Chagall.

Still in Vitebsk when this misfortune happened—just returned from Paris—I smiled to myself.

I was busy then with something else.

On the one hand, Jews of the "new world"—that world so hated by Litvakov—my shtetl alleys, hunchbacked, herringy residents, green Jews, uncles, aunts, with their questions, "Thank God, you grew up, got big!"

And I kept painting them. . . .

Chagall resented very much being labeled a "Jewish artist," even to the point where he once threatened to sue a publisher who wanted to include him in a book of Jewish artists. However, Chagall also wrote: "If I were not a Jew, I wouldn't have been an artist, or I would be a different artist altogether."

On the other hand, I was younger then by a hundred years, and I loved them, simply loved them. . . .

I was more absorbed by this, this gripped me more than the thought that I was anointed as a Jewish artist.

Once, in Paris, back in my LaRuche room, where I worked, I heard through the Spanish screen the quarrel of two Jewish émigré voices, "So what do you think, after all, Antokolsky wasn't a Jewish artist, nor Israels, nor Liebermann!"

The lamp was dim and lit my painting standing upside down (that's how I work—now are you happy?!) and finally, when the Paris sky began to dawn, I laughed at the idle thoughts of my neighbors about the lot of Jewish art, "O.K., you talk—and I will work."

Representatives of all countries and nations!—To you—my appeal. (I cannot, I remembered Spengler.) Confess: Now, when Lenin sits in the Kremlin, there is no sliver of wood, smoke rises, the wife is angry—do you now have "national art"?

You, clever German Walden, and you, various others who preach international art, fine Frenchmen, Metzinger and Gleizes (if they're still alive), you will answer me, "Chagall, you're right!"

Jews, if they feel like it (I do), may cry that the painters of the shtetl wooden synagogues (why am I not with you in one grave?) and the whittlers of the wooden synagogue clappers—"Hush!" (I saw it in An-ski's collection, got scared)—are gone.

But what is really the difference between my crippled Mohilev great-grandfather Segal who painted the Mohilev synagogue, and me, who painted the Yiddish theater (a good theater) in Moscow?

Believe me, no fewer lice visited us as we wallowed on the floor and in workshops, in synagogues and in the theater.

Furthermore, I am sure that, if I stopped shaving, I would see his precise portrait. . . .

By the way, my father.

Believe me, I put in quite a bit of effort; no less love (and what love!) have we both expended.

The difference is only that he took orders for signs and I studied in Paris, about which he also heard something.

And yet. Both I and he and others (there are such) are not yet Jewish art as a whole.

Why not speak the truth? Where would it come from? God forbid it should have to come from some fiat! From Efros writing an article, or because Levitan will give me an "academic ration!". . .

There was Japanese art, Egyptian, Persian, Greek. Beginning with the Renaissance, national arts began to decline. Boundaries are blurred. Artists come—individuals, citizens of this or that state, born here or there (blessed be my Vitebsk)—and one would need a good registration or even a passport specialist (for the Jewish desk) to be able to "nationalize" all the artists.

Yet it seems to me:

If I were not a Jew (with the content I put into that word), I wouldn't have been an artist, or I would be a different artist altogether.

Is that news?

For myself I know quite well what this little nation can achieve.

Unfortunately, I am too modest and cannot say aloud what it can achieve.

It's no small matter what this little nation has achieved!

When it wanted—it showed Christ and Christianity.

When it wished—it gave Marx and Socialism.

Can it be that it won't show the world some art?

It will!

Kill me if not.

Jozef Israels (1824–1911), one of the leaders of The Hague school.

Max Liebermann (1847–1935), the principal German Impressionist painter. He went to France in 1872 and was greatly influenced by the Barbizon school of painters, especially Millet.

The Tablets of the Law. c. 1955. Oil on canvas.
16 x 13 in. (40.6 x 33 cm). Private collection.

Chagall Remembers

August 29, 1936

Dear Pavel Davidovich,
I'm sitting at the "dacha" and I remembered you. Altogether, in this village you remember our native land all the time.

You see a tree and think, but our trees aren't like that: the sky's different, and everything is different. And as the years pass these comparisons begin, as they say, to play on your nerves . . . As the years pass, you feel more and more that you are yourself a "tree" that needs the land, rain and air it's used to . . . And I begin to think that somehow, I hope, I'll soon manage to come home and draw new strength from my native land and do some painting there. Most of all I want to break with Vollard. After all, he still hasn't published the books I did long ago, *Dead Souls* and La Fontaine's *Fables,* and the Bible I began years ago is still in preparation . . .

Ambroise Vollard, Chagall's publisher, died in 1939, and the works mentioned here were eventually published by E. Tériade.

Well, what's happening with you? what's new? How are things with the arts in the mother country? I would like to receive an art journal, any one.—To have any kind of contact, because I'm otherwise too forgotten and alienated. Write to me any time. Nobody writes to me apart from you.

Best wishes,
Yours truly Marc Chagall

From Chagall's Lecture at Mount Holyoke College

"Some Impressions Regarding French Painting"

August 1943

At my friend Venturi's request, I agreed to say a few words today. A few words which might not be very French, and which might concern me too much. I apologise in advance. Talking in front of an audience, rather than among intimate friends, or to myself, is not a common experience for me, I must admit. I am a painter, and if you will forgive the expression, I am a consciously unconscious painter. There are things, heaps of things in the realm of Art, for which it is difficult, particularly nowadays, to find the key words. Indeed, why try, so relentlessly, to break down those doors? It seems to me that they sometimes open all by themselves, effortlessly, without useless words. But at the same time do I not every year feel somehow guilty towards someone, towards myself. I am full of faults: human and especially artistic. How can I confidently speak of others' art? If I could at least speak about my own!

Finding myself in a new land—in this hospitable America—in spite of myself my thoughts turn to the country in which I spent several decades of my life; where I arrived still a youth, which I left, driven out by those, who by a tragic misunderstanding have a human face. . . .

I would like to point out here that my travels from country to country have always been solely dictated by artistic considerations. I would not say that like some other foreign painters, I could not adapt myself. On the contrary, in France they did me the signal honor of inviting me to take part in international exhibitions in the French pavilions.

And, if you will forgive such presumptuous comparisons—would Van Gogh have been Van Gogh if he had stayed in Holland, Picasso in Spain or Modigliani in Italy? In France I was fortunate enough to become close to a man such as Ambroise Vollard, whose entire life was made up of encouraging certain artists, myself included, to create new works, always newer, although he himself, alas!, abandoned those works to the mercy of fate.

I would also like to point out how very beneficial to me, artistically speaking, were my trips outside France to Holland, or Spain, to Italy or Egypt or Palestine, or quite simply to the south of France. There in the South, for the first time in my life, I came into contact with a flower-filled greenery such as I had never seen in my native city.

In Holland, I discovered that light which is like a prayer, familiar and lively like an unending day before sunset. In Italy, I found the peace of the museums, but brightened by a sunshine harbinger of life. In Spain, I was happy with the ardent mysticism of that betimes cruel past, and with the song of its sky and its people. And in the East, unexpectedly I found the Bible and part of myself. No matter how great my enthusiasm for the great masters I was nevertheless saddened at the sight of the realism, always the same, of the recent schools. It finally became clear that an enormous technical, visual revolution had really taken place.

Look at this: Delacroix, for instance, outraged, in a way underlined to the point of fear some of Rubens' dreamy visual liberties. And to such an extent that even the simple white tone, in Delacroix' studies, astound us by their unexpectedness. And I am not talking of his brushstroke, and this was before Manet, whose brush was not idle either. They both painted and drew with their brushes. And Van Gogh, who invites us to share the feast of his touches, in which there is something of Japanese etchings.

The appearance of Courbet, regarded as a second-rate master, signified in my mind, not so much the advent of a new ethical, social ideology of naturalism as of that of a visual ideology. Cézanne understood this, who in his first manner applied the colors with a knife. This enabled Cézanne to lighten, so to speak, his forms and his paint, so that, later, in Aix, as a contrast, he left some blank canvas and was able to paint this canvas like an unfinished watercolor.

The Impressionists themselves, taking as their model a yellowish light and greying shadow in Piero della Francesca, and having assimilated Helmholz' scientific theories, opened up the doors of art so widely that it is impossible not to consider Impressionism as one of the most remarkable discoveries, of a technical order, in the history of art. . . .

Cézanne drove the cubists to cubism.

But whereas Cézanne created his cubism from nature, the cubists tended more towards stylisation and thus, detached from nature, have mostly left behind them a series of techniques. On account of that, Cubism found its way into life, into its daily background. And I always feel that this is a terrible omen.

Manet, like Cézanne, learning brilliantly from Goya, felt in the latter the importance of his black tones and the polish of his flashes of color.

To that group of illustrious masters, obviously incomplete, I would gladly have added a whole series of modern masters. So, these various elements went from one to the other like divine gifts until quite recently when they all fused together to become that unique Gallery of Art in France which is close to being a miracle. To bring about this miracle, these masters gave their best efforts, their whole life, but other years came along, years full of responsibilities, also needing decisions, great strength, all of life. And what did we see? . . .

The relatively quick acknowledgment of specific movements in painting has always seemed to me rather strange. Cubism, for instance, and other movements, were more easily acknowledged than Impressionism. Unwittingly, one is reminded that Rembrandt, Greco and others waited a long time for a definitive acknowledgment. It seems strange that Art, which by its technique and essence, aspires to the walls of a museum, should have so many premature charms. On the contrary, really great Art does not have this immediate attraction. For instance, Rembrandt, Goya in some of his works, Chardin, Cézanne, Van Gogh and others. A language which is both simple and visually varied is already sophisticated in itself, whereas a language which is not simple becomes decadent and finally fades away.

On my return to Paris in 1922, I was agreeably surprised to find a new artistic youth—the Surrealist group—who were bringing back so to speak, the prewar term: "literature". . . And what had been an insult in 1910, was now practically encouraged. For some it was rather symbolic, but also it was really literary, at times. It is all the more regrettable that art at that time was not noted for the natural technical mastery which characterized the masters of the heroic time before 1914. In 1922, as I was not yet acquainted with their art, I seemed to find in them

Self-Portrait. 1913. Watercolor and ink on paper. 8 5/8 x 6 7/8 in. (22 x 17.4 cm). Collection Marcus Diener, Basel.

The Donkey with the Umbrella. 1946. Oil on canvas. 31 x 42 in. (78.7 x 106.7 cm). Private collection.

COLORPLATE 14

what I had obscurely and yet concretely sensed from 1908 to 1914. But why on earth, I asked myself, proclaim this so-called "automatism"? However fantastical or illogical the construction of my paintings might appear, I would be afraid to create them with a mixture of "automatism." If I put the dead body in the street, and the violinist on the roof in my 1908 painting, or if in another one dated 1911 *Me and the Village*, inside the big cow's head I put a little cow with a milkmaid, I certainly did not do this by "automatism." If through automatism some good paintings have been produced, and a few good poems written, this does not mean that it can be seen as a method. In the same way, all those who have painted trees with blue shadows cannot be called impressionists. Everything in Art must be in answer to the beat in our bloodstream, of our whole being, even unconsciously.

As for me, in any case, I slept very well without Freud. I must admit, I have never read a single one of his books and I probably never will, at this stage. I am afraid, in fact, that as a conscious method automatism will breed automatism. And if I thought that the realistic period due to technical renewal was declining, then the Surrealists' automatism would seem to me rather thin . . .

Some people are wrongly afraid of the word "mystical," they give it an overly orthodox religious meaning. We must strip this word of its old-fashioned, stale appearance: it must be taken in its pure form, intact, strong! Mystical! . . . How often have I had that word flung at me, in the same way that I used to be accused of being "literary"! But without mysticism, would there be even one great painting in the world, a single great poem or even a single great social movement?

174

Every organism—be it individual or social—deprived of mysticism, of feeling, of reason, would fade away, or die.

Sadly, I answer myself: they are wrong to pursue mysticism, it is precisely the lack of mystical feeling which nearly spelt the end of France. One must distinguish between different sorts of mysticism. And precisely, this war must have as its final objective victory over badly understood mysticism, exploited towards evil ends, cruel and one-sided, the enemy's mysticism . . .

People will reply, and I know it already, that the heroic times of French art before 1914 lived and flourished without benefit of mysticism. Yes, but a brilliant technique had achieved its highest peak. Those technical perfections had reached their highest point, but they could not replace for any length of time the missing interior heart. Forgotten and cast out like outmoded garments were the interior sources which, in the course of a long history, had given dignity and heightened awareness to people. So the soul had fled, and like an empty bag floated in the air before falling to the ground and being trampled on by the enemy's boots. Do not think that I am talking of politics. I have only seen art in it. Recently, I was given the opportunity of saying: "They are over, the good old days when Art was nurtured only on outside elements, form, line, color. Everything interests us—and not only the interior world, unreal, that of dreams and fantasy." I can never forget the portentous statement made by an artist who aspired to modernism: "You know, sincerity is not fashionable." If that were true, then everything becomes much simpler.

All the remarks about so-called pure Art, and about bad literary Art, easily led to the fragile positions of recent years, and even to the trips to Berlin of some, theoretically in order to promote loyal Art. Some French painters have decided to replace their lack of interior order by the military discipline of a soulless enemy. Which only goes to prove that the lack of humanism in Art—do not fear that word—was the ill-fated omen of our present predicament. The example of the great schools and great masters of the past teaches us that a true and authentic quality of painting and drawing cannot merge with anti-human tendencies, such as one can see in certain paintings of the so-called avant-garde schools.

The lack of a living bloodstream in fact often leads to a withered painting and a lifeless drawing. Of course, good intentions by themselves cannot give life to a color which is without talent. The young movement in French painting, I mean that which was born during the last decades, enchanted us precisely because it was thrusting towards something new. Why did this drop of fresh blood have to be spilled into an older and unlively body? Beforehand, French painters—Corot, Poussin—had gone so far as to leave their homeland to seek in other countries new revelations which they then set forth on their own native soil. In those days, the flag of a vulgar "nationalism" did not fly above their heads and every journey was fruitful for a painter.

I notice, after talking for so long, that in fact I said very little, and above all have I made it clear what is troubling me, what I wanted to say? No doubt about it, it is best to judge a painter on his works—and his words, I fear only cloud the issue. . . .

I do not know—and who can foretell?—what interior and exterior form will be that of future French art, when France, after such cruel trials, will be restored to herself. Will there be a progressive renewal of its admirable previous vision, and of her cult of form? Will there appear, instead of the previous one, a new interior vision, a whole different conception of the world, as well as new social and moral foundations? And this not only in France. After the closed circle of its great masters, France—just as before, I believe—will build new miracles. So long as the enemy does not starve to death the inventors of these miracles! Let us more than ever have faith in France's spirit. With all our soul, let us hope for her rebirth, a rebirth which will also be that of the entire world.

Chagall to Benois

February 6, 1940

Paris

Dear Alexander Nikolaevich,

How moved I was by your article. Never has the writing of any foreigner abroad, whoever they might be, so touched me.

Thank God that you are passionate, partisan even, and who knows—perhaps you are now the only person to be so in the Arts. That's why I'm proud that you have written about me. Please God, may I only justify it.—I'm glad you recognized that I am not "posing," and have not turned "snobbish" and so on. I come, after all, from a poor people.

I remember too well my father's calloused hands and the hopelessness of his life and work. So how could I, engaged in such "light work," "give myself airs." It seems I demand a lot of myself . . . as I do from others as well—you agree that I'm just a little aware of my *métier* in art. Yes, indeed. But as you noticed, it is impossible to find "laws and rules" in what I do. So much the worse (and more painful) for me. Still I do not feel myself a "child" but fully conscious of what I'm doing. You said much that is true, because you spoke honestly. At present, they have (for the time being!) taken our country away from us and will not let us breathe her air. Yet, despite all my tribulations, I have not broken my inner ties with her all through these years. So your profound Russian words have been a support and, believe me, I very rarely write others such replies.

Most sincerely and thankfully yours,
Marc Chagall

From *First Encounter*

Chagall's Tribute to Bella

1947

Bella wanted to work in the theater, and did work in the theater successfully. Then I came back from Paris and married her. We left for France, and that was the end of her dreams of the stage.

For years her love influenced my painting. Yet I felt there was something within her held back, unexpressed; that she had treasures buried away in her heart, like her "String of Pearls" misted over with love. Her lips had the scent of the first kiss, a kiss like a thirst for justice.

Why was she so reserved with friends, with me? Why that need to stay in the background?

Then came the day when she relived the exile of recent years; the time when the Jewish soul echoed in her once more and her tongue became the tongue of her parents again.

Her style in *Burning Lights* and *First Encounter* was the style of a Jewish bride in Jewish literature.

First Encounter *and* Burning Lights *by Bella Chagall were first published in Yiddish and later in English, German, and French.*

Blue Concert. 1945. Oil on canvas. 48 $^7/_8$ x 39 in. (124 x 99 cm). Private collection.

She wrote as she lived, as she loved, as she greeted her friends. Her words and phrases were a wash of color over a canvas.

To whom compare her? She was like no other. She was the Bashenka-Belloshka of Vitebsk on the hill, mirrored in the Dvina with its clouds and trees and houses.

Things, people, landscapes, Jewish holidays, flowers—that was her world, they were her subject.

Her sentences, long or short, written out or sketched, were now developed fully, now left indistinct like marks or lines in a drawing which must be divined rather than seen.

Toward the end I would often find her sitting up in bed late into the night, reading books in Yiddish by the light of a little lamp.

"So late! You should be asleep!"

I can see her now, a few weeks before her eternal sleep, fresh and beautiful as always, in our bedroom in the country. She was arranging her manuscripts—finished works, drafts, copies.

I tried to hide my fear.

"Why this sudden tidiness?"

She answered with a wan smile, "So you'll know where everything is . . ."

All calm and deep presentiment.

I can see her again from our hotel window, sitting by the lake before going into the water. Waiting for me. Her whole being was waiting, listening to something, just as she had listened to the forest when she was a little girl.

I can still see her back and her delicate profile. She does not move. She waits, and thinks, and perhaps already sees other worlds.

Will the busy men and women of today be able to enter into her work and her world?

Perhaps, later on, others will come who can scent the perfume of her flowers and of her art.

Her last words were: "My notebooks . . ."

The thunder rolled, the clouds opened at six o'clock on the evening of September 2, 1944, when Bella left this world.

Everything went dark.

From Chagall's Lecture in Chicago
"Art and Life"
February 1958

An intellectual asked me the following questions:

"What is the relationship between Art and Life?" Answer: Of course I can enjoy many things which are being accomplished in our life and in our present culture. And we cannot enumerate here all that is talked about in the newspapers . . . If I was a sociologist, I could, eventually, throw light on that state of things using material motivations. Sometimes, one withdraws into oneself with sadness to avoid hearing, and to avoid seeing. And one thinks of such and such a prophet lying on the sand and prophesying for himself and for the passers-by who were ready to listen to him.

He also asked me: "Have the natural sciences taught me anything useful for my art?" Answer: Art, in the last resort, is not something consciously scientific. An artist without his instinct is like a pendulum.

He also asked me: "Is religious faith necessary to an artist?" Answer: Art, in general, is an act of faith. But sacred is the art created above interests such as glory, fame or any other material consideration. We don't know exactly what kind of men Cimabue, Giotto, Masaccio, Rembrandt were. But very fortunate is the hour of our life when, facing them, we are moved to tears. For me, even Watteau is religious, with his flowers, his lovers, his bushes. If his paintings were placed in a religious temple, instead of being in the Louvre, the emotion felt would be even greater.

In the course of these last ten years, I have worked a great deal. Joy came to me in the form of books being edited, and among them, the Bible.

I have chosen to paint: to me it has been as indispensable as food. Painting appeared to me like a window through which I would fly away to another world. Speaking of that, you will excuse me for recalling the biblical image of Moses who, in spite of his stammering, was haunted by God so that he would do his duty. In the same way, we are all, in spite of our stammering, pursued by someone so that *we* will perform *our* duty.

I see again the poor house of my youth where, it seems to me, on the door and in the sky, until night, shone also a burning bush. But I was then only in the house of my parents. Around me there were, haunting me, the bustle of the household, my parents' worries, my life when I felt so lonely and saddened by my father's tiredness (my father fed and raised with difficulty his nine children). My head started to turn at the sight of his calloused and chapped hands, of his worn-out look. Haunted by all that, I left by another way which is, maybe, the same

Photograph of Marc and Bella Chagall in front of *The Fiancées,* c. 1939. Collection Ida Chagall, Paris.

way as my fathers who, on looking then at my drawings thought that they were a continuation of the wall.

Since that time, I have travelled a great deal. I have seen many countries. I have taken different roads looking for colours, looking for light. I have thrown myself into a certain observation of ideas, of dreams. But along that road, I have come up against wars, revolutions, and all that goes with them . . . But I also have met exceptional people: their creations, their charm, and their contact have often quietened me down, reassured and convinced me to carry on.

More clearly, more precisely, with the years, I have come to feel the relative righteousness of our ways, and the ridiculousness of anything that is not produced with one's own blood, and one's own soul, and which is not saturated by love.

Everything is liable to change in life and in Art and everything will be transformed when we pronounce, unconstrained, this word "Love"—a word which indeed is wrapped in an envelope of romanticism (but we do not have, for the time being, another word). In it lies the true Art: from it comes my technique, my religion; the old and the new religion which has come to us from far distant times.

Love should also be the basis of true politics which could bring real peace.

All the other things are a sheer waste of energy, waste of means, waste of life, of time, and can take us nowhere but to the limit which is close to disaster itself.

Art, without Love—whether we are ashamed or not to use that well-known word—such a plastic art would open the wrong door.

What is colour, what is painting? So few people know what it is. True art in painting is not reached when either the canvas or the picture, depending on the subject, is abstract or figurative; but how scarce are those who could answer that question.

The Kidnapping. 1920. Pen and ink on paper.
7 $^{1}/_{2}$ x 8 $^{5}/_{8}$ in. (19 x 22 cm). Musée National
d'Art Moderne, Centre Georges Pompidou,
Paris.

Prophets have been but few in history. Artists, composers, authentic painters are likewise but few, and religion and Love, rare.

Let us rejoice whenever we see signs of this somewhere and let us try to feed that flame, for it is the source of true Art and of Culture.

There cannot be any plastic message or, indeed, any other message, without humanistic values or without what we often call Love-Colour. Outside of that, there is no value whatsoever. Greatness is to be believed in only at that level. Thus Titian, in spite of his religious subjects, thus Gauguin, in spite of his anarchism, thus Monet, in spite of his belonging to the bourgeoisie of the time.

When we look at the first works produced by certain inquiring artists, it is striking to find that, if they do not reach a certain plastic level, as far as quality is concerned, it can be concluded that whatever they have rushed into in the hope of discovering later, something else is likewise to be not up to par as far as quality is again concerned.

It was not the same with Van Gogh. His early works can be compared with certain of Rembrandt's. Cézanne's debuts, in spite of their affiliation with Manet's and Pissarro's, are important too; likewise Seurat's, Gauguin's and those of a few others.

We are living on this planet only, and all the signs of our life, of our behavior, are for this planet only. No cerebrality, however great, be it Da Vinci, Mantegna's, Signorelli's, Cézanne's or that of any other can kill the values and the essential reason of our life on earth, which is, basically, like the joy of a plant and its natural growth.

That's why I speak often of certain qualities measured as if they were pharmaceutical products, exactly weighed. Such is the measure of life, but what is that measure?

This goodness and this Love of which I am speaking are in my own terms colour, light.

It is possible to be gifted in the handling of lines, even on the architectural level. But what is most important is the blood, and the blood is, for the artist, the colour. Colour and all its distinctions are the pulses of the organism. Colour is the pulse of a work of Art. The line, the architectural composition of the pictures may often look like the attributes of dummies. They can be lengthened, modified, distorted according to the mood. In my opinion it is simply unfair to call that drawing. But the best drawings are so-called unconcerned things, such as Rembrandt's. Those by Bonnard, for example, give the impression that he did not know how to draw and I have almost never seen any drawing by Monet.

Anniversary Flowers. 1946. Oil on canvas. 43 ³/₄ x 38 in. (111 x 96.5 cm). The Norton Gallery and School of Art, West Palm Beach, Florida.

The predominance of writing, of drawing, is the sign often of a certain weakness in the painting, of its lack of depth.

No speculation, no skeleton-like scheme can change the disposition and the flow of the born colours; thus a butterfly or a flower in its simplicity or its natural beauty.

I am often asked: what do you call colour and its chemistry? The same can be said about colour as is said about music: "The depth of colour goes through the eyes and remains within the soul, in the same way that music enters the ear and stays in the soul." It is interesting to remember Cézanne's words about Monet. He said: "Monet is an eye, but what an eye!" In the same way we can, very simply, seeing a piece of material over somebody's shoulders, gauge its quality, without considering the cut or the fashion. . . . Thus the Greeks, the Ancients, wore their robes freely, without shaping them, so full of distinction were their tints, their qualities.

Everybody knows that life will end one day. But this is not a good reason for us to let destructive elements take the lead in us. The more we criticize and reject this life, after the manner of some philosophers, writers and artists, the less we live ourselves—the number of years counting for nothing, of course—and the less life we give the others through our works.

Life is indeed a miracle. We are parts of that life and we pass, the years adding to the years, from one stage to another stage of life.

When I came first to Paris, I was instinctively against the realism which I saw everywhere. Upon my return to France, at the end of the war, I had the vision of glowing colours, not decorative and screaming ones, and I rediscovered Claude Monet, with his natural source of colours.

Now I feel the presence of a colour which is the colour of Love.

Chagall Accepting the Erasmus Prize

1960

Your Majesty, Royal Highnesses, Excellencies, Ladies and Gentlemen,
First, I should like to thank you all, and especially H.R.H. Prince Bernhard, for your kind words and your warm welcome.

I should also like to thank you for having founded the Erasmus Prize, which bears witness to the idealism of those who, together with the members of the Foundation Européenne de la Culture, wish, in our troubled times, to encourage people whose lives are spent in search of an ideal.

I think it was a very happy idea to have named this Prize after Erasmus, who was himself an idealist, thus commemorating his name and his thinking.

I thank you for your choice, and am deeply appreciative of the honour you have done me.

On a day like this, I cannot help reflecting on the future of Art.

A few weeks ago, I was in Italy. All of you, I am sure, have seen there works by Titian, especially the *Descent from the Cross* and the *Miracle of San Lorenzo*. How strange it is to think that Titian and Erasmus were almost contemporaries.

Except for Rembrandt, I wonder whether there was ever a greater master, and at the same time a greater man, than Titian, who is so much in keeping with our own period and our own artistic preoccupations.

For, after so many revolutions in the plastic arts, do we not seem to be orphans, lost in a planetary solitude?

Fifteen years ago, when I returned from America, to which I had emigrated, I was amazed to discover Claude Monet. He fulfilled my dreams, for in him I found a source of chemically-pure colour that proceeded from the soul.

But it seems to me now that he indulged in a brilliant form of plastic chemistry: as Cézanne put it: "Monet is no more than an eye—but what an eye!"

Today, when the world, like ourselves, seems to grow old, we are looking for some deeper meaning. In the course of our search, we come upon Titian, a man who has been neglected by the fashion of the past two or three centuries. He seems to us to resemble nature, and his grandeur is written upon his face. He is like a God. A child of nature, he dedicated his art to nature.

In fact, when we are in a mood of doubt, we can always find aesthetic satisfaction in contemplating the Art of nature herself. But if we turn to gaze on the creations of man, we hope to find there the cosmic prolongation of nature.

How bitter we become if we find all kinds of things in that creation, but fail to be permeated by the natural chemical grandeur, the majestic rhythm with which Titian expresses himself.

It is the meaning of Art and of life that communicate a certain tranquillity, a feeling of love.

I do not forget that, beside the Titians I saw, were hanging a Crucifixion by Cimabue, frescoes by Giotto, Masaccio, and Carpaccio.

One of them heroically freed himself from Byzantinism, while another began to pave the way for Realism.

Titian quietly took his place in the Renaissance, which, I may say in passing, forced upon him the humanistic ideas of the period.

But these are mere historical details. What links them is man and nature.

All those who, like Tintoretto, and even Michelangelo and Caravaggio, did something to accelerate the tranquil and natural greatness of the human pace, have now withdrawn into a certain twilight.

I have always thought, and even more so latterly, that man is theoretically weaker than, let us say, God himself. But if man "sings," he is comparing himself to God in some way.

Of course, there are various keys of song: there are Leonardo da Vinci and Bach, and there are Mozart, Watteau and Schubert. There are Rembrandt,

Landscape; I'Ie Adam. 1925. Oil on canvas. 39 5/8 x 26 3/4 in. (100.7 x 70 cm). Collection Ida Chagall, Paris.

Vermeer and Titian or, in our own day, the douanier Rousseau and Paul Gauguin.

It is exceptional for theoretical discoveries to be completely satisfying; in the long run, mankind has rarely rejoiced over them.

One feels like saying, in the silence: "Let us be simple, let us not hide our faces." But it is very difficult to be simple.

One would like to say to oneself, again: "Our unhappy life on this earth is not a masquerade, so there is no need to wear a mask. Those who do are wasting their time."

We cry at birth and we weep when we leave this life.

The only thing left to us is to be as simple as a tree or, as Mayakowsky, the Russian poet, said: "simple as a cloud."

It is up to us to shorten the duration of all types of inflation, be they cultural, artistic, social or physical. It is up to us to bring joy to the hearts of the coming generation and those who wish to live worthily.

For in this inflation, that has lasted so long, there is neither love, nor religion, nor values, nor freedom, nor peace: there is nothing but an existence of frightened sleepwalking.

Sometimes one feels it better to be a voice in the wilderness than one of those multitudes who howl their approval from fear of seeming late for something.

"Late for what? For whom?"

The Dairy. 1933. Watercolor and gouache on paper. 8 x 10 in. (20. 3 x 25.4 cm). Musée National d'Art Moderne, Centre Georges Pompidou, Paris.

But they forget, not to be late for themselves.

Let us not play at being geniuses, pretending that, before us, the world did not exist.

Mankind, today, is living in fear and even in a certain apathy.

In our childhood, we did not know that fear; and our father's house, despite the family's slender means, was intact.

Today, the family roof has, as it were, been torn apart for the children. We parents coddle our children, and even spoil them.

What effects will this have on Art and Culture?

Many people have, quite consciously fled in Art from the visible world, or have deformed the world until it is unrecognizable. The result is a total divorce.

It is no excuse to say that the visible world with all its forms of humanism is going bankrupt.

Nature has been living for centuries: she will never be bankrupt unless man—God help him!—ruins Nature for a long time to come.

Why, then, should a part of nature—that is to say the human race—be going bankrupt?

As far as I can see from looking about me, the animals are *not* bankrupt!

Truly, man can be brought to despair by the realization that cultural and scientific discoveries do not exclusively better the circumstances of his life, but may also frighten him, or even destroy him for the so-called benefit of future generations.

Truly, man can be brought to confusion by foisting an outlook upon him, or even a new ideology; not because of its moral strength, but simply by show of force.

Truly, man can be saddened by the sight of one or other of his fellow human beings behaving unworthily.

But I have no wish to continue with these themes, which could lead us very far.

COLORPLATE 55. *The Three Acrobats*. 1926. Oil on canvas. 45 ⁷/₈ x 35 in. (116.5 x 89 cm). Private collection.

COLORPLATE 56. *Clown on a White Horse*. 1926–27. Gouache on gray paper. 24 $^{7}/_{8}$ x 18 $^{7}/_{8}$ in. (63 x 48 cm). Private collection.

COLORPLATE 57. *The Circus*. 1937–38. Watercolor, pastel, and pencil. 25 ¹/₂ x 20 in. (65 x 51 cm). Private collection.

COLORPLATE 58. *Clown on a Horse*. 1927. Gouache on paper. 26 x 20 in. (66 x 51 cm). Private collection.

COLORPLATE 59. *The Juggler*. 1943. Oil on canvas. 43 1/4 x 31 in. (109.9 x 79.1 cm). The Art Institute of Chicago.
Gift of Mrs. Gilbert W. Chapman. Photograph © The Art Institute of Chicago. All Rights Reserved.

COLORPLATE 60. *The Purple Rooster*. 1966. Oil on canvas. 35 x 30 ³/₈ in. (89 x 77 cm). Private collection.

COLORPLATE 61. *The Circus Rider*. 1969–73. Oil on canvas. 25 $\frac{1}{2}$ x 31 7/8 in. (65 x 81 cm). Private collection.

COLORPLATE 62. *The Circus.* 1962. Oil on panel. 16 x 20 3/4 in. (41 x 53 cm). Private collection.

Snow-Covered Church. 1928–29. Gouache on paper. 26 ¹/₂ x 20 ¹/₄ in. (67.3 x 51.4 cm). The Detroit Institute of Arts. Founders Society purchase with funds from The Friends of Modern Art. Photograph © The Detroit Institute of Arts.

May I, in closing, express a wish? Let us remember the life of Erasmus, whose memory we honour here with the members of the Erasmus Prize Foundation—that seeker after truth who dreamed of a better life for men: let us, like him, express our belief in the genius of Man.

Chagall's Address at the University of Notre Dame

April 16, 1965

I find it hard to tell you, on this occasion, how deeply touched I am by your kindness.

It is a strange and affecting experience to have passed like a cloud under a bank of clouds, for one who, before the coming of the airplane, had known flight only in his paintings.

This is not my first visit to this country. I have lived and worked here for a long time, and I am grateful to the United States for its hospitality.

In response to your invitation, here I am at the University of Notre Dame, in this seat of American culture.

I said once, speaking of Art, that there is such a thing as the color of light. If that is true, then this color has other components as well: freedom, poetry, and everything else that gives meaning to Art and life.

When I was young, I did not strive after fame, or wealth, or honors. I merely wanted to be a simple man and an artist, in the meaning I gave to that concept.

I wanted to be unpretentious, like my father.

That does not mean that I was passive. I did not fight with other men, but I fought with myself.

My only ambition in life was to love: love what is worthy of love, believe in whom one can believe.

It is only to love, I think, that men will open their hearts; it is only through love that union and peace can come to them.

With age, I have gained a clearer understanding of this idea: that a man can have but one end. Long ago I decided, I chose, to proceed to that inevitable end with love in my life, in my art, and in everything I do.

The Art that is rooted in love continues to live.

I think that Art should speak to the spirit rather than, through various theories, to the brain. That kind of Art grows increasingly blurred as time goes on.

On the other hand, we feel closer to it and it plays a greater part in our lives as if it is an intense representation of the inner life of the artist.

Let us not be afraid of words like these, or of ourselves, or of the human spirit, in this day and age. The human organism has lived like this for thousands of years, and for thousands of years it has needed love.

I am happy to be among you, in this University whose work is founded on love of men.

I lay no claim, however, to having chosen the right path in life and, like many others, of course I have my faults.

To me, Art and life itself are like a ship on the high seas.

Who has the gift of knowing where to steer this ship and how to steer it?

Leaving aside scientific facts, there are many sources of intuitive knowledge concealed within us.

I often think of the birds, which translate their life into song so naturally and with such art.

The world has known artists like that: Mozart, Rembrandt, Masaccio, the later Titian.

In everyday life, I see people and things as if through tears. I try to offer them, as best I can, a plastic reflection.

The more sincere you are, the more people respond to you, and seem to expect an answer.

I do not believe in technique. It is within us.

There is no such thing as technical perfection.

Technique is acquired with age, and then it is something other than so-called perfection: by then it is made up of what is in the heart.

One listens with pity to those theories which sound like a case being presented in court and which miss the essential and the continuous in the realm of Art. Art which has the smallest drop of pride in it or which lacks feeling for others has nothing to offer that can feed the spirit.

This is the goal I have aimed at all my life, and whatever may be said of me or of my Art, I have always affirmed and reaffirmed that the qualities of Art are only in ourselves, and not in the outside world.

But it is very difficult to recognize the signs. Could that be the source of tragedy and the cause of certain crises?

Today we seem to be drowning in quantity, and we cannot save the world or ourselves except by moving towards quality.

There is no law, there is only an inner harmony between all the elements of our inner world and the external world.

Let us look back in the realm of Art.

Cézanne's theory did not make Cézanne; theory did not make painters of Seurat and Gauguin.

Impressionism did not make Monet.

Similarly, a Rembrandt or a Mozart, without a theory to back them, took whatever they could use wherever they found it. That did not prevent them from being very great.

But this is hardly the time to speak to you of Art at any length.

In concluding these brief remarks, I wish to pay tribute to your work and to the cultural life of this great American university.

I also wish to express my gratitude for the great honor you have done me.

"A Painting is Born"

A painting is born into the world like a child or like the first quickening moment of love. A child is conceived in a second; thus in a fraction of time is a painting conceived in the mind of the artist. But before and after this moment, years must pass! Years of gestation, of perfecting, perhaps, as each idea grows from theory to reality. And all this has had its starting in a single second: a second of time that is our eternity, or rather not our eternity alone, but that of our ancestors, and perhaps, that of generations yet to come. A work of art which has not been tested, shaped, empowered in this way, can never hope to move the heart of another human being . . .

Chagall painting his *Introduction to the Jewish Theatre*. 1919–20. Collection Ida Chagall, Paris.

THE CIRCUS, THE BALLET, AND THE OPERA

LOUIS ARAGON

Chagall's Circus

1968

Louis Aragon (1897–1982), French poet, novelist, and journalist who became a militant communist in the 1930s and edited the communist newspaper Le Soir. *He was a close friend of Chagall and wrote about him often.*

There are many painters of the circus: Seurat, Lautrec, Rouault, Léger. I should like some day to see their canvases alongside of Chagall's. Not by way of competition or classification of masterpieces, not to give one a higher rating than another, or bestow a prize. But to compare the variety of attraction the circus

exercised over them. One would perceive with a certain surprise that perhaps only in Chagall do all the senses play a prominent role, and that for him the smell of the horse and of the woman, amid the glitter of the ring, is as disturbing as the brilliant light and the spectators in the gallery are for us. Acrobats, tightrope walkers, clowns, all seem to be assembled here only for the glory of the bareback-rider, her scintillation, the incitement of her revolutions. In the Chagallian circuses, indeed what makes them incomparable is that we are caught up in the movement of the woman circling the ring, she whose beauty is the beauty of danger, waiting for her to come around again, until all the men watching with bated breath reach the point of being jealous of the horse.

MARC CHAGALL

"The Circus"

1967

For me a circus is a magic show that appears and disappears like a world. A circus is disturbing. It is profound.

I can still see in Vitebsk, my home town, in a poor street with only three or four spectators, a man who had come with a little boy and a little girl.

Before starting his act, he laid a dirt-colored rug on the ground, raising a cloud of dust. He produced a ten- or twelve-foot pole which he held propped against his belt.

The boy, completely naked under his pink leotard, climbed up the pole. When he got to the top, he bowed over like a snake. He did not smile, and his face had a grayish tinge. You might have thought he hadn't shaved for a long time, even though he was still far too young.

Like many artists before him, Chagall loved the circus. His publisher and dealer Ambroise Vollard provided Chagall with permanent tickets to the circus whenever it came to town, and Chagall could often be found in the audience sketching and drawing.

Below, costumed as an acrobat, the father held the pole against his belly, then hoisted it up to his face, then into his mouth where you caught a glimpse of yellowed teeth. The boy came down. Then it was the little girl's turn to climb up: a child with two small pigtails, in a multicolored dress, so tiny and tired-looking . . .

She slid down the pole and nothing moved in the street, nor at the height she'd come from. I don't know if anyone gave them so much as a penny.

And it seemed as if I had been the one bowing and bowing up there . . .

Another time I saw another little girl. She looked to me like a bareback rider without a horse. In the nakedness of the courtyard her transparent body stocking glistened. I was struck dumb with fear, dreaming of her at night. These visions have transfixed me, although the transparent girl, as well as the boy, evaporated long ago. Where can they be? Where will they end their days? Like them, I add up my age, year by year.

These clowns, bareback riders and acrobats have made themselves at home in my visions. Why? Why am I so touched by their make-up and their grimaces? With them I can move toward new horizons. Lured by their colors and make-up, I dream of painting new psychic distortions.

Alas, in my lifetime I have seen a grotesque circus: a man roared to terrify the world, and a thunder of applause answered him.

A revolution that does not lead to its ideal is, perhaps, a circus too.

I wish I could hide all these troubling thoughts and feelings in the opulent tail of a circus horse and run after it, like a little clown, begging for mercy, begging it to chase the sadness from the world.

Yet, if I have made pictures, it is because I remember my mother, her breasts so warmly nourishing and exalting me, and I feel I could swing from the moon.

It is a magic word, circus, a timeless dancing game where tears and smiles, the play of arms and legs take the form of a great art.

But what do most of these circus people earn? A piece of bread. Night brings them solitude, sadness. Until the next day when the evening flooded with electric lights announces a new old-life.

The circus seems to me like the most tragic show on earth.

Through the centuries, it has been the most poignant cry in man's search for amusement and joy. It often takes the form of high poetry. I seem to see a Don Quixote in search of an ideal, like that inspired clown who wept and dreamed of human love.

I have drawn lions, on King Solomon's throne, at David's feet, on the arch of the Temple. I have seen their image on the robes of high priests, on palace carpets.

All my life I have drawn horses that look more like donkeys or cows. I saw them in Lyozno, at my grandfather's, where I often asked to go along to the neighboring villages when he went to buy livestock for his butcher shop.

At the sight of horses, who are always in a state of ecstasy, I think: are they not, perhaps, happier than we? You can kneel down peacefully before a horse and pray. It always lowers its eyes in a rush of modesty. I hear the echo of horses' hooves in the pit of my stomach. I could race on a horse for the first time and the last time, to the brilliant arena of life. I would be aware of the transcendence, of no longer being alone among the silent creatures whose thoughts of us only God can know.

These animals, horses, cows, goats among the trees and hills: they are all silent. We gossip, sing, write poems, make drawings which they do not read, which they neither see nor hear.

I would like to go up to that bareback rider who has just reappeared, smiling; her dress, a bouquet of flowers. I would circle her with my flowered and unflowered years. On my knees, I would tell her wishes and dreams, not of this world.

I would run after her horse to ask her how to live, how to escape from myself, from the world, whom to run to, where to go.

The Circus. 1961–62. Gouache on paper. 22 $^{1}/_{2}$ x 21 $^{5}/_{8}$ in. (57 x 55 cm). Private collection.

Card Players. 1917. Watercolor, tempera, pencil on paper. 15 x 19 ½ in. (38 x 49.5 cm). The Los Angeles County Museum of Art. The Mr. and Mrs. William Preston Harrison Collection.

I have always thought of clowns, acrobats and actors as tragically human beings who, for me, are like characters in certain religious paintings.

Even today, when I paint a crucifixion or some other religious scene, I experience almost the same emotions I used to feel painting circus people. And yet, there is nothing literary in these paintings, and it is very hard to explain why I find a psycho-plastic resemblance between the two kinds of work.

VIRGINIA HAGGARD

From *My Life with Chagall*

Stravinsky's *Firebird* Soars

1960

Virginia Haggard McNeil was Chagall's companion for seven years after the death of his wife Bella. She is the mother of his only son, David McNeil.

One day Marc told me that he had been commissioned by the New York City Ballet to design the sets and costumes for Stravinsky's *Firebird,* with Balanchine's choreography. Ida decided to rent a large house in Sag Harbor on Long Island so that he could combine work with pleasure. A real holiday was something unknown to him; his sojourns in country places always turned into opportunities for work.

COLORPLATE 72

Ida asked me to accompany them with Jean, and the prospect filled me with pleasure. Ida packed heavy suitcases with household linen and groceries, and Marc, in a short-sleeved shirt with green and mauve checks, a straw hat perched on his fuzzy hair, picked them up without effort and carried them onto the train. I admired his brawny arms and youthful energy.

Jean, Virginia's young daughter from her marriage to artist John McNeil.

The house had vast rooms with threadbare carpets; an oak staircase at the head of which dusty stuffed sea gulls and cormorants perched; and a wide balcony that linked all the bedrooms together. Often, when everyone had settled down for the night, I would slip out of my room and into Marc's. One night, Jean woke up and, finding me gone, screamed in fear. I ran back to my room just as Ida was coming out of her's, and we bumped into each other with embarrassment. I wish we could have laughed instead!

Ida was kind to me, but our relationship was bound to be delicate. I admired her strong personality, her excellent intellect and her sense of humor, but she made me feel ill at ease. Sometimes she scrutinized me until I was completely out of countenance and blushed hotly. She was seductive and charming, but I didn't know what she was really thinking. I was awkward, naive and inhibited; she was emotional. Marc avoided speaking about me, and Ida was discreet.

Marc and Ida spoke together in Russian, and I could tell by the winsome tone of her voice when she wanted to please him (the charming way she had of calling him "Papochka") and her indignation when he was hard and unyielding. There were sometimes passionate quarrels, followed by kisses of reconciliation. Marc shouted, Ida protested tearfully, but there was no sulking; everything blew over quickly. As she was deeply attached to her father, Ida needed frequent demonstrations of affection, and these were not always forthcoming, especially when they were most needed. It was not easy being a famous man's daughter. As a child she was adulated, spoiled perhaps, but not always loved the way she needed to be loved.

For days, Marc listened to the *Firebird* music in a huge bedroom, with three windows looking out over Long Island Sound. At once he began to float in Stravinsky's music, thoroughly tuned in to its powerful archaic rhythms. He started sketching feverishly, jotting down ideas, sometimes in color, sometimes in pencil. They were barely more than abstract shapes or colors, but they contained the living seeds out of which would grow birds, trees and monsters. He let them soak in pools of color until something started moving. First, a bird woman emerged with outstretched wings of awesome beauty, sweeping into a sky of ultramarine; then a mysterious forest emerged where trees grew upside down and the bird was a twirl of gold caught in its branches. In the third scene the bird became a cloud-palace with a ladder leading up to it. Finally there was a celestial wedding scene in reds and yellows where the canopy, the cakes and the candles exploded joyously to the last majestic chords of Stravinsky's music. Everything was flying in Marc's *Firebird;* the dancers would have to be celestial.

Everything that happened at Sag Harbor was full of shattering contradictions: the promised bliss with Marc—the growing suspicions of John (when Jean and I paid him fortnightly visits in Manhattan); Marc's astonishing eyes that had regained their former brilliance, his sun-browned, radiant face; Ida's watchful eye, her unrestrained enjoyment of picnic parties on the beach with amusing friends, her full-blown beauty; Jean's fascinated discovery of the sea and her bewildered fear each time I was out of sight; and, dominating everything, the *Firebird* designs that grew in intensity with our love. Michel came occasionally, and was kind to me. One day, I put too much salt in the soup, and he called to the kitchen teasingly, "They say that when you put too much salt in the food, it means you're in love!"

*   *   *

Marc and Ida got to work immediately on the sets and costumes of *Firebird* and I was employed in helping to sew the costumes. There I met a theater friend of my brother's, Elizabeth Montgomery, a member of the Motley group of theater designers. Before the war my brother, Stephen Haggard, had been a well-known actor in London. From acting he had turned to writing plays, and one of these, with Peggy Ashcroft and himself in the leading parts, was playing when war was declared. He had been sent to the Middle East in the intelligence service and was killed there in 1943. Elizabeth and I spoke with deep nostalgia of those prewar years when Stephen and the Motleys had made the sparks fly in the London theatrical world.

Chagall and Virginia McNeil, 1951.
Photograph © Lipnitzki-Viollet.

Balanchine blew in and out of the costume studio, as were the New York City Ballet's principal dancers, Maria Tallchief and Francisco Moncion, who came with the corps de ballet to try on their costumes. It was good to be back in the theater world again. I had worked in a scene-painting studio in London when I first left my parents' house, and it was there that I had met John McNeil.

Marc supervised the execution of the back drops at the Metropolitan Opera House for two arduous weeks, wielding the long-handled brushes expertly and adding brilliant finishing touches that made the whole thing come alive.

Ida was following in the footsteps of her mother, who had supervised the costumes of the ballet *Aleko* in 1942. After Ida had dressed the dancers, Marc came to inspect them; sometimes he took a brushful of aniline color and dabbed it directly onto their costumes, breaking up a line here and there, flicking a few dots or heightening a tone.

When I saw the ballet a few days after the triumphant opening, the moment of greatest intensity was, strangely enough, the prelude, before the dancers appeared—the first spine-shivering bars of music in the darkened theater, the slow parting of the curtains and the dazzling apparition of Marc's celestial bird. Never had music and painting been so miraculously one. As soon as the dancers appeared, the spell was broken. But the magic returned when the monsters tumbled onto the stage, and the music exploded in a whirl of greens and purples.

When the Yiddish novelist, Joseph Opatoshu, saw the ballet, he exclaimed, "Marc, you must be in love!" Marc chuckled and kept his secret, but a month or two later, we took Oppen, as he was called, and his wife Adele into our confidence.

Reviews of Chagall's Work for the Ballet

1945

From The New York Times: *"Decor by Chagall Dominates Ballet," by John Martin*

Twice in recent years Marc Chagall's familiar painted world has come to life on the stage; he designed two enchanting picture stories, the gypsy-drama *Aleko* and the Russian legend *Firebird*. Both spectacles, now in Ballet Theatre's current repertoire, have been acclaimed with an enthusiasm reminiscent of Diaghilev's glorious times. The scope and surety of the public reaction, however, suggest a significant change of attitude during the last two decades. While Diaghilev's distinguished designers found appreciation only with a limited and rather exclusive circle of connoisseurs, Chagall's ballets are popular with those unprecedented masses which crowd ballet performances every night of the season.

In these beautiful ballets, the perfection and finality of the artist's scenic designs permit little further elaboration in terms of either movement or enacted drama. While the dancers still compete successfully with the décor in *Aleko*, they are in *Firebird* reduced almost to insignificance. But for the congenial quality of Stravinsky's score, but for the fleeting memory of Markova's glittering and brilliant fairy-bird, *Firebird* is a painter's triumph. For there is neither much need nor much opportunity for the ballet's essential medium: the dance. Thanks to one miraculous front curtain, three delightful back drops and some thirty costumes, the spectator is royally entertained, and thus barely misses the ballet. Let us be frank: such triumph, though gratifying and legitimate in the realm of the fine arts, demands a good deal of sacrifice and self-denial on the part of the choreographer and the performers. The magic width and transparency of the scenery has no counterpart in human scale and matter, the weightless flight or suspension of Chagall's painted creatures mocks the leaps and lifts of the dancers, and the marvelously organized diversity of Chagall's imagination is not equalled in a choreographic pattern.

From The New York Herald Tribune: *"Chagall in Wonderland," by Edwin Denby*

Aleko may still with some reason claim to be a genuine ballet. *Firebird*, but for the fortuitous presence of the dancers, turns into a dramatized exhibition of giant paintings, "surpassing everything Chagall has done on the easel scale" (Jewell). In size and substance a breathtaking experience, but hardly one to be expected in the theatre. Or, we may also ask: should we revise entirely our conception of the theatre, surrender the drama to the genius of painting? The importance of the problem grows with the stature of the artist and thus justifies this little investigation. Chagall may have visualized a moving drama, gradually unfolding its enchanting reality in living images; yet he starts out with so overwhelming an optical climax that it is hard to equal, let alone surpass, in any subsequent scenic developments. That, precisely, is the danger; for it is almost impossible to conceive of a choreography which would live up to the ideal demands of the artist's vision. Massine's uncanny skill and empathy which qualified him for the effective staging of such strange imagery as Dali's *Mad Tristan*, also enabled him to organize the ballet proper toward choreographic integration with Chagall's conception of *Aleko*. Adolph Bolm, less fortunately endowed for an adjustment to alien and essentially esthetic requirements, fought pathetically against an imagination too subtle and too powerful to be matched by a conservative rendition. However, the

COLORPLATE 73
COLORPLATE 72

From *Aleko: Scene I, Zemphira.* 1942. Gouache, watercolor, pencil, brush, and wash on paper. 21 x 14 1/2 in. (53.3 x 36.8 cm). The Museum of Modern Art, New York. Acquired through the Lillie P. Bliss Bequest. Photograph © The Museum of Modern Art, New York.

Multi-colored Circus Figure. 1978. Ink, oil, pastel, and collage on canvas. 15 x 11 ³/₄ in. (38.1 x 29.8 cm). Private collection.

patent failure of the choreography is not due to an inadequacy of the ballet idiom but rather to a total lack of balance between two different artistic media. If the specific medium in which the choreographer works sets definite limits for the creative use made of it, the same should apply in costume and decor. This is not to suggest an obvious agreement, between several contributing arts, merely on general esthetic or physical premises. The principle involved concerns the essential logic, the "coherence of imagination" (Venturi) which makes a world of art intelligible and acceptable *in terms of its own medium.* In the case at issue it is ideally neither dance nor painting but the creation of a unified art work of a new category. Chagall's own medium is painting exclusively. He lives in a wonderland of his painter's creation which is valid only within its own esthetic laws. This world is absolutely self-sufficient. If a theatrical production may be summarily defined as the creation of a valid reality in scenic terms, it implies a creative process of transformation. Chagall's imaginary world, as so marvelously revealed in his paintings, is entirely real to him; it does not require, nor even permit, any form of reinterpretation in other terms. Thus the esthetic imperfection of the scenic realization amounts not so much to a question of proportion and integration, nor to a problem of coordination and interpretation, but to a conflict between two different concepts of reality.

Aleko and *Firebird* are not Chagall's first contribution to the theatre. A quarter of a century ago Granovsky invited him to the Jewish Theatre in Moscow in the capacity of stage designer. It soon became obvious that so strong and original a creative imagination as Chagall's transcended the requirements of the stage. The result was both exquisite and incongruous. The irrational reason of his imagination enabled him to maintain his identity and integrity even in an alien medium. But no performer should be expected to sacrifice this identity for the sake of painting. Faced with the concrete problems of the stage Chagall remains essentially a painter. Indeed it is hard for us to visualize him timing his magic on cue and translating his fluid fantasy in terms of rigid stage mechanics. And again in his new ballets Chagall is successful primarily on the strength of his artistic stature and authority, and one may argue whether in such perspective the question of theatrical validity does not become irrelevant. It is a relevant problem, however, for the performers and for the directors of our theatre, lest the conception of art for art's sake and the nostalgic memory of Diaghilev's legendary productions revive artificially a ballet theatre without the life-blood of dancing.

From *Aleko: Scene IV, Rooster.* 1942. Gouache, watercolor, pencil, brush, and ink on paper. 16 x 10 ³/8 in. (40.6 x 26.3 cm). The Museum of Modern Art, New York. Acquired through the Lillie P. Bliss Bequest. Photograph © The Museum of Modern Art, New York.

MARC CHAGALL

At the Inauguration of the Ceiling of the Paris Opera

1964

Two years ago André Malraux asked me to paint a new ceiling for the Paris Opera. I was troubled, touched, and deeply moved.

Troubled, because I dread working at someone else's behest, dreaming all the while of doing monumental works, and touched because of André Malraux's confidence. I doubt myself, my work. Certain opinions only reinforced my doubts, until one day my wife said: "Try to make a few sketches and you will see." I doubted day and night. I thought about the whole structure of the opera. I profoundly admired the genius of Garnier's building and Carpeaux's inspired sculpture.

I wished to reflect, as though in a mirror high above, in a bouquet of dreams, the creation of actors, of composers, to recall the colorful movement of the audience below. To sing like a bird, without theory or method, to render homage to the great composers of opera and ballet.

Sometimes, what one thinks is inconceivable is possible, what seems strange is obvious. Our remote dreams are only starved for love.

I wanted to be among and with those of today, to pay lasting homage to Garnier.

I labored with all my heart, and I offer this work as a gift, in gratitude to France and her school of Paris, for without them there would be no color, there would be no freedom.

When André Malraux asked Chagall to paint the ceiling of the Paris Opera it was received with mixed emotions and much criticism from conservatives who objected to the fact that Chagall was not a native Frenchman.

COLORPLATE 71

SIR RUDOLF BING

Commissioning the Murals for the Metropolitan Opera

1971

Sir Rudolph Bing, general manager of the Metropolitan Opera in New York from 1950 to 1972. It was he who commissioned Chagall to do the sets and costumes for The Magic Flute *as well as the two murals at the entrance to the opera house.*

When I was a very young man about 1919 or 1920 in Vienna, I worked in a bookstore and just about then a thin volume on Marc Chagall appeared. I saw for the first time these flying cows and blue horses with the half-moon somewhere at the bottom of the picture and a little cockerel in an upper corner. It was then that I fell in love with that childlike magic world of Marc Chagall. It never occurred to me that I might ever meet the painter. Here I was, a young man in Vienna, and Chagall—I did not even know where he lived at that time.

Frankly, I never thought of the man behind all these strange figures—but as time went by I—all of us—saw and heard more and more of and about Marc Chagall.

I got married to my wife Nina, a Russian dancer, and we moved to Berlin where we met a charming young Russian woman: Vava Brodzky. Vava and Nina became great friends and after a while we all met again in London. Years went and the war came. We all went through hard times. Vava too did not have it easy, but we always kept in close touch and in spite of all the terror and worries, we laughed a lot together.

Then the war came to an end. I started the Edinburgh Festival and eventually in 1949 went to America. Naturally contact with Vava slipped a little but we kept in touch and met in Paris from time to time. For a while we did not hear from her and then came the sensational news: Vava was to be married to Marc Chagall. And soon we met him and were great friends ever since.

Chagall is the kind of man one either knows well or not at all. After the first ten minutes I felt as if I had known him all my life—and even after a year's absence one feels as if one had met only yesterday.

We met almost every year in Paris, in Switzerland, in their house in Vence, and in New York. Naturally we talked often about music, about ballet and opera; I knew.

I started thinking about the repertory for the first season in our new House at least three years ahead of time; I had some years before produced a *Magic Flute* in the old House, but I had not been happy with that production, even though Bruno Walter conducted it at the time. I was determined to do this—one of my favorite operas—again, and it occurred to me that Chagall's magic world might be the right foil for Mozart's magic. I had engaged Günther Rennert, the eminent German stage director, for the production and he enthusiastically endorsed my suggestion. So I approached Chagall and he showed great interest, but also great concern.

He knew this was a great challenge—he had never done sets and costumes for an opera—but also a great responsibility. I told him that I thought he would enjoy working with Rennert, that we had an excellent painter—a Russian (Volodia Odinokov)—as the head of our paint shop and that we would give him all the help and support he might require. Then I asked Rennert to visit him in Vence and as I had hoped and expected he soon was deeply involved and drew and painted sketches from morning to night.

We soon reached agreement. He had several more meetings with Rennert, then he came to New York, met the painters, the tailors and saw the stage and the result is now history.

At the same time the new House was being built and there were two large areas on the Grand Tier foyer that required artistic treatment. Wallace Harrison,

Sir Rudolf Bing, general manager of the Metropolitan Opera, invited Chagall to produce sets and costumes for Mozart's *The Magic Flute* and proposed the Chagall murals at the opera house. Photograph: Metropolitan Opera Archives.

our distinguished architect, gave it a great deal of thought together with the Art Committee of our Board under the chairmanship of Mr. Robert Lehman and innumerable ideas were advanced and discarded.

So I suggested the possibility of two large Chagall murals and eventually everyone concerned liked the idea. Chagall was again invited to come over. He inspected the site, he met the Art Committee and finally he was commissioned to paint these murals—a commission made possible by the generous contributions of funds by Mr. A. Chauncey Newlin on behalf of the Doherty Foundation, just as Mrs. John D. Rockefeller, Jr. had made it possible for us to produce *The Magic Flute.*

COLORPLATES 76, 77

So here we are with a *Magic Flute* designed by Marc Chagall, the only Opera House in the world that can boast a Marc Chagall production and two huge Chagall murals—and I for one am proud of it.

COLORPLATES 74, 75

EMILY GENAUER

From *Chagall at the Met*

Conceiving the Murals

1971

Emily Genauer, an American art critic and author.

It is no secret that Chagall was invited to paint the murals after the opera house had been designed and, in fact, when its construction was already under way. Initially he was asked, back when the Metropolitan Opera Company still functioned in its old building on Broadway at 39th Street, to design a new production for *The Magic Flute* in its new home being constructed at Lincoln Center.

It was after *The Magic Flute* was completed that Rudolf Bing asked the painter if he would like to paint the opera house murals as well. It was an inspired choice. Chagall is, of course, an artist of incomparable genius and, with Picasso, the last surviving master among the pioneers of painting whose experiments, almost sixty years ago in Paris, changed the course of art history. Murals by Chagall, permanently installed at the Metropolitan Opera House, were bound to enhance the structure enormously, making it one of the most distinguished art sites in New York. They would have special point in a city he loves deeply, where he lived for years and did some of his best work, and to which he returns frequently. They would also be his only major works on free and virtually continuous view (curtains are drawn over them at certain hours to prevent their fading under the bright sun) to a large general public which has long responded to his art with a very special warmth accorded to no other living painter. . . .

Back in America for a conference with the Rockefeller family about a set of eight stained-glass windows he was executing for the family church at Pocantico Hills, New York, Chagall went to Lincoln Center to examine the site. He found an opera house too far along in its construction to allow for any changes he might suggest for the placing of his murals, but still too far from completion for him to visualize how the allotted space might work.

It took him a year to make up his mind. Several factors finally persuaded him to accept the commission, despite some serious misgivings.

First, it would be a rare opportunity to execute what he describes as "exterior" murals which would, since only a glass wall would separate them from the public, be visible to every passerby, as only an occasional ancient mural is on church exteriors or in public squares in Italy.

Chagall and the choreographer Serge Lifar reviewing the designs for the ballet *Daphnis and Chloe*, Paris, 1958. Photograph © Lipnitzki-Viollet.

Second, even with visibility of the murals less than perfect, he would be no worse off than the great painters of the Renaissance whose poorly lighted works the public must strain to see in most Italian palaces and churches.

Third was the fact that the murals would be his first permanent, public work in New York (a magnificent stained-glass window which he did for the Secretariat building at the United Nations as his own gift in memory of its secretary-general, his friend Dag Hammarskjold, is in an area open only to delegates and special guests).

Fourth was his old and continuing affection for New York, plus the stimulus he found here.

Fifth was the beauty, gaiety and special excitement engendered at Lincoln Center when thousands of people come for performances each night in a festive, buoyant mood of anticipation.

Sixth was his idea that the murals might be a tribute to Mozart, an extension, in effect, of the designs he had already completed for *The Magic Flute*, a kind of pictorial epilogue for the opera. Later he changed his mind about this, expanding the idea so the murals embrace all of opera. Mozart remains, however, a powerful motif in the panel called "The Sources of Music," where the largest single figure, larger even than David-Orpheus, is identified as "The Angel Mozart."

COLORPLATE 76

What Chagall could not have anticipated was that the glittering glass facade, ascending almost a hundred feet to end in five great arches, and offering to viewers across the open plaza a spectacular panoramic view of its grand, sculptural, circling double-staircase, its red and gold decorated foyer, and its glistening chandeliers, would also place between viewers and murals a strong physical barrier. . . .

What he could not have realized was that while the glass wall, broken up into busy rectangles by a bronze framework, was going to make seeing any murals behind them extremely difficult from outside the opera house, the problem of seeing them from inside would be equally difficult. He did not know that the promenade space would be too narrow to offer any perspective for viewing panels beginning at a point thirteen feet from the floor. And he did not know that this condition would be compounded by the construction of a public bar directly under the south panel and the placing of dining tables and chairs under the north panel, where the wall turns the corner to become the grand tier restaurant that extends along the Metropolitan's north facade, and overlooks the Vivian Beaumont Theater and its gardens.

On November 18, 1965, after the first press tour of the still unfinished structure, I wrote to Chagall at his home in Vence, in the south of France. As an old, respectful friend, I was troubled. I still have a copy of my letter to him. After describing the magnificently soaring walls his murals were to occupy, I described the shallow promenade and the distractions of the barred glass wall.

"If you worked geometrically, like Léger, for example," I wrote, "I can see how the bars might be embodied somehow into the composition. But with your lovely, flowing, airy figures, what will happen? It would set my uneasy mind at rest if I could be certain that you know about this situation, and if I had some notion of how you plan to handle it. It would break my heart if the murals weren't given an absolutely magnificent setting."

By November 30, I had Chagall's reply. "I have made the first sketches and models, but I cannot deny the uncertainty which envelops me in thinking about and starting this work. Nevertheless, remembering and encouraged by all the sympathy I always encountered in America, I accepted the commission to do this enormous job. It seems to me that I can still make my murals harmonize with the facade of the opera house, and that the paned windows need not necessarily hamper the window's transparency and the murals' visibility. What I really hope, in effect, is to so charge the murals with movement that they will be able to divert attention away from the window grid."

In a later conversation he enlarged on his plans, explaining that he saw two possible approaches for a painter working in so unaccommodating a space. One was to pattern his panels very boldly, adjusting them not only to the barred glass

From *The Magic Flute: Homage to Mozart.*
1966–67. Gouache on paper. 22 x 18 ¹/₂ in.
(55.9 x 47 cm). Musée National d'Art
Moderne, Centre Georges Pompidou, Paris.

but also to the huge rectangular masses of the architecture of the opera house and
of the two buildings flanking it to establish the plaza. In view of the flowing,
undulant rhythms of Chagall's style, this would obviously be impossible for him.
In any case, such an austerely geometric conception would be soaked up by the
architecture and altogether lost.

The other way was neither to submit to the architecture nor to fight it, but to
conceive of the murals as something quite separate, having their own existence,
enhancing the architecture precisely because they hold their own against it, as
well as against the constantly moving crowds on the plaza and inside the opera
house as well.

"I decided, therefore, not to paint 'pictures' at all," says Chagall. "I would
make something more like flags. I had to create something that would also move,
if not like a flag, then like the rustling leaves of a tree. A tree doesn't fight buildings. It has its own life alongside them, making them even more beautiful.
I wanted the murals, painted in strong bold colors, to function like trees."

He talked with the architect, Wallace Harrison, and with the design committee for the building, asking for ideas and a reaction to his own approach. He
showed them colors, and they approved his suggestion that since the panels and
the space between them would be seen as a single unit when viewed from across
Lincoln Plaza, their basic color scheme should be harmonious but varied, to avoid
monotony. Red was agreed upon as the dominant color for the panel at the north
side of the wall, yellow for the panel at the south side.

When Chagall came to New York to supervise the installation, the red panel,
"Triumph," had already been installed—but on the wrong side of the wall. It had
been his intention that the trumpeting angels were to face north, their music pour-
ing out to the world at large beyond the opera house and Lincoln Center. The yellow of "The Sources," with its gentle, central figure of David-Orpheus playing his
lyre, was to be at the south end, its compositional movement directed to the opera
house itself and its audiences.

When he saw the error, Chagall recalls, "I yelled as I never have before. My
mother, when she gave birth to her children, didn't yell as much. I could doubtless be heard all over Lincoln Square."

It remained for Rudolf Bing, the company's extremely persuasive general
manager, to resolve the issue. Chagall, recalling the event, says he asked, "Why
do you want the music to go out of the theater and into the world? Perhaps destiny was behind the error, and the heralding angels *should* play for the people

COLORPLATE 77

207

who have come to the opera house, because they do love music." Chagall, studying the situation, eventually decided that the unintentional rearrangement was not only workable but possibly even an improvement, and a crisis was averted.

MARC CHAGALL

At the Unveiling of the Murals at the Metropolitan Opera

September 8, 1966

At this moment when my two mural paintings are shown in New York at the Metropolitan Opera, may I say a few words.

COLORPLATES 76, 77

I should just like to express the general idea which surrounded this work.

Yet, all questions and their answers can be seen in the paintings themselves. Everyone can see them his own way, interpret what he sees, and how he sees.

Often there are hidden in paintings more utterances of silence and of doubt than words can express. These utterances pronounced often diminish the essential and lead away to other roads.

I have worked as if for myself, day and night, searching and doubting. But this self often separates itself, multiplies itself in the mass of people of whom I am aware around myself.

And I ask myself whilst I work these questions: For whom do I paint? From where do I come? Towards what do I go?

As always, I want to appeal not only to the eyes, but to the very heart of the others, so that this way of work surpasses all the cerebral means with all their theories; and which one calls the technique, for the technique is automatically embodied in the message.

If the message is authentic, the technique is authentic, too.

My friend Rudi Bing and the Committee of the Metropolitan Opera approached me to make these mural paintings. And now, on these walls are reflected my feelings and my plastic dreams wanting to express the dreams of art and of our tumultuous times.

I lived here in America during the years of the inhuman war which made humanity desert itself. One has shielded me from danger in making me come here. I have seen the rhythm of life. I have seen America fighting with the Allies. I have seen the wealth that she has distributed to bring relief to the peoples who suffered the consequences of this war.

I accepted what the Committee and its director proposed, and I have worked with joy to express also my thanks.

I thought that only love and uncalculating devotion towards others will lead to the greatest harmony in life and in art of which humanity has been dreaming so long. And this must, of course, be included in each utterance, in each brush stroke, and in each colour. Always there returns to my mind, like the stars to the sky, an echo of the authentic cultures of art created in bygone times. They must unite with the dreams of today's culture, if they are worthy of them, and become together like one faith and like one song. I believe that with those that contain human pity and love for one's neighbor, we can progress towards the ideal and leave behind the creations of our time. If our voice is a voice in the desert, it must, because of this, be truer than certain calculations which fade like an echo further and further away.

COLORPLATE 63. *The Rooster*. 1947. Oil on canvas. 49 ⅝ x 36 in. (126 x 91.5 cm).
Musée d'Art Moderne, Centre Georges Pompidou, Paris.

COLORPLATE 64. *The Ebony Horse* from *The Arabian Nights*. 1948. Lithograph.
14 1/2 x 11 in. (37 x 28 cm). Collection Jacob Baal-Teshuva.

COLORPLATE 65. *Julnar the Sea-Born and Her Son King Badr Basim of Persia* from *The Arabian Nights*. 1948.
Lithograph. 14 ¹/2 x 11 in. (37 x 28 cm). Collection Jacob Baal-Teshuva.

COLORPLATE 66. *Window to the Village*. 1949–50. Gouache and pastel on paper. 24 3/8 x 22 1/2 in. (62 x 57 cm).
Private collection.

COLORPLATE 67. *Green Landscape*. 1949. Gouache on paper. 30 3/8 x 22 in. (77 x 56 cm). Collection Marcus Diener, Basel.

COLORPLATE 68. *The Blue Bird*. 1945. Oil on canvas. 30 x 20 ¹/2 in. (76 x 52 cm). Private collection.

COLORPLATE 69. *Freedom*. 1937–52. Oil on canvas. 66 1/8 x 34 5/8 in. (168 x 88 cm).
Musée National d'Art Moderne, Centre Georges Pompidou, Paris.

COLORPLATE 70. *Sunday.* 1953–54. Oil on canvas. 68 1/8 x 58 5/8 in. (173 x 149 cm).
Musée National d'Art Moderne, Centre Georges Pompidou, Paris.

And as I speak thus, I see that the children of all the peoples while playing watch us. The trees and the flowers in the fields await us, too, in the silence of eternity. Like these children, who smile stretching out their arms, all would ask for the happiness which is their hope. If I were asked to explain, I should reply: "Ask these children. In their eyes you could, perhaps, read the answers to your questions." We want the happiness in the clear colours, free of the turmoil of the earth, so that art may enter into a paradise, as was once realized in the introduction to the *Magic Flute* of Mozart. I wished to surround myself with colour and with music, with those characters whose faces retain the smile. This smile which calms, though the soul might often be covered in a nostalgic cloud.

I have tried to do my best in expressing all this on these walls. On them are to be found these heroes of music; the singers, the dancers, who have wanted and who want to play the contents of the dream of their lives for all of us. I am among them with the means given me not only by the academies, but by the hard life of my parents, and the affectionate esteem of my friends. I do not know how many will accept my utterances, my colours, and these rhythms on these paintings. I wanted to transmit this to those to whom my soul listened in this world and in the other world. Therefore, I leaned on these fantastic heroes who possessed the voice of nature like nature itself.

CHAGALL'S GRAPHIC WORK

AMBROISE VOLLARD

"How I Came to Publish La Fontaine's *Fables*"

1952

Ambroise Vollard (1868–1939), renowned French art dealer and publisher of many of the leading artists of the early twentieth century.

When I began as a publisher, one of my most dogged ambitions was to put out an edition of La Fontaine with illustrations worthy of the text. With Chagall, I have finally been able to achieve this long-cherished aim. I leave it to the public to judge whether or not, with the *Fables,* I have succeeded.

Believe me, I have not done this for the vain pleasure of adding yet another edition to all those that already exist. Some of them are utterly remarkable; several are masterpieces, both typographically and artistically. It is not that I didn't appreciate their worth, but rather that I had my own notion. It seemed to me that none of the interpretations of the fabulist's work gave him to us whole, did not, for example, express the magnificence, restrained sensitivity, and deep lyrical resonance of certain verses . . .

On the whole, I said to myself, the illustrators of the *Fables* usually retained only this quality or that, often just a secondary one. Some saw in La Fontaine only an amiable raconteur, others, the cruel observer of the human comedy; the former, a carping wit with some talent for caricature, a dilettante with a strain of

Jean de la Fontaine (1621–1695), French scholar and poet, most famous for his revival in verse of traditional Aesopian and Bidpai Indian fables.

217

From *The Fables: The Miller, His Son, and the Ass.* 1926–27. Gouache. 19 3/4 x 15 3/4 in. (50.1 x 40 cm). Private collection.

bourgeois moralism, the latter, one who loved what was picturesque in nature and in episodes of rural life, a satirist, a describer, an animalist. Every interpreter diminished him, reduced him to one or another of these viewpoints, as if they didn't understand that he was all these things, and more. He was discussed solely under one or another of these aspects, while all the rest was neglected or ignored. Thus, it seemed to me that he was being cheated of his very essence, that is, a profound unity, disguised by his variety of incident. In any case, no one, in my opinion, had thought to render what is as evocative as it is plastic in this "one-hundred-act play" that comprises the *Fables,* nor to make us feel that an artist is adding his sorcery to a great poet's inspirations.

This is why I believed that it was both desirable and possible to attempt a less literal, less fragmentary interpretation of La Fontaine's work, an interpretation that would be just as expressive and more synthetic . . . And whom should I ask for this transcription if not a painter, and furthermore a painter gifted with a creative imagination, prolific in vivid inventiveness.

"That's all very well," you may say, "but what an odd fancy, or, rather, what a long shot, to go seeking out a foreign artist to interpret the work of so specifically French a genius, to illustrate a *Champenois.*"

I find it entirely reasonable that La Fontaine be perceived as nothing more than the authentic representative of the French spirit, and that he be presented only as such. But, again, I believe that this is to diminish him, to truncate a part of his glory, to curb the power of a genius who knows no limit in time or space to his radiance. I am inclined to say that to consider La Fontaine a characteristic writer of the Great Century is to wrong him. For, if we savor him as much as we do today, it is not for documentary reasons, but for our own reasons, just as his contemporaries did not give him his proper due, for *their* own reasons. To be sure, the great poets partake of their time, but they go beyond it, and through time every age responds to them, not as ancients, but as living and current. It is all well and good to say that Racine paints a picture of Louis XIV's court, but if that were all his achievement, he would be admired only by scholars. We love Racine, we love La Fontaine, but this is no veneration for the archaic, but for the particular way they speak to the intelligence and sensibility of our time.

Similarly, La Fontaine knows no geographical limits. He has become a universal genius whose name, or at least influence, is everywhere evident. Is the public aware, for example, that in Russia, in the first half of the nineteenth century, Kriloff translated or adapted most of the fables so felicitously that he is practically a national fabulist? That his work is a classic in the schools, where most of the students don't even know La Fontaine existed? I said earlier that we twentieth-century French have our reasons for admiring La Fontaine, but I am no less persuaded that every people admires him for its own motives, and that there are reasons to like him—or even dislike him—that are Scandinavian, English, Belgian, Italian, Spanish . . .

In short, whatever is specifically Oriental in the fabulist's sources—Aesop, and the Hindu, Persian, Arab, even Chinese outlines from which he borrowed not only his subjects, but at times even his settings and the atmosphere of his adaptations—led me to think that an artist whose origins made the marvellous Orient familiar and natural to him would be the best one to do the right plastic transcription of them.

Now when I am asked "Why did you choose Chagall?" I reply: "Well, precisely because his aesthetic seems to be so close, in a sense, affinitive to La Fontaine's, at once ingenuous and subtle, realistic and fantastic!"

La Fontaine is so bewitching! Chagall is so bewitching!

SYLVIE FORESTIER

"The Engravings"

c. 1990

Sylvie Forestier, chief conservator and director of the Musée National Message Biblique Marc Chagall, Nice, France.

"I am sure that Rembrandt loves me!" exclaims Chagall in the final pages of his autobiography, *My Life*. These words are indicative of the degree to which the child from Vitebsk came to identify with the great Dutch master from both a visual and a spiritual standpoint, starting in 1922 when Chagall produced his first etching in Berlin. He was thirty-five years old and had already produced a significant body of work when he left Russia for good in 1914 and went to Berlin. "Come back to Europe; you are famous here," his friend the poet Rubiner had written to him. Chagall had experienced deep pain and disillusionment in Russia. In addition to the problems of daily life, he had been deeply hurt by his bitter disagreement with Malevitch. Although it was a wrenching experience, his departure was inevitable. During the summer of 1922, bringing with him the manuscript of *My Life*, the painter left his native land, the Russia he had loved so passionately and which had inspired his work so profoundly.

So Chagall, who was soon followed by his wife Bella and his daughter Ida, went to Berlin, "a veritable caravanserai, a meeting place for everyone traveling back and forth between Moscow and the West," he wrote. An entire colony of artists of every nationality: painters like Georges Grosz, sculptors like

Archipenko, experienced the fever of those troubling times. Frida Rubiner, wife of the poet who died in 1920, translated the first monographs, the ones by Efros and Tugendhold dedicated to the artist. Chagall found a friendly environment in which people knew and admired his work. However, it was meeting Paul Cassirer which was to cause his art to develop in a new direction. Cassirer wanted to publish *My Life* in an edition to be illustrated by Chagall himself. This presented an opportunity to become involved in a new technique, engraving. Thus, through Hermann Struck, Chagall was to broaden his means of expression considerably, and the fact that this meeting took place in Germany, the country of choice for the art of engraving, is not without significance.

An initial portfolio of twenty engravings was produced. In them, Chagall demonstrated astonishing skill. Even more astonishing for an artist who up until then had been accustomed to the fluidity of the brush, was his ability to understand the specific functions of this new technique, thereby establishing himself as a true "master engraver." "The drawn line and the engraved line are basically different," he said. Indeed, the copper plate is resistant to the creative act [of drawing]. The work springs from the material itself; in a single decision, with no possibility of going back, the creative will is etched into the copper plate before being revealed against the whiteness of the sheet of paper. With this technique, the power of the imagination anticipates and foresees its effects. It truly opened up a world of new visual possibilities for Chagall. This painter who was already known for his lavish colors was now to reveal himself as a master of black and white, a master engraver for his period, the legitimate heir of Rembrandt.

The initial project, that is the publishing of the illustrated edition of *Mein Leben (My Life)* could not be completed. There were problems with the translation of Chagall's text, which was poetic, tender, tragic and full of humor. However, in 1923 Cassirer published an album of the twenty-six initial dry-point engravings from *Mein Leben (My Life)*. The French version was published in 1931 in Paris with Bella Chagall's translation.

In Berlin, in addition to line-engraving, with Budko Chagall discovered lithography and xylography. In the case of xylography, or wood engraving, it is interesting to note that beginning in the Berlin period, Chagall went back to a traditional medium, one which he knew perfectly, the Russian folk print. The "Loubok" contributed its vigorous shapes and vivid colors to the painter's vision. A few woodcuts were produced for *My Life*. Much later, Chagall would go back to wood engraving for the illustrated edition of his poems produced in 1968 by Gérald Cramer. As it turned out, the work produced for Cassirer marked the beginning of a major period in terms of his work as a whole.

As for the fall of 1923, Chagall settled in Paris and mastered a complex technique in all its diverse forms including etching, dry point and aquatint. Up until World War II, Chagall remained partial to this medium.

At that point, with the encouragement of Ambroise Vollard, the well-known merchant and art publisher, he began working on a larger scale. He produced three monumental collections, three masterpieces: the illustrations for Gogol's *Dead Souls*, for the *Fables* of La Fontaine and finally for *The Old Testament*.

The collection for *Dead Souls* was produced between 1923 and 1927: ninety-six dry point etchings which recreate with power, devastating humor, wit and tender inventiveness the world of rural Russia which Chagall knew so well. "This is the most faithful and accurate visual representation ever produced of that bygone Russia which has now disappeared," wrote Jacques Lassaigne. It is also a portrait gallery of human types, ruthlessly depicted in Chagallian lines, fierce reflections of acute psychological observation. There is a remarkable sense of connivance between Gogol's text and Chagall's illustrations of it. Although the details are realistic, they are not naturalistic. The freedom of the lines recreates the movement of the narrative, and the visual inventiveness of the blacks and whites recreates its poetic balance by adjusting the space on the page.

Vollard was delighted with the book, which was published much later, however, in 1948, by Tériade. But his business sense detected in Chagall a contemporary master engraver. His unfailing instinct led to a new and paradoxical commis-

The Rider on the Red Horse. c. 1960.
Lithograph. 24 x 20 in. (61 x 50.8 cm). Private
collection. A tapestry of this subject was
executed by Madame Cauquil Prince.

sion: the illustrations for La Fontaine's *Fables*. Nothing is further removed from
Chagall's wild fantasy world than the poetry of Jean de la Fontaine, that quintessential reflection of the French spirit, the essence of moderation, modesty, distance and light irony. One could say of his poetry that it was well guarded as it
had come to represent the archetypal value, the collective property of the nation.
Vollard was harshly criticized for choosing Chagall to illustrate the *Fables*. It was
even contested in the House of Deputies. Vollard explained his reasons, and one
cannot help admiring his intelligence and sense of discernment: "All that is
specifically Oriental in the sources of this author of fables, Aesop, the Hindu,
Persian, Arab and even Chinese storytellers . . . has led me to think that an artist
whose origins are such that glamorous Orient seems familiar and natural is better
equipped than anyone to render it in appropriate visual form. And if I am now
asked why I chose Chagall, my answer is precisely because his aesthetic sense
seems to me quite close and in a way related to that of La Fontaine, being at the
same time naive and subtle, realistic and fantastic."

Chagall therefore undertook the job, which he hoped to produce in the spirit
of the engravings of the eighteenth century. He felt that color was necessary, and
using a method to which he was to become accustomed, he did a series of
gouaches as a preliminary step. In this case, a color version preceded the work
in black and white. Unlike *Dead Souls*, Chagall wanted color illustrations.
Discovering the French countryside in its softness and diversity in Provence and

Homage to Gogol. 1917. Watercolor.
15 1/2 x 19 3/4 in. (39.3 x 50.1 cm). The
Museum of Modern Art, New York. Acquired
through the Lillie P. Bliss Bequest. Photograph
© The Museum of Modern Art, New York.

Auvergne and at Lac Chambon gave him a feel for the fundamental presence of nature. Flowers, trees and animals reveal the compelling strength of the vital flow which unites all living things. The gouaches produced during his stay at Lac Chambon in 1926 reveal the spontaneity of his vision. Chagall draws directly with the brush, which seems to follow the vivacity and instantaneousness of feeling—nervous and vibrant splashes of color which translate, as Franz Meyer stated so well, "the lushness of the plant world as well as the great quiet strength of the animal world."

The plates for the *Fables* were engraved from 1927 to 1930. Because of the difficulty of color engraving, Chagall treated the copper plate in a more pictorial manner than in *Dead Souls*. Several methods are used simultaneously: direct engraving, then touching up with varnish, fairly dense hatching, lines and counterlines for rendering half tones and gradations from white to black. Colors are then actually transposed visually: bright whites, dark blacks, subtle and tender greys containing all the nuances of chiaroscuro.

The last of the one hundred engravings for the book was completed in 1931, but Vollard was not the one who published it. As was the case with *Dead Souls,* it was Tériade who produced and published the book in 1952.

Chagall had barely finished the *Fables* when Vollard ordered a third work from him, the *Bible*. These one hundred and five engravings are among the best examples of the art of engraving. They were done in the same manner as *Dead Souls*, starting with a series of dazzling gouaches directly inspired by the landscape of Palestine.

Interrupted by the war, Chagall gave in to his daughter's entreaties and moved to the United States in 1941. New York was burning with the same intellectual and artistic fever as the Berlin he had known in the twenties. Among those who sought refuge there were Max Ernst, André Breton, André Masson, his friends Jacques and Raissa Maritain, and Pierre Matisse, the son of the painter, who quickly arranged the first exhibitions.

Chagall also found engraving again in the person of Stanley William (Bill) Hayter, who was already working on the problem of printing colors simultaneously. Chagall worked in the famous Studio 17 and engraved a few plates between 1942 and 1945. But it was lithography which rekindled his interest. Chagall would come to prefer it as a medium. If etchings made up a significant portion of his creative work between 1922 and 1945, after the end of World War II lithography would carry the painter's message and convey his genius throughout the world.

The lithographic work is considerable and significant. A decisive step was taken in 1950 when he met the best practitioners of it—Fernand Mourlot, Georges Sagourin, and the person who was to be his artistic companion up until the end, Charles Sorlier. Lithography became art in the fullest sense and, thanks to Chagall, contributed new masterpieces to the history of printmaking.

Chagall's lithographic works are among the most significant of the twentieth century. These admirable illustrated books—*Drawings for the Bible, Daphnis and Chloe, The Circus, In the Land of the Gods, Odysseus, The Tempest*—which do honor to the great publishers of the period, including Tériade and Aimé Maeght, as well as the independent lithographs, established the painter as the master of color and the poet of form.

COLORPLATE 78

Chagall's message is conveyed throughout his etchings. It is a message of peace and love revealing the highly unusual nature of an outstanding artist, an artist of "Light and Freedom," he who "created the circle of incandescent color which calls forth the creative goodness of the world" (Max Ernst). Chagall—poet, prophet—Chagall "in the ladders of light". . .

MARC CHAGALL

On Engraving and Lithography

1960

It seems to me that something would have been lacking for me if, in addition to color, I had not, at one time in my life, worked at engraving and lithography.

Already, in my earliest youth, when I first began to use a pencil, I looked for this thing that would be capable of spreading out like a great river towards inviting, distant shores.

When I held in my hand a lithographic stone, or a copper plate, I believed I was touching a talisman. It seemed to me that I could entrust them with all my joys, all my sorrows . . . Everything that has crossed my path, throughout the years: births, deaths, marriages, flowers, animals, birds, poor working people, my parents, lovers at night, the Prophets from the Bible, on the street, in my home, in the Temple, in the sky. And, as I grow older, the tragedy of life that is inside us and all about us.

Chagall's lithographic oeuvre of about 1,100 lithographs fills six volumes.

When I handle all these tools of the trade, I feel the difference between lithography, engraving, and drawing. It is possible to draw well and yet not possess in one's fingers the lithographic touch; this is a matter of feeling. Not to mention the fact that, in general, there should emanate from each line a particular spiritual quality that has nothing in common either with "know-how" or with knack.

But I shan't go into this at length.

It is real suffering for me to speak of myself. And yet my friends the publishers have asked me to say a few words. But for me, it's the same thing as walking on water . . .

The longer I live, the less I like to talk about myself.

ROBERT MARTEAU

Robert Marteau, French writer and art critic.

"Chagall as Engraver"

1982

The Bible is unquestionably Chagall's masterpiece so far as engraving on copper is concerned, and no doubt it is the single greatest masterpiece of engraving of our age. It becomes plain that everything previous to *The Bible* found its fulfillment in the Old Testament pictures. The anecdotes and observation of *My Life*, the spontaneity and perspicacity of *Dead Souls*, the understanding and technical knowledge of *The Fables of La Fontaine:* these all come together in *The Bible*, and the flowering is complete. Looking at these 105 eau-fortes, you would think Chagall learned how to engrave in Berlin with the one intention of going back to the source of the Hebrew soul; you would think he had been building up his strength for years in order to respond to the Word of his people and bring his contribution to the Book. Elsewhere he could show only facets of his spirit; here spirituality itself unfolds, the mighty breath of the poet-prophets. Fable takes on its real dimension, in the origin and creation of the world; to speak is to create; the word is lightning; the poem is made of stars, nights, days, dawn, water, woman; the man-shepherd receives the divine Word, comes down from the mountain, and transmits it. The living God reveals himself, the dove is the winged symbol from whom salvation is looked for; the angels, stilling their white wings, grow visible to Abraham's eyes, and the earth is present all around them just as they themselves are truly present without old Melchisadek the priest showing any sign of surprise; yes, they have taken on the reality which is now there in the hand that Abraham raises in front of his face, in *Abraham Mourning Sarah.* Then there is Joseph, full of music and sun like the shepherd Apollo, in the middle of his flock, a premonitory figure of the one who, like himself, is to be sold. The prophets are afraid at their vision, or afraid at the Word which they alone hear; God is the only witness of their solitude and suffering; the heavens open, Jerusalem perishes, and the living are clearly one with the dead, left standing upright only to weep. Chagall makes the great drama and the tribulation his own; and the tempest that shakes him is transmitted to the paper in its violence, its gravity, its amplitude: what is happening here and now, around this well, amid this flock, is at the epicenter of the great theater of the world.

We can really understand, then, that he truly did go to Holland as a pilgrim, to Rembrandt; he went to pay homage to the man who, like himself, had the gift of making the divine acts find access to the visible world. Complete mastery of technique leads the hand in this work to respond to every vibration of the soul. All is softly bound together. The eye searches the surface as though with hands, is enthralled, and cannot tear itself away.

The Cellist. 1976. Lithograph. 23 5/8 x 18 7/8 in. (60 x 48 cm). Private collection.

From this moment on, as though he had the intimate conviction of having reached a summit in this art and in this technique, and that no wave could lift him higher and no river carry him further on, as the work began to be finished Chagall turned more than ever to color, and required of lithography that it should answer to another side of his painting. He had made 13 lithographs in New York for *Four Tales of a Thousand and One Nights.* He renewed the link with Paris again by making nine other lithographs published in 1954 in the review *Derriére le miroir* under the title *Paris.* In the same year he made his second visit to Greece and painted several gouaches. The plates for *Daphnis and Chloe* were to come out of these gouaches. The choice of the Greek text, full of fresh, sensual poetry, and his first visit to Greece, date from 1952.

COLORPLATES 64, 65

COLORPLATE 78

Chagall always found it essential to walk over the ground of whatever country he had chosen for a work, and to see, feel, test the light and colors, and get to know the people. He did not undertake *The Bible* without visiting the land of his people, and he did not allow himself to decide on the colors for *Daphnis and*

Chloe without first having had physical contact with the light and the sea and the land of Greece. True poet that he is, Chagall always works from what is concrete. That is where he found the life-giving joy that breaks through naturalistic appearances, causes forms to burst open like undreamed-of flowers, splashes color on the sky and the fields and in the fathomless depths of the sea, so that the soft sounds of grasses, rivers, trees and lambs commingle with the lovers.

A set of lithographs was published by Tériade in 1967 with the title *The Circus*. Chagall wrote the accompanying text-poem. In a sense it was an extension of *My Life,* which in 1922 was itself the point of departure for his engraved work.

This reminder comes quite naturally, for *The Circus* is not a work simply illustrating the circus in words and pictures. Perhaps above all else it is a secret testament, in which Chagall gives free play to the telling of his secrets. Again, it is a journal, or a fresco in which the human comedy is made to unfold and is denounced for what it is, or a mirror in whose greatly reduced space is reflected everything that becomes exhausted or dissolved in day-to-day living. It is a way of saying that for Chagall the circle of the circus ring is magical only in so far as it encloses what is essential: each gesture and attitude being raised to the level of sign and symbol. For nothing is natural here, though all seems to be, thanks to an art and artifice based on the precise observation of instincts, habits and behavior. Is not the circus, by its very form, a replica of the universe, a world in which the impossible is still about to be annihilated at any moment? The girl on the trapeze goes from star to star; the horse and its rider make poetry spring from its source; men and animals begin to converse with each other again . . . Childhood marvels at a daylight that is almost the pristine light.

No, it is not a dream; only a reality slightly beyond the exchanges of every day. Chagall knows in a flash how to disclose this reality to us, by a surreptitious displacing of objects and people and a substituting of the true color for the expected color. In this way he creates relationships of enchantment, surprise and play, where what is grave banishes what is merely serious; passages and crossing places where comedy, drama, grace and humor are suddenly swallowed up; planets where what is imaginary is part of reality, not an effort to escape.

CHARLES SORLIER

Working with Chagall

January 1990

Charles Sorlier worked in the Paris Atelier Mourlot for thirty-five years as an engraver and lithographer for many of the major twentieth-century masters including Picasso, Matisse, Léger, Dufy, and Chagall.

I met Chagall in the beginning of 1950. I was very impressed by this first encounter with a painter whom before I had deeply admired. I never had thought that I would find myself face-to-face with him one day. I didn't realize at that time that a very deep and reciprocal friendship was being borne.

From 1950, I had the opportunity of watching the creation of all the original lithographs of Chagall, which meant of more than a thousand. Occasionally, I have been asked what was my part with regard to these works. The present script gives me the opportunity to explain myself.

Traditionally, well-known artists have had assistants who were also their disciples. Chagall has been no exception to this rule and he never made a secret of it. To insinuate that his original lithographs were produced to a large extent by myself is a myth created in the mind of naive people. When one compares his original lithographs and my engravings of interpretations even the slightest doubt

From the Bible series: *Rebecca at the Well.*
1936–56. Etching. 11–12 ¹/₂ x 8 ⁵/₈–9 ¹/₂ in.
(28–31.7 x 22–24 cm). Private collection.

is erased; the technique used as well as the final results are completely different.

Chagall felt a great joy in working on stone or on zinc. He considered himself as an artisan and was proud of it. This artist has never—or at least very seldom—recopied an already existing work of art, with the exception of some book illustrations requiring a close context to the poetry. He worked out of imagination related to the lithographic technique to create a work of art he would never have achieved using any other means. This procedure is, from my point of view, the essential criterion of an original lithograph.

Chagall would first sketch a composition in black, on stone, on zinc or on transfer paper according to the requirements of the individual work. This black sketch was in most cases the heart of the piece of art. After various proofs had been made, he added water color of pastel, thus having the choice between different versions. When he had designed his preparatory drawing, he prepared the plates in different colors. Then, we printed on a hand-press the proofs and submitted them to him. Almost always he corrected them and added other shades. New proofs, sometimes two or three, were necessary before they were completed. Only when he was totally satisfied he would sign the r. t. p., in general for fifty drafts, if not, he destroyed all compositions.

It was my duty as his assistant to supervise the work of the printer, sometimes to touch up the plates according to the indications of the painter and sometimes, upon his request, to add one or two colors. In particular, this procedure allowed him to avoid frequent trips between the Côte d'Azur, where he lived, and Paris.

Then, I supervised the completion of the editions and of the exact quantity of prints. To avoid any fraud, I numbered these prints before they were signed by Chagall. Additional proofs remaining were destroyed. The artist did not have to spend days—or even months—in the printery to take care of the technical aspect; this would have meant a loss of time for him and he trusted me completely.

Additionally, I often had the pleasure of engraving works of interpretation after paintings of Chagall. Before 1956, I have not signed these lithographs as the engraver. Only when the number of buyers had increased, certain less scrupulous merchants declared my engravings of interpretations as original works of the painter. These are the malpractices which have caused the myth, that Chagall didn't design his lithographs himself. To avoid any confusion, he insisted at that time that my name was shown on all works I had engraved. . . .

One of the remarkable features of Chagall was his fidelity to himself and to his familiar themes. Due to his genius, he was able to make us see these themes in a new form as if for the very first time: Everything being different to our own expectations.

Chagall had the rare privilege of seeing the newness of each morning: This day to him was the very first day, the orange the sweetest one, the flower the brightest one and woman the most beautiful one.

It has been a marvelous experience to watch him discover life day-by-day: Chagall, renewed eternally, remaining himself, bringing us his message of joy and hope. . . .

CHAGALL'S CERAMICS, SCULPTURE, AND STAINED GLASS

MARC CHAGALL

On Ceramics

1952

Ceramics are the work of the hands and the heart. The theories only come afterwards, when the work is done. They result from the work, but they are not its source. . . . The ceramic art is nothing more than the alliance of fire and clay. If what you offer is good, the fire will give you something in return; if it is bad, everything is smashed, nothing remains and there is nothing you can do about it. The test of fire is pitiless.

* * *

Madonna and Tree. 1951. Ceramic bowl. 16 1/8 x 13 in. (41 x 33 cm). Collection Daniel Malingue, Paris.

These few pieces, these few samples of ceramics are a sort of foretaste: the result of my life in the south of France, where one feels so strongly the significance of this craft. The very earth on which I walk is so luminous. It looks at me tenderly, as if it were calling me. I have wanted to use this earth like the old artisans, and to avoid accidental decoration by staying within the limits of ceramics, breathing into it the echo of an art which is near, and at the same time distant. It suddenly seems to me that this earth, so radiant, is calling from afar to the deaf earth of the city where I was born—Vitebsk.

But this earth, just as the craft of ceramics, does not give itself easily. The fire returns my efforts at the oven door sometimes gratifyingly, sometimes in a grotesque and ridiculous form. The fire and the earth remind me only too well that my means are modest.

Marvelous examples of this occidental and oriental art often occur to me. During these threatening times, one is especially eager to attach himself to this earth, to mingle with it.

Whether I am speaking of ceramics, of engraving, of sculpture, or of painting, all my words are centered on the material, which, because of its very characteristics, is abstraction, provided it maintains a certain aloofness. But even if this material were imbued with an excessive sensitivity, is it not better to devote oneself to this, rather than to be lost in a world where automatism and prideful insensitivity prevail?

JACQUES THIRION

"The Flowering of His Art"

1982

Chagall's research in this field of the kiln arts coincided—and this is significant—with his settling in Provence in the old city of Vence in 1950. In this country, near Greece and the Promised Land, privileged by its light, the austere majesty of its landscapes, its leafy vegetation, its fields with silvery olive trees, the blue horizon of the sea, the artist who is a poet, attentive to everything that covers the earth and populates the sky, even the humblest creatures, found, more than elsewhere, the beauty, even the sacred character, of one of the oldest and most rustic arts: that of the potter. It is there that he became fully conscious of its necessity. "In Provence," Chagall said, "the earth burns your fingers." The renown of Vallauris, made famous by Picasso, also rang in his ears. Chagall, always curious about techniques—he also worked at the same time on stained-glass windows and tapestries—feels that the ceramic art can only be approached successfully in an age of maturity and synthesis. We know the importance he attributes to what he calls "the chemistry" of painting. Ceramic work requires, from a technical point of view, special care. With the baking, waiting, drying, coats of varnish, it imposes constraints on the hand as well as the mind. The artist can be victorious only if he is in full possession of his capabilities. It is good, the perpetually uneasy Chagall believes, that these new servitudes work as an antidote for the temptation of facility to which every artist in his zenith is prey. Finally, for him, sculpture and ceramics are not mere diversions nor simple exercises to keep the painter "in form." It is the flowering of his art.

Indeed, there is not the slightest breach between Chagall's paintings and his ceramics. The latter are only a prolongation of the former. They realize them perfectly. Gifted with the third dimension, they will live, henceforth, in space and are

enriched, thanks to the caprices of the kiln, by new tactile attractions. They give us a desire to touch them, to caress them. . . .

Chagall began his ceramic experiences in a pottery works in Antibes in 1950, with a series of plates illustrating the *Fables* of La Fontaine that were exhibited shortly thereafter in Maeght's Gallery. Then he made a large, hand-sculptured vase for his daughter Ida, incrusted plates, very pale in color, with Biblical subjects (they fill a marvelous glass cabinet in his villa in Vence), painted tiles for the decoration of Assy, and many pots, using the kilns of various pottery works in Antibes, Vence, Biot, Valbonnes, and Vallauris. The most recent vases were created in 1962, in Vallauris in Madame Ramier's studio. For each of his works Chagall made several precise drawings, using colored pencils to determine the harmony of color and the rhythm of each object of which only one example was

Chagall and Picasso working in the Madoura ceramics studio, Vallauris. Photograph © R.A./Gamma Liaison.

COLORPLATE 89

made. One can well imagine with what care he watched over its manufacture.

Chagall's ceramics are extremely original, both in form and color. From the point of view of form, one can distinguish two groups: simple vases with traditional lines; and pitchers, pots and vases where the artist gave free rein to his imagination.

For the vases, Chagall was content to make the most of their rounded sides, with marvelous ease and skill, enlivening them with undulating and fluid compositions that give the whole a pleasant gyratory movement. The viewer has the impression that the vase is going to revolve; he cannot resist walking around it in order to follow the dreamlike figures that curve around the sides: languid naiads with pearly bodies; moonlight reflected on marine currents of subtle shadings, clear or golden, azure or emerald; delicate bouquets of flowers—roses or mimosa—inhabited by fabulous birds whose gentle songs of love seem to hypnotize, long, nostalgic profiles in a summer sky on the *Vase with a Mermaid and Face*. Occasionally there is a more slender vase with a high neck to make room for figures of more affected gracefulness. Examples of this form are *The Woman with the Blue Donkey*, where, in a balmy Oriental night, a donkey with a muzzle as caressing as a kiss watches over a woman in love, lost in her dreams. In these delicate works, all treated with nuances, the forms are sometimes underlined by hollowed out lines.

The pots and pitchers, by their exuberance, are different from the modest forms of the vases: here, the abundance of handles and spouts has nothing to do with utility; these outgrowths are, above all, a prolongation of themes which thus find a tumultuous and chatoyant development. They rise, overflow, bend like a statue: some of these ceramics are veritable sculptures, such as *The Rooster*. But they also stand out by the delicacy of their colors, their generally light harmonies, their tender, mat surfaces, as fragile and precious as Mycenaean potteries. This soft, velvety aspect is the result of the artist's most recent research. Nothing could be more different from the shiny varnish, often a little vulgar, of most contemporary ceramic works. Instead of reflecting exterior light, Chagall's potteries seem, to the contrary, to absorb it or, rather, their phosphorescent colors seem to spring from the clay itself under the effect of some mysterious transpiring, due to the magic of dark light. They are illuminated from within just as his paintings transmit the image of an interior reality, the poet's own, and the reality that surrounds us.

In the very special universe of his studio, Chagall's ceramics are very naturally impregnated with his familiar myths, a little bit as the color of flora in the ocean depths leaves its mark on nearby amphorae and shells. His vases reveal the majority of subjects that the Master of Vitebsk never tires of reinventing: *The Blue Donkey*, tenderly ironic as in the fable, serves as a figure-head, with its luminous coloration—for a pitcher of rustic inspiration—ochre, brown, dark green, black—on the sides of which, blithely, dance houses in a village with its rooster and tender lovers.

The Peasant at the Well with its cheerful, pale yellow harmony—symbol of Provençal light—brightened by pale blue, green, brown and black—celebrates just as naively the happiness of country life. It depicts a peasant in a firm stance serving as a spout, next to the familiar view of Vence, the "new Vitebsk," where Chagall has found, after torment, "the heartbreaking joy of living." Vence is also profiled on the other side of *Two Women* who are smiling at each other, holding a bouquet in a graceful movement that is closer to sculpture than to the potter's art. It is significant that these pitchers tell a story on each side. On the other side of *Two Women*, an hallucinating crucifixion floats in the sky while a donkey drinks under a very definitely malefic moon. The colors themselves—red, ochre, bluegray, black set off by white—illuminate these figures with their tragic gleam. The *Two Heads*, glowing from beautiful red clay, enhanced by dashes of white, black, yellow and green, are even more extraordinary: they exalt Provence, of course, but are also disturbing memories of Russia with the intoxicated village bristling with bulbar towers and their two resigned faces overlooked by a comical and melancholy donkey. As for the decorated *Sculptured Vase* in a very "baked" red-

Woman with the Blue Donkey. 1962. Ceramic vase. 15 3/4 x 7 3/4 in. (40 x 19 cm). Collection Daniel Malingue, Paris.

dish paste, of a feminine figure, as fascinating as a Cretan idol, it is almost more a sculpture than a vase. The same is true of the *Rooster*, as fantastic as a Ming bronze. Its very pale paste is tattooed with a pair of lovers sketched in bister with a light touch. . . .

In Provence, not only the earth "burns the fingers." There is also the stone, as polished as marble, and all sorts of smooth, flat rocks. Chagall, who feels almost physically the call of this antique country, has found on its soil the emotions he experienced during his voyage to Greece in 1952, during which he admired the archaic statuary of the Museum of Athens and the sculptures of Olympia. For this reason, he feverishly began to sculpture between 1952 and 1958. He first sculptured, at the request of Father Couturier, using themes from verses of the Psalms, small bas-reliefs in marble for the Assy baptistry. Then he made small statutes in marble that are clarified transpositions. They remind one, more than of archaic Greece, of the spontaneity and enigmatic power of the first Roman age. They are inspired by his familiar themes, in particular the couple: *The Couple and the Bird, La Vague à l'Ane or Lovers*, a two-sided sculpture.

Among the most striking, let us mention *The Couple with the Goat*, a charming image of a juvenile embrace, with supple arabesques, sheltered by foliage and flowers, and with the sole complicity of the moon and a tender young goat—or the *Two Heads*, this time detached from the base and which is one of the purest, tenderest and most spell-casting representations of the kiss that has ever been

COLORPLATE 71. *The Ceiling of the Paris Opera*. 1964. Oil on canvas. Approximately 2,367 sq. ft. (220 sq. m).
Photograph: Jacques Moatti. Courtesy Explorer.

COLORPLATE 72. From *Firebird*: *The Enchanted Forest*. Scene design for Act I. 1945. Gouache on paper. 15 x 24 7/8 in. (38 x 63 cm). Collection Ida Chagall, Paris.

COLORPLATE 73. From *Aleko: A Wheatfield on a Summer's Afternoon*. Decor for Scene III. 1942.
Gouache, watercolor, wash, brush, and pencil on paper. 15 ¹/₄ x 22 ¹/₂ in. (38.7 x 57.1 cm). The Museum of Modern Art,
New York. Acquired through the Lillie P. Bliss Bequest. Photograph © The Museum of Modern Art, New York.

COLORPLATE 74. *The Magic Flute*. 1966. Lithograph. 39 3/8 x 25 5/8 in.(100 x 65 cm).
Private collection. Photograph: Christie's, New York.

COLORPLATE 75. From *The Magic Flute*. 1967. Set design at The Metropolitan Opera, Lincoln Center, New York. Photograph: Winnie Klotz, The Metropolitan Opera.

COLORPLATE 76. *The Sources of Music*. 1967. Oil on canvas. Approximately 36 x 30 ft. (11 x 9 m).
The Metropolitan Opera, Lincoln Center, New York. Photograph: Winnie Klotz, The Metropolitan Opera.

COLORPLATE 77. *The Triumph of Music.* 1967. Oil on canvas. Approximately 36 x 30 ft. (11 x 9 m).
The Metropolitan Opera, Lincoln Center, New York. Photograph: Winnie Klotz, The Metropolitan Opera.

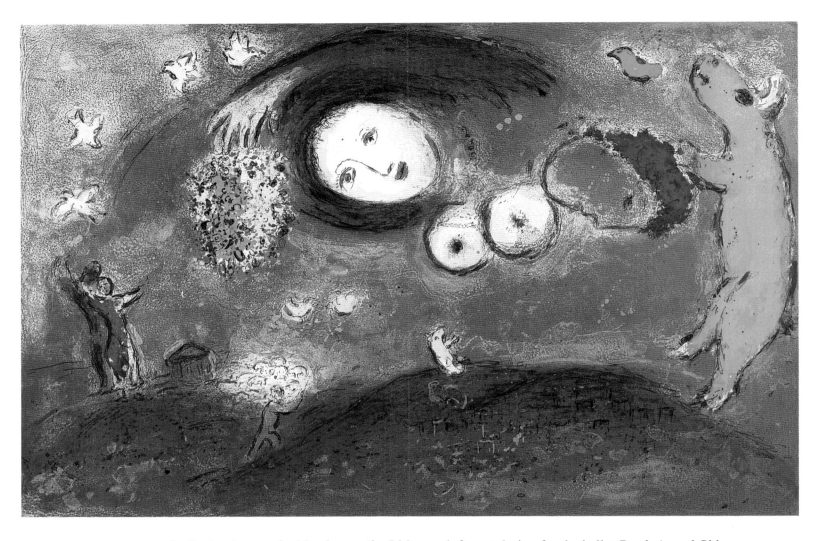

COLORPLATE 78. *Springtime on the Meadow*. 1961. Lithograph for set design for the ballet *Daphnis and Chloe*. 16 1/2 x 25 1/4 in. (41.9 x 64.1 cm). Private collection. Photograph: Christie's, New York.

The Lovers. 1952. Marble. Approximately
23 ¹/₂ in. (59.7 cm) high. Private collection.

sculptured. What reserve and what intensity in their longing for each other, in that mute complicity protected by a caressing hand!

Chagall loves his neighbor but he also loves himself, which is very natural, and his wife Valentine at the same time. Thus, he depicted himself humorously, accompanied by a redeeming feminine silhouette in an amazing chiselled medallion, its style reminiscent of Gauguin with the subtle lines and majesty of an Aztec emperor.

But Chagall's most astonishing sculptures are, without a doubt, his terra cottas and his bronzes cast by Susse in very small quantities. Capturing the third dimension, they are an autonomous reality and no longer a complementary transposition.

Two Women. 1957. Ceramic pitcher.
Approximately 12 ½ in. (31.7 cm) high.
Private collection.

The Donkey, a demoniac animal in this case, with its troubling profile, a vehicle in its flanks and a limping walk, is a haunting figuration of the couple.

The Mother Holding Her Child carries him to her bosom in a wide gesture, a symbol of pride and protection, her face proud and anxious at the same time. She evokes by her buxomness the blooming of the robust divinities of the art of Aurignac. *The Bathing Woman* recalls the vigor of the vineyardists of Roman art who also splashed in their vats (how can one not think of the wine-harvesters on the Autun tympanum?), with its gyration accentuated by the circular tub from which she emerges, her beautiful, inflected torso, broad, granular, and seeming to shine with soap. It is one of the most striking bathers in contemporary sculpture.

The simplicity, the frankness, the power of these sculptures merit reflection. They are a flat contradiction to all those who would like to consider Chagall as a colorist only. If he makes objects fly about, if he envelopes them in colored vibrations according to his reveries, he nevertheless possesses a very sure instinct for construction. Nature is liberty but it is also harmony. Movement should not be confused with gravity. The Ferris wheel in a country fair turns and creates an impression of vertigo: it is nonetheless solidly built. The purified images that Chagall's sculptures offer are admirable proof of his vitality and equilibrium.

MARC CHAGALL

On Stained Glass Windows

A stained glass window has a different fate from a painting. Because of the setting, the eye does not look at it in the same way as a collection of paintings. The eye of a man at prayer is simply part of his heart. For me a stained glass window is a transparent partition between my heart and the heart of the world. Stained glass has to be serious and passionate; it is something elevating and exhilarating. It has to live through the perception of light. To read the Bible is to perceive a certain light, and the window has to make this obvious through its simplicity and grace.

CHARLES MARQ

"When Chagall Hears the Angels Singing"

1982

Chagall first met Charles Marq, a master glassmaker, at his studio in Reims when he was commissioned to create the stained glass windows for the cathedral in Metz, France. Chagall "apprenticed" himself to Marq and the two collaborated on all of Chagall's stained glass windows. A great friendship developed and in 1973 Chagall recommended Marq to become the first director of the Musée National Message Biblique Marc Chagall in Nice, France, where he served for a short time.

I remember our first conversations. Chagall had just been commissioned by Robert Renard to create the stained glass windows for the Metz cathedral. After the two small windows of Assy, this was quite another thing: a world of color and an immense space in the Gothic cathedral that he had to grasp and fill in. We spoke of the orientation of stained glass windows, of the way forms are reduced in a Gothic edifice, but above all, we talked of the light passing through the work, ready at any moment to make it explode with color, exalting the radiance of tones, transforming forms according to their transparency or their opacity, that sovereign power on which form and color depend. There was no question of technique, of lead, of the size of the glass . . . dead frameworks in which life itself would have wilted. Chagall was wrapped up in his vision, waiting for work to give it form.

A short time later, before the large models of the windows, I experienced the same feeling. How could I transmit that modulation, that luminous song of color? A thousand difficulties, even impossibilities, confronted me but I was conscious only of a deep desire to carry it out, of an ardor to give the painter's vision to the world. . . .

After showing the model—the painter's first proposition—Chagall then awaited my own proposition, made this time in glass and lead. When he says, "Now show me what you know how to do". . . it is actually an appeal to your freedom, to that faith in our poor hands, capable, God willing, of transmitting to creation. He shows with humility that his genius is greater than he, so great that it can also inhabit others.

How I admire his manner of being outside of himself when he arrives at the studio. My work is there, a window that concerns him in every way but for which he is not responsible. With what force he enters into that dispersed, stammering, skeletal reality! "I'll take everything," he says, not lingering over criticisms but knowing that he can make his own all those forms, those colors although they are still foreign to him. He harmonizes the pieces of glass, examining, correcting, touching on only a few essentials but with astonishing precision. And perhaps his love for France is so deeply rooted in that spirit of clairvoyance that it carries him into unreality.

Now the window is ready to be "done." The glassmaker, like Adam's clay, has fashioned the glass, the masses, the possible forms, the weight of color required, but the window is there like a lifeless being awaiting that first breath of life.

Chagall then begins to work before our dazzled eyes.

He enters the studio with the punctuality of an artisan who knows that work alone allows one to accomplish something, sometimes also with the precision of those tight-rope walkers whom he loves and who float up there in gravity by the grace of an immense daily labor.

An artisan finding life by the contact with materials, as poets or "poor men" by a contact with flowers. A material which, he says, "is a talisman . . . to touch this talisman is a question of sentiment." Thought always says too much or too little and the intellect, for him, is left outside the door of the studio.

"In the soul there is a sort of intelligence, but in the intelligence there is not always a soul."

He paints. The grisaille, by the sole power of its value and of the line, permits him now to justify everything . . .

Form, that is his soul. In it there is neither an idea, nor a symbol, nor even reminiscence. I see a curve become, according to his inspiration, a plant, a flower, a face, an animal or a moon . . . or simply remain a curve.

An intensity of spirit that makes a new form spring forth. Infinite boundaries between order and disorder. He looks, moves away, rejects, begins again, going mysteriously towards a new image that he does not yet know.

The feeling he has about a subject dictates a line to him, a certain touch, and that touch enlightens him on his subject. The painting explains itself to the painter.

And in this ceaseless back and forth movement the window is born and gradually finds its form. There is no question of subject, technique, sentiment nor even sensitivity . . . only a mysterious relationship between light and eye, between grisaille and hand, between space and time . . . as if biological, as if molecular, becoming visible in rhythm, color and proportion. When the glass appears to have received its exact weight in grisaille, its proper quantity of life, the hand stops as if restrained by another hand. But any form that has not received all the painter's blood, dies, wilts, fades and disintegrates.

Chagall speaks of chemistry . . . No need to back away, this touch discloses the whole picture and this glass the whole window. Everything is there, everything is reassembled in every way in a living work. A touch born in a flash, produced by millions of years of accumulated forces or by a slow maturation of a gesture eternally repeated, an obscurely ripened deposit of effort. "Look at Rembrandt, look at Chardin, look at Monet—each has his own chemistry."

How, then, can one speak of technique when the "how to do" becomes the "how to be"? How can one speak of reason when I see the sublime fatigue of work destroy all determination to become only "color, light, liberty"?

Color . . . The impassioned weight of red, the infinite exchange of blue, the great repose of green, the dark mystery of violet, the implacable limit of yellow— here it is exalted in all the plenitude of its richness—and Chagall likes that color. But his color is something else.

"Ah! This isn't mere coloring. No question of red or blue there. Find your color and you've won the battle." The grisaille is spread in sheets, in accents, ordering, orchestrating by value until the moment when that sonority of color-sensation is perceived.

Light . . . "You kill it or it kills you and that's not it." Light that passes directly through the work to be painted, that animates it and gives it life; but light that must be tamed, directed, imprisoned in glass, allowed to live where it belongs.

"Stained glass is not easy. You must take it as one catches a mouse: not in a cage but with the hand. There are no 'in-betweens,' it is yes or no."

Chagall scrapes, washes, repaints, becomes angry.

"What a nightmare! One must struggle with the lead: struggle, struggle, and then perhaps we'll win out."

"Ah! I don't know how to draw . . . One doesn't need to know how to draw. A line, that the good Lord knows how to do perfectly. When it's X or Y, it's still a line, it is not God. And so I make little dots, pricks, like that, full of little things of no importance."

His hand races over the glass, placing spots, lines, tints, stamps and marks for a whole hour . . .

"Ah! I have forgotten everything. Where am I?"

Liberty . . . the eternally repeated instant, a childhood that is his source and his goal. A childhood from which he emerged whole, from which he still draws his strength. As a painter he is like a newborn child. His anxieties, his torments, his long life of work have turned his hair white but for him painting begins at the break of day.

"The sign of a masterpiece is its freshness."

The inspired freshness of a Mozart, of a Schubert, whom he adores and who revive him after long hours of work.

A Schubert quartet . . . "That is what Art must be. Ah! Schubert, he cried because he had no friends, no love, nothing but look at what he has done to the whole world. Listen to the way he cries. I love that . . . Ah! How he suffered!"

He goes on working, becomes moved and thinks out loud. "One must caress. Nothing is given for free. Even the love of a dog must be won with a lump of sugar."

A quintet by Mozart . . . "Where did he unearth that? Someone whispered it to him . . . sing it . . . sing it, and he sings, he listens to what the angels tell him . . . that gift is not given to everyone . . . he does anything he wants, whether here or there, and it's right, always right."

Chagall continues his creation; his work accompanies him, and in the dazzling light of the creation I cannot distinguish one from the other.

This poet's dream of an ever new and luminous subject is perhaps what forces him to leave his completed work so quickly in order to go out and find the street and life—and to await the birth of a new dream tomorrow.

MARC CHAGALL

At the Dedication of the Jerusalem Windows

1962

COLORPLATES 93, 94

How is it that the air and earth of Vitebsk, my birthplace, and of thousands of years of exile, find themselves mingled in the air and earth of Jerusalem.

How could I have thought that not only my hands with their colours would direct me in my work, but that the poor hands of my parents and of others and still others with their mute lips and their closed eyes, who gathered and whispered behind me would direct me as if they also wished to take part in my life?

I feel too, as though the tragic and heroic resistance movements, in the ghettos, and your war here in this country, are blended in my flowers and beasts and my fiery colours . . .

The more our age refuses to see the full face of the universe and restricts itself to the sight of a tiny fraction of its skin, the more anxious I become when I

The Twelve Tribes of Israel were Chagall's only stained glass windows produced for a synagogue. All of his other windows were commissioned by churches and museums.

Chagall at work on *Tribe of Dan*.
Photograph Courtesy Hadassah Medical
Relief Association.

consider the universe in its eternal rhythm, and the more I wish to oppose the general current.

Do I speak like this because, with the advance of life, the outlines surrounding us become clearer and the horizon appears in a more tragic glow?

I feel as if colours and lines flow like tears from my eyes, though I do not weep. And do not think that I speak like this from weakness—on the contrary, as I advance in years the more certain I am of what I want, and the more certain I am of what I say.

I know that the path of our life is eternal and short, and while still in my mother's womb I learned to travel this path with love rather than with hate.

These thoughts occurred to me many years ago, when I first stepped on biblical ground preparing to create etchings for the Bible. And they emboldened me to bring my modest gift to the Jewish people—to that Jewish people which always dreamt of biblical love, of friendship and peace among all peoples; to that people which lived here, thousands of years ago, among the other Semitic peoples. And this, which is today called "Religious Art" I created while bearing in mind the great and ancient creations of the surrounding Semitic peoples.

My hope is that I hereby extend my hand to seekers of culture, to poets and to artists among the neighbouring peoples. . . .

I saw the hills of Sodom and the Negev, out of whose defiles appear the shadows of our prophets in their yellowish garments, the colour of dry bread. I heard their ancient words . . . Have they not truly and justly shown in their words how to behave on this earth and by what ideal to live.

I draw hope and encouragement from thinking that my humble work will remain in their land, your land.

MARC CHAGALL

At the Dedication of the *Peace* Window at the United Nations

September 17, 1964

COLORPLATE 95

While I was working on this project, in my studio at Vence and, later on, at Reims in the studios of Jacques Simon and of Charles Marq, with their generous cooperation, I heard within me, as it were, an echo of man's destiny in the past and now, in our own troubled times.

I took advantage of my visit to New York last year to meet some of you and to hear your views; and this gave me greater confidence in my work. Together we discussed various possible ideas for a memorial. Finally I recalled this prophetic legend on the theme of peace, and I can think of no more poetic legend, or one of more universal significance.

I thought, on showing you a few sketches, that I sensed in you an echo, and this gave me great joy, because with all my soul I wanted to convey the extent of my inspiration and the inspiration of Dag Hammarskjold and of all those who died for Peace. For that was the very purpose for which the United Nations was founded.

These colours and these forms must show, in the end, our dreams of human happiness, as we conceive it today. On the right-hand side of this panel you will see mankind, with its yearning for peace, its prophets and its victims. In the

Marc Chagall discussing the stained glass *Peace* window in the United Nations, New York, with former Secretary-General U Thant and a member of the staff Memorial Committee, 1964. Photograph: The United Nations, New York.

247

centre is the symbol of peace itself. On the left, above and below, are depicted motherhood and the people who are struggling for peace.

The main thing is not to see it but to feel it.

In doing this work, I was far from any current theories.

I should like people to be as moved as I was when I was engaged in this work, which was done for the peoples of all countries, in the name of Peace and Love.

CARLTON LAKE

"Artist at Work: Marc Chagall"

July 1963

Carlton Lake, an American writer and art critic living in Paris.

I got down to the lobby at ten minutes to eight the next morning, but I found Chagall and Charles Marq waiting by the entrance. When we reached the studio, the light had barely begun to filter in through the high windows, and the two lancets were not much more than faintly visible from the back of the atelier. Chagall walked over to the lancets. "What time does the light come in?" he called out.

"In about half an hour," Charles Marq said. Brigitte, in black stretch pants, was vigorously preparing Chagall's paint on a small rectangular table between the two lancets. Chagall took off his coat and suit jacket and pulled on a black-and-white-checked lumber jacket. He fumbled unsuccessfully with the zipper. "It's modern. No buttons," he grumbled. Brigitte came over and zipped him up.

Charles Marq, now at the little table, tested the paint. "It's much too liquid, Brigitte." Brigitte returned to the table and worked at the solution to bring it to the proper consistency.

Propped up on a large easel at the left of the two lancets was Chagall's final maquette for the window, which was painted in gouache on a one-to-ten scale and arranged against a white background, framed, and covered with transparent-plastic protective sheeting, showing the design the window would take when installed at the Cathedral of Metz. The maquette as a whole had the pointed-arch form of a Gothic ogive. The main body of the window was composed of four parallel lancets at its base, separated by white strips representing the stone into which they would eventually be set.

Chagall, half a dozen brushes in his left hand, saw me studying the maquette and came over to join me. "That one" — he pointed to the lefthand lancet — "is 'The Sacrifice of Abraham.' The one next to it is 'Jacob Wrestling with the Angel'; the one next to that, 'Jacob's Dream'; and the fourth one, on the far right, 'Moses before the Burning Bush.'"

Directly above the four lancets were two smaller units of the design, each in the shape of a heart, but having, like the lancets, an ogival point at the top. The one on the left showed a boy with a sheep in front of him. "That's Joseph," Chagall said. "And on the right is Jacob, weeping for Joseph." He pointed up to two similarly shaped but longer parts of the design that were set in between the two heart-shaped pieces but rose almost to the top of the maquette. They were crowded with a variety of human and animal figures. "Noah's Ark," he explained. "And on top" — he pointed to another element above them that formed the very tip of the maquette and had the same form as the two lower heart-shaped parts — "that's Noah after the Flood." Over Noah's head was a rainbow, and over the rainbow an angel. Set into the white areas that separated all these elements, from the points of the lancets to the top of the maquette, were eighteen curved-sided triangular shapes of varying sizes that filled out the design. "The whole window will be a little over twenty-three feet high," Chagall said.

The two lancets that were set up on the metal racks were, on the left, "Jacob Wrestling with the Angel" and, on the right, "Jacob's Dream." Each one was about ten feet high and forty inches wide, divided into three rectangular panels and a fourth one, higher than the others, that ended in a point. Their metal edges were secured to the framework with clothespins, and black cloths draped around them allowed the light from the studio windows behind them to enter the room only through the stained glass itself. The left-hand lancet showed Jacob down on one knee, struggling with a larger-than-life-size angel whose form, together with Jacob's, filled the central area of the lancet and whose wings, a pale yellow flecked with brighter tones, swept upward into the point of the lancet. The flesh tones of the angel and the blue of Jacob's body were sharpened by the warm red of their background. Behind Jacob was a small bouquet of flowers.

"I finished 'Jacob's Dream' last week," Chagall said, "but there's a lot of work to do on the other one still." He went over to the lancet that showed Jacob wrestling with the angel, sat down on a low stool beside his table, selected a small brush from the ones in his left hand, dipped it into the paint, and started to work.

Brigitte, I saw, was working with two wide brushes over the surface of "Jacob Wrestling." With one, which she dipped frequently into the grisaille — the black liquid paint she had earlier been mixing on the table — she was covering the upper panels with broad strokes. With the other, apparently dry, she removed the excess and whatever clung to the leads, giving in this way a fairly uniform thin grayish film to the surface of the glass. Her long legs and arms were moving efficiently around Chagall, who seemed planted in front of his lancet like a tree rooted in the ages. Utilizing the film of grisaille that Brigitte had already washed over the lower panel, he was painting in accents, small figures, and flower and leaf forms.

He had begun, lightly and gently, in the lower left-hand corner, until then populated chiefly by Jacob's and the angel's right feet. Now he had worked over to the right center, near the spiky bouquet, and was working faster. The glass rattled in its frame. One of the clothespins popped off onto the floor. Chagall stopped, studied the bouquet for a moment, then picked out, with a finger, areas between some of its clusters where the grisaille was still wet, to vary the effects of shading. He painted in new forms, neither animal nor purely vegetable, through whose presence what had been colored glass became matter in movement. He was working rapidly now, ranging widely from the bush to Jacob's beard to the angel's aureole and back to Jacob's beard again. Behind us, in the center of the atelier, the high old-fashioned coal stove had swung into its stride, too, and in spite of the twenty-five-foot ceiling, the temperature was rising by the minute. Chagall peeled off his lumber jacket and tossed it onto a chair. Almost in the same sweep of his arm he returned to the glass and attacked the angel's wings.

"Charles," he called out, "my glasses are steamed up." Charles Marq came over, lifted off Chagall's glasses, wiped them clear, and replaced them. Chagall didn't stop working. He sat down on a small chair near the painting table and began to pick out, with his finger, some of the shaded areas around the bouquet. The deep-blue central stem and the dull garnet of the background began to glow with new warmth.

Charles Marq came over with a young fellow in a long gray workcoat.

"Ah, bonjour, Michel," Chagall said. "You were very nice to come in on your day off."

"You aren't doing anything more on 'Jacob's Dream,' are you?" asked Charles Marq.

Chagall shook his head. "No, I think it's all right the way it is. I'm leaving it like that — at least for now. If I did anything more on it, it would be in a different spirit, so I'd better leave it alone."

"Good," said Charles Marq. "I want to get it into the kiln. If you want to make any additions, you can do that afterward." He and Michel started to dismantle "Jacob's Dream," which was principally in warm tones of rose and red with touches of blue, green, and yellow. They removed first the bottom panel, about two and a half feet high by three and a half wide, with the figure of a bearded Jacob asleep. They then removed the panel next above, which, with a similarly shaped panel above it, and the point of the lancet above that, showed the angels of Jacob's dream ascending and descending the ladder. In the center, to the right of the largest angel figure, was a crescent moon in which Chagall had painted a worn peasant figure with a pack on his back. Underneath, on a branch of the bush at Jacob's head, was a tiny bird. They removed the third panel and then the point. They stacked them against a wooden rack at the rear of the studio.

Chagall, I saw, was picking out, with the wooden tip of his brush, spots of light in the grisaille around the perimeter of the bouquet behind Jacob. I asked him why he was digging into the grisaille like that, making hundreds of tiny marks in the film. "That makes it vibrate," he said. "And it makes a marriage between the bouquet and the upright composition in the center — Jacob wrestling with the angel. It brings them together. You'll see."

Charles Marq came over to us. "If the bottom panel is done," he said, "you might as well sign it so we can take it downstairs." Chagall moved from his chair onto the low stool, dipped a brush into the paint, and signed his name in the lower right-hand corner.

"That's too low," Charles Marq said.

Chagall rubbed it out and wrote it in a bit higher. "You're sure it won't run, your ink?" he asked.

"That's too small," Charles Marq said. "You're too modest."

Chagall looked up at him. "How do you spell 'Reims'?" he asked.

"R-e-i-m-s," Charles Marq answered.

Under his name, Chagall wrote *R-i-e-m-s.*

"Not like that," Charles Marq said.

Chagall looked up at him. "What do you mean?"

The Prophets Abraham, Jacob, and Moses.
1962. Maquette for the stained glass windows
at the Metz Cathedral. 56 1/4 x 36 5/8 in.
(143 x 93 cm). Collection Ida Chagall, Paris.

"Nothing," Charles Marq said. "That's all right. It makes no difference." He
moved the painting table aside, knocked over a glass, and spilled water onto the
floor. He cleaned up the mess, pushed the table out of the way, and spilled the
water again.

"Don't touch my color," Chagall said.

"Matter in revolt," Charles Marq said. "Rebellious neutrons." Chagall went
back to work on Jacob's head.

Michel came in with the sections of another lancet and began to set them up
in the frame that earlier had held "Jacob's Dream."

"This is 'The Sacrifice of Abraham,'" Charles Marq said to me. "Chagall
hasn't seen it yet." He and Michel mounted the four panels onto the frame, pinned
them against the supporting wires with clothespins, and draped the black cloths
above and on each side to shut out the light. Chagall left Jacob to the angel and

walked over to study Abraham. The central figure, a hesitant and grief-stricken Abraham, holding a long knife in his right hand, stood over the naked body of his son Isaac, ready for the sacrifice. Behind Abraham was a flowering tree; over his head, a small figure of Christ carrying His cross, and looking down on Him from the point, an angel. After a minute, Chagall went back to his maquette, looked at it carefully, then returned to the new lancet, which was mostly in blue except for the naked body of Isaac stretched out at his father's feet.

"It needs more warm tones, Charles," he said. Charles Marq suggested adding more yellow to the body of Isaac. "That's not enough," Chagall said. "I want more in other places than just that body." He pointed to two pieces of purple glass on the lower right. "That's too dark. I don't need that," he said. "Put in another lead there with something warmer. And a touch of green."

Charles marked with a grease crayon the pieces of glass Chagall had asked him to change.

"It needs more light up there at the top, Charles, near the angel."

"I'll put in a more intense red," Charles said.

"And more light up there on the angel's wing. And calm it down in back. Poor man. I make you suffer, no?" Chagall kept studying the lancet. "We've absolutely got to have three pieces of green up there in the left shoulder," he said. "We have to light up all those blues. And three pieces of warmth in there, too. And take out that violet. I don't need it."

Charles Marq looked over at Chagall's maquette. "It's violet on the maquette," he said.

"Something warmer," Chagall said. "A little more red. And up there, on the left, in the tip, behind the angel, it needs to be broken up. Another lead, no? It's a little monotonous, all that. And it's too dark."

"All right," Charles Marq said, "we'll take care of that. I'll engrave it. That will lighten it."

"And give it more warmth," Chagall said. "It looks a little too much like Matisse, as is."

"You're right," Charles Marq said. "It's a little flat — Montparno."

Chagall shook his finger. "If it's done very, very, very, very, very well, that's all right. If not, it's no good." He ran his hand down Abraham's robe to his feet. "I want there to be some warmth, a sort of envelope, right down to his feet. That's all. Good-bye." Charles Marq and Michel took the panels down to the workroom below to make the changes.

Chagall walked back to the Jacob lancet and began to brush on vigorously more of the grisaille in the area around the angel's head, then removed some of it with the dry brush. He reversed his brush and began scraping with the wooden tip to heighten the nuances in the shading of Jacob's body. The glass rattled and squeaked and squealed. I began to wonder just how resistant it was. Chagall sighed, grunted, and groaned, then pressed his left index finger against Jacob's left cheek to lighten a blue area. He pulled away the grisaille from the rose of the angel's body and then from the pale-blue shadows of its face and ran his finger glancingly down the shading of the angel's right thigh. He stopped, inspected his work briefly; then with the palm of his right hand modified the imprint of his finger and smoothed out the impact of his earlier shading along the entire thigh. He then moved over onto the angel's left arm, first with two fingers and then with his fingernails, lightly, caressingly.

"You see how it is," he said. "Stained glass is like the body of a woman. It needs loving attention over every square centimeter." . . .

It was now 10:45. Brigitte came in with a tray of coffee things and set them down on a long table on the far side of the studio. She called to Chagall. He kept on working. After a minute or two he stopped. "Oh, well, I didn't get very far. *Tant pis.*" He threw his checked lumber jacket over his shoulders and sat down at the end of the table. Brigitte sat at the coffee tray, and I between them.

"It's not too strong?" Chagall asked as she began to pour.

"Just the way it always is," she said. She handed us steaming cups of coffee

Brigitte Simon with Chagall at the studio in Reims, c. 1971. Courtesy Charles Marq.

and spread slices of toast with butter and honey and passed them to us. Chagall took a bite, sipped his coffee for a minute, then turned to me.

"Well," he said, "you're present at the *accouchement.*" I told him this was one *accouchement* I was enjoying.

"I never let anyone into the atelier while I work — never. But now you're seeing the whole damned cuisine. As you see, I don't have any method. As soon as art becomes method, it's finished. I just do what I have to do, what I feel here" — he touched his heart. "It comes down here" — he ran his left hand down his right arm onto the right hand. "Like an idiot, maybe, or like a child, like your little boy who does whatever comes into his head, without reflection. It's childlike, but not childishness. Isn't that right, Brigitte? As children go, I'm a child." Brigitte smiled and poured us more coffee. Chagall stirred in a lump of sugar. "Nobody's more of a child than I am," he said. "All the others, compared to me, are people who struggle." Brigitte spread another *tartine* with honey and handed it to him. *"Voilà, mon enfant,"* she said.

Chagall finished his coffee and *tartine.* We walked back to Jacob. "Jacob is wrestling with the angel," he said. "I wrestle with Jacob *and* the angel." He picked up his brushes and went back to work on Jacob. "Everybody has been after me to write the second volume of *My Life,* to bring it up to date from 1923. I'd like to, but I'm tired. I have no more strength. Besides, it's not my métier. Maybe I'm lazy. I just don't get to it. I go on pecking away, pecking away. It's a form of madness, idiocy. But what else can I do? On this little planet, in our little world, probably the smallest of all, of millions of others, what makes sense? Friendship, a woman to love, making a child, not piling up too much false intellectuality and pride of life. Look at Gide. He died like a dog, and nobody reads him anymore. Nobody but a few pederasts. Look at the Spaniard. He spits on God. God will spit on him soon. God, who made all the millions of planets, will spit on him because He's the stronger. Yes, the Spaniard with all his millions and all his Kahnweilers and all the rest, God will spit on him, just the way He'll spit

"The Spaniard" refers here to Picasso, with whom Chagall had a volatile personal relationship.

on Khrushchev. But He doesn't spit on children, like your boy. The child is the genius, not all the knowledge a man piles up, because God is always stronger."

Charles Marq joined us at the Jacob lancet. "Well, Charlot," Chagall said, "how goes it down below?"

"It's coming along," Charles Marq said. "A little time, that's all."

"I wondered if you weren't pulling something on me," Chagall said.

Charles Marq laughed. "Oh, no. Not this time. Every once in a while I rebel, though."

"But you like it, don't you?" Chagall said.

Charles Marq smiled. "Of course. There's always a purpose in the changes you have me make."

"He's a wonderful boy, that Charles," Chagall said. "He knows I'm a child, and I know what I want. A child always knows what he wants, even if it's just a piece of bread and butter."

"That's the way it goes," Charles Marq said. "We show him the work. He says, 'I want this, that, and the other.' Then afterwards it's still not right and —"

Chagall interrupted him. "I like to listen to other people's opinions. I don't always follow them, but I listen. The only man I wouldn't listen to is the Spaniard. I would never listen to him."

Michel came in with the lower panel of "The Sacrifice." Chagall looked over it, dubiously. "What's this little bit here?" he asked, pointing to a touch of red at the end of the fagots beneath Isaac's body. "Can't you get rid of that?"

"Oh, no," Charles Marq said.

"You'd better put in a lead there, and I'll make you a gift of the color."

"But that corresponds to what you've shown on the maquette."

"You don't need a big piece," Chagall said. "You give me something warmer. Look, *mon petit,* that can continue on — ah, no, there's no lead there. Well, you put in another tone, warmer." He coughed, like a lion roaring, and returned to the Jacob lancet. He began painting along the right-hand border. "No still lifes with a bottle here," he said. "I make flowers because they're divine." Chagall chuckled. "'A great artist, where he belongs.' That's funny, you know, because my wife is against my specializing in Palestine. She's not nationalist. And I'm not either. But I love the Bible, and I love the race that created that Bible. And I'm not going to buy myself a place in the French Panthéon by refusing to work for those poor people in Israel if they want me.

"In any case, the French will say the same thing about me whether I work for Israel or not. Chagall belongs there, they'll say. It's in their blood. That's the way they are. And I'm not going to do something or refuse to do something else in the hope that the French will think more of me for it. I do all this for nothing. I give paintings free to the Musée National d'Art Moderne, for France, not for other countries. And what happens? It's a little like Don Quixote. Of course, they sugared the pill a little. At least they said, 'A *great* artist' — but over there, in Israel, where he belongs."

*   *   *

During lunch we settled the affairs of Russia, China, India, Venus, Mars, and the moon. Chagall checked his watch against mine and decided it was 1:45. "All right, let's get back to work," he said.

"Why don't you settle down now and take a little rest?" Brigitte suggested.

Chagall shook his head. "Work to be done. Let's go."

"No, no," said Charles Marq. "You stay right here. There are still a few changes to be made in 'The Sacrifice,' and there's nothing for you to do just yet, so relax."

Brigitte threw back the comforter on a day bed behind Chagall's chair. "Why don't you lie down here?" she said.

Chagall sighed. "Maybe. For a few minutes." He stretched out on the bed. I could see he wasn't really resting, though. He seemed to be listening. In a few minutes he was back on his feet. "I hear Michel downstairs. He must be bringing in the panels now," he said. We followed him down to the atelier. Michel was

Chagall with Virginia McNeil and their son
David in Cannes, 1951. Photograph ©
Lipnitzki-Viollet.

fitting the reworked panels of "The Sacrifice" into the right-hand frame. When he
had finished, Chagall picked up a long pointer and tapped an area in the foliage of
the tree to the left of Abraham's head.

"I want it more pale in here, Charles," he said.

"But no," Charles Marq said. "We changed that because you said it was too
pale. That moves around just right now. I changed that whole area around for
you."

Chagall shook his head. "I'm not completely happy about it, all the same. It's
too stiff. It needs just another little piece in there."

"Well," said Charles Marq, "I could replace that blue above the tree by a
warm reddish rose. That will bring it closer to the maquette. With a bit of silver-
stain yellow."

Chagall nodded. "All right. That's enough for that. Now," he said, pointing
down to the form of Isaac in the bottom panel, "I want something warm along the
side of his leg here."

"I'll put in a strip of yellow on neutral," Charles Marq offered. "Will that
make it right?"

"That's what I'll see," Chagall said. "Now, here," he said, tapping Isaac's
right arm with his pointer, "I'll make you a present of this. I don't need it. And
this."

Charles Marq groaned. "Oh, no. Not that."

"Oh, yes," said Chagall. "Get rid of it, you understand? And I want more yellow on the right side of Isaac's face. And I want the blue of Abraham's head continued so it will replace the dark-blue shadow behind it." He tapped the tree to the
left of Abraham. "I want three spots of green — maybe four — in here." He
moved over to the right and studied the small group of figures above Abraham's
head: Christ carrying His cross and four or five other figures sketched in roughly
in black. "I can't see the Christ carrying His cross," he said. He looked at the
maquette. "It's not readable. I want to *see* Him carrying His cross."

Chagall reached up with his pointer and tapped the violent red area on the right side of the angel's chest, in the point of the lancet. "This is good, but over here" — he tapped the left side — "it's too dull. I want a more revolutionary red. Frankly revolutionary. And here, down by Abraham's foot, you'll put in a piece of the same green as up there. Now, have you got all that marked down in your head, Charles?" Charles assured him he had. Just to make sure, Chagall recapitulated rapidly each one of the changes.

"Perfect, perfect," Charles Marq said. He climbed up on the ladder and tested a piece of red glass against the angel's chest, then left the atelier. Michel removed the upper rectangular panel of "The Sacrifice" and then the point of "Jacob Wrestling."

Chagall sat down. "Maybe I make them work too much," he said, "but you have to know what you want, and when you do, then you have to see that you get it. Every orchestra needs a conductor. If I ask for the maximum, it's because it's really the minimum."

HOMAGE TO CHAGALL

VIRGINIA HAGGARD

From *My Life with Chagall*

1960

IN CHAGALL'S COMPANY

Marc always had a superstitious preference for the number 7, having been born on the seventh day of the seventh month, 1887, and although he'd said, "It *could* be that my father lied about my age and gave me two extra years so that I and my younger brother, David, would be exempt from military service," he preferred to stick to the official date of 1887, because of the magic number, and the mystery remained. I never managed to clarify the matter; his answers became more and more vague whenever I questioned him about it. He simply didn't know. What he did know, however, was that he had been frightened of adolescence; he wanted to go on being an innocent child. Perhaps he was launched into adolescence a little too early because of these two extra years. But later, he enjoyed the thought of having two suspended years to play with.

Marc was pleased when he discovered that I was also born in the seventh month, and when the day came, he presented me with an inscribed copy of *Ma Vie,* containing a watercolor of an artist at the easel, half-man, half-faun, a revealing version of the self-portrait.

I took home the Venturi book before it was inscribed and showed it to John, but I left *Ma Vie,* with its telltale painting, hidden away on Marc's shelf. John was impressed by the beauty of some of Marc's pictures, but the next day he said something unkind about Jews. Was he beginning to feel a bit jealous?

COLORPLATE 79. *King David*. 1951. Oil on canvas. 78 x 52 ³/8 in. (198 x 133 cm).
Musée National d'Art Moderne, Centre Georges Pompidou, Paris.

COLORPLATE 80. *The Red Roofs*. 1953. Oil on paper mounted on canvas. 90 $^1/_8$ x 83 $^7/_8$ in. (229 x 213 cm).
Musée National d'Art Moderne, Centre Georges Pompidou, Paris.

COLORPLATE 81. *The Flying Fish*. 1956. Oil on canvas. 34 ⁵/₈ x 52 ⁵/₈ in. (88 x 133.7 cm). Private collection.

COLORPLATE 82. *Quay of Bercy*. 1953. Oil on canvas. 21 5/8 x 25 1/2 in. (55 x 65 cm). Private collection.

COLORPLATE 83. *Pont Neuf.* 1953. Oil on canvas. 39 3/8 x 31 7/8 in. (100 x 81 cm). Private collection.

COLORPLATE 84. *The Tree of Jesse.* 1960. Oil on canvas. 59 x 39 ³/8 in. (150 x 100 cm). Collection Marcus Diener, Basel.

COLORPLATE 85. *The Bay of Angels*. 1962. Lithograph. 30 3/4 x 22 1/2 in. (78 x 57 cm). Private collection.

COLORPLATE 86. *The Woman Bird*. 1958–61. Oil on canvas. 42 $\frac{1}{2}$ x 62 $\frac{1}{2}$ in. (108 x 159 cm). Private collection.

The Mermaid. 1952. Gouache on paper.
37 3/4 x 26 in. (96 x 66 cm). Private collection.

Ida certainly sensed the change in her father and the easy friendliness
between us, though we were careful to show as little familiarity as possible, and I
continued to address Marc as Monsieur Chagall. But his eyes could hide nothing
from Ida, nor could mine. She had a way of looking at me, kindly, but with a certain insistence, until I felt uncomfortable.

I seldom saw her husband, Michel Gordey, who was a journalist with the
Voice of America and rushed in and out of the house all the time in tremendous
haste.

Sometimes a cheerful crowd of young friends blew in, some in G.I. uniforms,
and the lunch table was often the scene of lively conversations in French, English
and Russian. The months following the end of the war in New York were charged
with tremendous vitality. The G.I. Bill was creating a vast movement of learning,
a thirst for culture, and the European exiles had brought and received a powerful
stimulus.

Fernand Léger and Piet Mondrian were quickly assimilated to New York; it
was their element, and it made their art flourish. The sculptors, Ossip Zadkine,
Amédé Ozenfant and Jacques Lipchitz also developed in very positive directions
under the strong impact of New York.

Pierre Matisse organized an exhibition of illustrious exiles in 1942 in his New York gallery. A photograph shows them all together: Max Ernst, Kurt Seligman, Ozenfant, André Masson, Piet Mondrian, André Breton, Léger, Zadkine, Yves Tanguy, Lipchitz, Pierre Tchelitchew, Eugene Berman, Roberto Matta—and Chagall.

In the photograph, Marc appears severe and rather ill at ease. He avoided his famous colleagues in New York as much as he did in Paris. His contacts with other painters were always difficult. Against his fear of being misunderstood was the inevitable conviction of his own superiority. In short, he had an inferiority-superiority complex.

As for painters of Jewish origin, he was even more distrustful of them, and when the less successful ones showed him friendliness and admiration, he imagined they sought to be associated with him so as to take advantage of his prestige. He was particularly anxious not to be considered a Jewish artist, but a universal one.

At the luncheon parties on Riverside Drive, Marc was usually gay and talkative. I occasionally caught snatches of conversation when I was passing dishes. Sometimes he was teased about his various aversions, and once when someone mentioned Moise Kisling and Mané Katz, two other exiled Jewish artists, he made a comical grimace of disgust, and everyone laughed.

Virginia was originally hired by Ida Chagall to be a domestic helper for her father after Bella's death. Virginia and Chagall soon became intimate.

Marc had a more friendly relationship with poets and writers. Among the exiles were Jacques and Raissa Maritain, excellent friends of the Chagalls for years. Jacques was a Catholic philosopher, and Raissa was a Russian Jewess converted to Catholicism by Jacques. They, in turn, converted Pierre Reverdy, Jean Cocteau, Max Jacob and Georges Rouault, but their fervent proselytizing had never been aimed at the Chagalls, who were all too obviously not interested.

Another couple, Claire and Ivan Goll, both poets, had been friends of Bella and Marc since the twenties. Marc illustrated their *Poèmes d'amour.* Yet while in New York they were still living their chaotic, romantic lives; still faithful to their communist principles, especially Ivan, who often gave vent to solemn sermons of political faith. Communists, Marc thought, were even worse than devout Christians in their desire to convert everyone.

Marc also became friendly with André Breton after the publication in New York of a text in which Breton stated that the Dada and surrealist movements had underrated the importance of Chagall.

Marc was very proud of this homage, since Breton's prestige was enormous. But it amused him to be considered a forerunner of the surrealists, with whom he felt he had little in common.

CHAGALL'S ADVICE TO YOUNG PAINTERS

In those days young painters occasionally came to the door with an armful of paintings to ask Marc for advice. They were mostly foreigners; the French painters never imagined they could come unannounced. Marc enjoyed these impromptu visits and received the young artists kindly. His faculty for seeing with the vision of others and understanding their problems was remarkable.

A young Italian painter, grave and earnest as a priest, once appeared with paintings that were full of dark violence. He was absorbed in obscure theories and used elaborate terms to explain them. Marc said, "You are far too preoccupied with theories when all that matters is quality, and one is born with that. There may be quality in your work, but it is obscured by schools of thought. If your cloth is not of good quality, your suit will be worthless, however well it is tailored. Any part of a good picture is good, like a fine piece of cloth. All that matters is the plastic value, the form comes of itself. Klee is an artist of quality because of the purity of his plasticity; Mondrian, too."

Street Scene with Clock. 1952. Oil on canvas. 25 ¹/₂ x 21 ¹/₂ in. (64.7 x 54.6 cm). Private collection.

The young man said that what he admired in Chagall was not his plasticity, but his poetry. Marc replied that without plasticity, poetry didn't exist.

"Don't you think," said the young man, "that in this atomic age, our plasticity should be full of atomic energy?"

"Mon cher," Marc smiled, "if you possess atomic energy, well and good, but if you don't, it's no good searching for it! Say what you have to say without troubling about the manner in which you say it. Whatever qualities you possess will then be evident."

To a Scandinavian painter he said, "Don't confront nature with a knife, but with a prayer. Don't bother yourself with texture. Perhaps the 'cuisine' of Braque and Matisse doesn't suit you. You're not French. Search for your weltanschauung, your personal conception of the world."

Another painter showed him a very violent painting and Marc asked him, "What gave you such a shock?" The man explained that his wife was very hostile to his work.

"Never mind," said Marc. "You must be patient and steadfast. Be calm, don't search so far away. Do a chair or a bowl of fruit. All this fantasy is foreign to you. In any case, it's banal fantasy."

To a Dutchman whose paintings were heavy, obscure and confused, he said, "You must wash your paintings just as you wash your body."

To two Americans he said, "You must reevaluate your currency. You need a dollar that has one hundred percent value. Your values, your talent, your chemical qualities, *these* are your capital."

One of them asked whether it was advisable to study in an art school, and he replied, "If you have a small talent, you will lose much, but if you have a big talent, you will lose nothing. I advise you to forget about poetry, feelings, love—you won't lose those. Concentrate on your plastic quality while you are young. The older you grow, the less spontaneous you will be. A child paints with passionate intensity, that's the quality you must preserve. Above all, don't think too much about your direction. Daumier never had time to think about his direction, he had to earn his living. But he found his direction quite naturally, because he found his true value."

To one very young painter he urged, "Don't exhibit, because if you are successful, you will be tempted to repeat your success. Your painting is too fragile, don't use it as a means of livelihood, you might destroy it completely. Earn your living any other way. Keep your painting innocent."

One time he held court with a group of painters who had arrived: "Don't wait for ideas, they come with production. If you prepare yourself too much, you might never be ready. Creation is itself a preparation. I have been producing like a madman ever since I was sixteen. Don't be afraid to do inferior things, the first fruits are always small and sour. You must work a lot, it clears the brain."

Vence: The Painter and the Model. 1952. Oil on canvas. 26 x 21 ½ in. (66 x 54.6 cm). Musée National d'Art Moderne, Centre Georges Pompidou, Paris.

FRANÇOISE GILOT and CARLTON LAKE

From *Life with Picasso*

1964

Françoise Gilot (b. 1921), French painter, author, and illustrator who lived and worked with Picasso from 1946 to 1953. She is the mother of two of his children, Claude and Paloma.

Most of the writers and painters who had left Paris to spend the war years in America returned to France as soon as they could after the Liberation. Chagall was one of the last to come back. Bella, his wife, had died in New York in 1944 and some time later he met an English girl named Virginia and had a son by her, born just a few months after Claude. Chagall wrote to Pablo from America saying that in a few months he would be back in Europe and was looking forward to seeing him, and he sent Pablo a picture of his son. Pablo was rather touched, I remember, because he pinned up the photograph of Chagall's son in our bedroom.

One day Tériade came to see Pablo about the illustrations for his edition of Reverdy's *Chant des Morts,* and Pablo mentioned Chagall's letter to him. "I'll be happy to see him," Pablo said. "It's been a long time." Tériade said that Chagall's daughter, Ida, was over at his place at the moment and that she would enjoy seeing Pablo. So a week later, along with Michel and Zette Leiris, we went over to Tériade's place in St.-Jean-Cap-Ferrat for lunch and there was Ida, who had prepared a sumptuous Russian meal for us. She knew Pablo's wife, Olga, was Russian and she must have thought he had a taste for Russian food. She put on all her charm for Pablo, and told him how much his work meant to her. That was music to his ears, of course. She was rather well set up, with curves everywhere, and she hung over Pablo almost adoringly. By the time she had finished, Pablo was in the palm of her hand, and he began telling her how much he liked Chagall. So Ida finished off what her father had begun: she made Pablo want to see Chagall even before he had returned.

Several months later, Chagall arrived in the Midi. One of the first things he did was send word that he wanted to make pottery at the Ramiés' and he came over, prepared to go to work. That was too much for Pablo. His fondness for Chagall wasn't built to withstand that and he showed it. Finally Chagall stopped coming. There was no quarrel; it was just that Pablo was much less enthusiastic once Chagall was back. But officially they were good friends.

Thinking of Picasso. 1914. Ink on paper.
7 ¹/₂ x 8 ⁵/₈ in. (19.1 x 21.6 cm). Musée
National d'Art Moderne, Centre Georges
Pompidou, Paris.

About a year after that, Tériade invited us to lunch again. This time Chagall
and Virginia were there. Virginia had a very pretty face, but was exceedingly thin
and so tall as to tower over Chagall and Pablo and everyone else. Pablo, I could
see, was aghast at her thinness. In addition she was, I believe, a theosophist and
her principles prevented her from eating meat and about three-quarters of the rest
of the food on the table. Her daughter, about ten, was there too, and followed the
same dietary laws. Pablo found that so repugnant he could hardly bear to eat,
either. I, too, was at the absolute limit of thinness for Pablo at that moment.
Surrounded by skinny women he was in a bad mood and he decided to put it to
good use. He started in on Chagall, very sarcastically.

"My dear friend," he said, "I can't understand why, as a loyal, even devoted,
Russian, you never set foot in your own country any more. You go everywhere
else. Even to America. But now that you're back again and since you've come
this far, why not go a little farther and see what your own country is like after all
these years?"

Chagall had been in Russia during the revolution, and had been a commissar
of fine arts in Vitebsk at the beginning of the new regime. Later, things went sour
and he returned to Paris. In the light of that experience, he never had any desire
either to return to his country or to see the regime flourish anywhere else.

He gave Pablo a broad smile and said, "My dear Pablo, after you. But you
must go first. According to all I hear, you are greatly beloved in Russia, but not
your painting. But once you get there and try it a while, perhaps I could follow
along after. I don't know; we'll see how you make out."

Then suddenly Pablo got nasty and said, "With you I suppose it's a question
of business. There's no money to be made there." That finished the friendship,
right there. The smiles stayed wide and bright but the innuendos got clearer and
clearer and by the time we left, there were two corpses under the table. From that
day on Pablo and Chagall never set eyes on each other again. When I saw Chagall
quite recently, he was still smarting over that luncheon. "A bloody affair," he
called it.

Not long after that visit at Tériade's, Virginia left Chagall. One evening soon
after that, we were at the ballet and met Chagall's daughter, Ida. She was very
upset about Virginia's leaving. "Papa is so unhappy," she said. Pablo started to

laugh. "Don't laugh," Ida said. "It could happen to you." Pablo laughed even louder. "That's the most ridiculous thing I've ever heard," he said.

But in spite of his personal differences with Chagall, Pablo continued to have a great deal of respect for him as a painter. Once when we were discussing Chagall, Pablo said, "When Matisse dies, Chagall will be the only painter left who understands what color really is. I'm not crazy about those cocks and asses and flying violinists and all the folklore, but his canvases are really painted, not just thrown together. Some of the last things he's done in Vence convince me that there's never been anybody since Renoir who has the feeling for light that Chagall has."

Long after that, Chagall gave me his opinion of Pablo. "What a genius, that Picasso," he said. "It's a pity he doesn't paint."

In fact, Françoise did end up leaving Picasso after several years of emotional abuse by the artist.

HENRY MCBRIDE

From *The New York Sun*

"Chagall at the Museum of Modern Art"

April 13, 1946

Henry McBride (1867–1962), American writer, critic, and illustrator who was an early champion of Modernism. He wrote criticism for The New York Sun *and* The Dial.

More than most artists who have had one, Marc Chagall profits by the retrospective show of his paintings in the Modern Museum. He has never entirely lacked appreciation in this city for his works came with the stamp of Parisian approval upon them and collectors promptly appeared with sufficient courage to buy them, but the single pictures in occasional shows never quite explained the artist to a public that is always just a bit afraid of fantasy—his specialty.

With this big exhibition, where the artist carries you right out of this world into the realms of imagination where everything is as startling as it was to Alice in Wonderland and where anything can happen and does happen, he takes you with him easily. It is likely he will take most of us with him this time, not even those escaping who used to be known as the "lower classes," for really Chagall isn't above the heads of anybody and plays continually with the elementary mental pastimes of humanity.

When his first examples appeared here there was some skepticism about the cows leaping over house-tops, about the figures with two faces and those with none at all, about the drunken fiddlers at the weddings, and the candelabra and other things floating in the air. It was thought to be an effort at eccentricity, and especially since the colors were raw to the point of barbarity.

But the complete showing vindicates the artist. It is curious to note how thoroughly it does so. The artist, it seems, is a poet. He is a first-rate colorist. He is an expert painter. He does whatever he sets out to do, and if there should be any trouble in the doing of it, he manages to conceal the effort from the spectator. The repetition of the cows, roosters and fiddlers up in the air is no more wearisome than the aspect of Fujiyama in the background of the Hokusai prints, for the symbol is not so much the real things in the picture as the presence of the artist invisibly but persistently there. He is charmed with the jugglery he is able to do with his toys; his excitement is catching, his behaviour as a painter alluring.

What amazes and touches the beholder is the Russianism that this artist carries with him into distant lands. His latest pictures, after five years of New York, are as undiluted Russian as the earliest known ones, and though I had occasion to

Mother and Child, Birds and Lovers. 1963. 45 x 45 in. (114.3 x 114.3 cm). Private collection.

remark only a few weeks ago that the new pictures had an increased suavity in the brush-stroke that might be a concession to our rage for refinement, nevertheless the essential matters in the work were as Russian as Gorki. And if you ask how we Americans can assay the true Russian atmosphere, I can only say that we always do. Genuineness may be recognized when nothing else is. New Yorkers laughed with instant glee at the drunken peasants in the Shostakovitch opera, *Lady Macbeth From Minsk*, done some years ago, knowing them to be the real thing. If you remember them at all, you must recall how perfectly Chagall they were. Chagall corroborates all the Russians.

CHAGALL to ETTINGER

En Route to America

November 22, 1947

On board ship

Dear Pavel Davidovich,
How are you? I'm writing from the ship that is carrying me back to America. I'm going there to "wind up" everything so as to return once and for all to France in a few months' time.

A large retrospective exhibition of my work over almost 40 years, 1908–47, is now on show in Paris.

As the press are saying, it has been an enormous success. It is the first time they have ever made an exhibition of a living artist in an official Museum, not to say a Russian artist. And although I have been forced to live and work far from my native land, I remain loyal to her in my heart. I'm glad that I could in this way be of some little help to her. And I hope I'm not considered a foreigner in my motherland. Am I right?

The exhibition at the end of December will be in the Amsterdam Museum. Then from February 1948 it will be in a London Museum (Tate Gallery). Before, it was in America. Please pass this letter on: my native country will probably be pleased about it. It's unnecessary for me to tell you that it would be a great day for me if such an exhibition were to be shown in my native land. It's true that 3/4 of the pictures belong to museums and collections in various countries. . . .

Write to me anytime. Best wishes.

Yours truly,
Marc Chagall

LOUIS ARAGON

The Miracle of Chagall

1968

I was scarcely more than a child when I first came on the painting of Marc Chagall, and I didn't know quite what to make of it. Just as, at that age, the outrageous beauty of some women is both disconcerting and at the same time alluring enough to make you lose your head. Marvelous creatures, to be painted, mingling the colors of nature, not doing anything *the right way,* reversing night and day, and the suns at their feet; I was fearful of boring them by walking like everyone else, by coming in by the door, or obeying the laws of perspective, fearful that every sentence I uttered was a leap in the dark. I'd have turned bandit if they had asked me to.

When I came on the painting of Chagall, I fell in love with it as I love women, for its disguises, its disorder, its unreasonable quality. What are you to think of someone who makes you lose your head? You're dazzled, that's all. And since you've lost your head, with what can you think? When I was growing to manhood I had been taught by prudent teachers to look at things in a certain way, in a certain sequence, to seek for the balance that had long been prescribed. The miracle of Chagall is that he makes you forget what you have been taught; thanks to him nothing had to be in its proper place, one went to bed in the sky, the size of the figures no longer depended on distance, animals played the violin, the order of the elements was reversed, it was like the end of a perpetual banquet. The painting of Chagall was a timeless lesson which taught you to see the world differently, to live differently, to be different. It gave me a taste for vertigo. It was the forbidden fruit, wine and travel, the joy of being disobedient and the adventure of using my eyes before I was twenty. And then the war came. It was a kind of painting in which everything was called into question, nothing was quite like what we were told. People had tried in vain to impose on us their view of events, according to their way of thinking, with all the words in their proper order; if blood was being spilled like water, death was explained according to the historical texts, everybody in uniform, the rules of the game slightly changed, but always

morality in action. People had tried in vain to offer us their idea of life, to give us a military version of springtime, moving little pins on the map every day to show our battle position; we had stopped believing them, we were searching for other teachers, we belonged to the party of indiscipline, we rejected the vision of our elders, we were overturning the scenery, we sneered at the symbols, even to doubt seemed childish to us. I am too incredulous not to believe in phantoms, was what Jarry said in a way.

I recall that I tacked up a copy of a Chagall on the bedbug-stained wall of my barracks; the N.C.O.'s burst into loud guffaws when they saw it. It was the painting known under the title of *I and My Village*, but since 1917 I have never called it by any name other than that written, fortunately in small letters, at the bottom of the reproduction I had displayed so insolently: *Ich und das Dorf.* I recommend it to you.

Not all the cares of life have changed me. Despite the passage of half a century, I feel the same as the boy who used to wait impatiently for the week to pass in order to see the next installment on the silent screen of *The Vampires*, starring Musidora, dressed like a hotel thief in black tights, who was for me the Virgin and the Saints. Rimbaud always makes my heart beat faster. And when I am alone at night, prey to the modern monsters of 1968, I renew the conversation never entirely suspended between Vauvenargues, Isidore Ducasse, and myself. I find again the paths of my youth. I enter the places then forbidden. Chagall's sun sits down beside me like an old friend.

Two or three years ago I wrote twenty-five poems, if I have counted correctly, inscribed to Chagall. It was no mere game, any more than earlier when my lips were innocent of kisses. Not a game but a delight, not a game but a gesture of revolt. For me the attraction of his work has not declined over the years but has swelled as from a deep spring. I have other eyes, as well as the same eyes. Chagall too.

COLORPLATE 14

ALFRED WERNER

Chagall in Exile

1970

Perhaps nobody knows how popular Chagall is all over the globe better than the postmen of the Riviera hill-town near Nice, where Chagall has a villa, or those of the Ile Saint Louis, in the heart of Paris, where Chagall occupies an apartment in a centuries-old, stately house. In 1967 in particular, they had ample reasons for regretting his popularity, as the mail addressed to the artist was heavier than ever before. Secretaries, as well as Madame Chagall, were kept busy for days opening the letters and parcels that came from all over the world to hail the master on his eightieth birthday.

It is doubtful that much mail came from Russia, not even from the artist's birthplace, Vitebsk, where he had been Commissar of Art for a short time. Chagall wrote in 1922, shortly before his final departure for the West—"Neither Imperial Russia, nor the Russia of the Soviets needs me, they don't understand me, I am a stranger to them"—and the words hold true to this day. His work was outlawed under Stalin and, despite the post-Stalin thaw, it cannot yet be displayed in Russia. However, some of Chagall's finest works from the 1914–1922 period are held there in museum vaults and occasionally—for instance, for the Grand Palais retrospective of 1970—they may be lent out for a show abroad.

Even those who stress the ramified origins—and the universal appeal—of Chagall's art would concede that the artist and his work would have developed in a totally different way had Feige-Ita *Chagal* (as his parents spelled their name) not given birth to Moshko in that particular year in a provincial town far from all art centers. Born in the 1880s, Chagall shared with Spain's Pablo Picasso, Italy's Amedeo Modigliani, Germany's Ernest Ludwig Kirchner, and Austria's Oscar Kokoschka, the ferment of unrest that swept that whole generation.

RENÉ HUYGHE

"Chagall or Inner Reality"

1977

René Huyghe (b. 1906), French art historian, critic, and museum administrator.

Art is not born of a doctrine; it is even less the result of a search. It is born of necessity, of an inner need experienced by the artist, confronted spontaneously, transformed and woven into the adventure of a life's work. At least that is the case of all great artists. None of this applies to any of those modern day attempts, of which there are far too many and which are nothing more than mental exercises or ponderous applications of doctrine. Innovation never comes from a recipe, no matter how ingenious; it comes from a force inside oneself which demands to be heard, and once it finds its voice, it compels recognition, if only because of its disturbing effect.

In the rush of painters now crowding the contemporary scene, rare are the masters who meet this criterion. Bonnard, Rouault, Braque and Max Ernest belong among them in every sense of the word; also Matisse and Picasso certainly, but with less purity. Lively, ageless and prodigious enough to justify a show devoted only to the last ten years of his work, Chagall has won his place among them.

As much as he despises theoretical verbiage, he cultivates the lucidity of the intelligence; this is clear from his writing. "Everything in art," he proclaims, "must spring from our vital force, from our entire being, including the unconscious." That is true of his work and of the work of all great painters. Indeed his work grows and moves upward with the irresistible force of a tall tree with its living logic. He plunged his roots into the nourishing soil where fate had planted him: into the earth of both Russia and Israel. Born in 1887 to a humble Jewish family in Vitebsk, he grew up steeped in two sets of traditions, both equally rich in ritual and popular poetry. Then he grew into the light; he found it in France, where he moved in 1910. The brightness of Paris, and the dazzle of Impressionism and its aftermath added warmth and light to the innate chromatic scale of the Slavic painter. Then with the spring the tree was covered with brilliant blossoms which would later unfold with the discovery of the French Riviera, where he moved in 1950.

But the tree was not spared its share of storms and many branches were broken. The death of his first wife Bella affected him deeply; and he left Russia, where the Revolution, which had at first allowed him to flourish, quickly become a disappointment, for Art was made to submit to political dogma, and the freedom he had hoped to gain from it was soon systematically stifled. In 1941, the rise of Nazism and anti-Semitism led to his exile from France to the United States.

But the tree kept on growing and spreading its branches. Now Chagall's inner life, the source of all inspiration, no longer contained only the melancholy musings of memory. It revealed its true nature, so different from that of the outside world and its realistic constraints. "What I wanted was a [kind of] realism, if you will, but psychic, and therefore quite different from a realism based on objects or on geometric figures." He constantly brings this up. His eyes "turn inward"; he seeks a "fifth dimension—the psychic dimension."

Of this he is well aware—inspiration can be triggered by "a tangible initial shock—the sight of things, flowers, a landscape, a woman's face," or by a spiritual jolt "from memory or from a specific recollection," for example. But that is merely the impulse which allows it to take flight, the trampoline from which the acrobat is thrown into the air. Then he leaps forth into poetry, music and the magic of the dance. In 1945, he did the costumes and sets for *Firebird*; in 1965, he was inspired by *The Magic Flute*; in 1966, by *Daphnis and Chloe* for the Paris Opera, for which he had done the ceiling two years before, as he would soon paint the one at Lincoln Center for the New York Met.

All that remains of the tree are the songs of birds and the beating of wings. But still it must follow its destiny to climb higher and extend its pinnacle. The sap drawn from its native soil is destined to rise, pushing the tree trunk toward the sky. Stretched out beyond music and poetry are the infinite spaces bearing only the wings of the spirit as it reaches out for the divine. By combining the dual inspiration of Judaism and Christianity, the foundations of western civilization, Chagall illustrates the Bible, and, starting in 1960, takes up mosaics and stained glass so that his colored lights now stream forth in Jerusalem, Metz and Rheims, in synagogue and cathedral alike.

I was at Rheims a few days ago, where I marveled at that stained glass window way at the back of the nave in the half-light, showing the crucified Christ borne up in a halo of colors. Thus the most winged of the cathedrals, encircled as it is by angles quivering in flight, now has achieved its final meaning through its own distinctive mark, just as others achieve it through the slenderness of a steeple.

It has been the fate of few artists to rise in such continuous fashion that the same dreams, which seem like repetitions, are actually pushing each other ever higher.

Some people criticize Chagall for not having cultivated form or visual discipline. He has admitted it: "I am not interested in the formal aspect of paintings." But this lack of interest is significant in and of itself. Shape defines matter and

COLORPLATE 71

The Couple. 1956. Wash drawing. 8 x 10 in. (20.3 x 25.4 cm). Private collection.

275

The Painter's Head. 1915. Wash and ink drawing. 10 x 8 in. (25.4 x 20.3 cm). Musée National d'Art Moderne, Centre Georges Pompidou, Paris.

mass. Chagall has a bent for winged figures, for light and for bursts of color. He dematerializes the world. In so doing, he joins a long line of truly revolutionary artists, whose continuity and influence will one day be discovered. From Giorgione and El Greco, from Rembrandt to Delacroix, Art has attempted to escape from the confines of materialism, positivism and objectivity in which our civilization has allowed itself to become entrapped and in which it is stifling. The modern revolution has accentuated this movement by pulling away from concrete reality and by remolding it according to the dictates of feeling, as in Fauvism and Expressionism, or of the unconscious, as in Surrealism, or even by rejecting it, as in abstract art. For the past three centuries, Art, like literature, has focused all its energy on acting as a counterweight, and it is in this sense that it may be deemed revolutionary, and not in the sense of provocation or useless destruction. At a later time this will be understood, and Chagall will be counted among the greatest of them all.

JAMES JOHNSON SWEENEY

"An Interview with Marc Chagall"

1946

CHAGALL: A painter should never come between the work of art and the spectator. An intermediary may explain the artist's work without any harm to it. But the artist's explanation of it can only limit it. Better the understanding that grows from familiarity and the perspective that will come after the artist's death. After all, it is better to judge a painter by his pictures. His words, I am afraid, do nothing but veil the vision.

SWEENEY: But your work is well known to the art-public in this country. It has enjoyed an extremely wide appeal. You are regarded as one of the leading fantastic illustrators of the present century—a reactionary from cubism and abstract art, a sympathizer with the emotional emphases of German expressionism and a forerunner of surrealism in its irrationality and dream-character. Thanks to the exhibition of major work such as *Moi et le Village* and *Paris par la fenêtre*, and to large retrospective exhibitions in New York, your name brings to mind at once certain images. The constant recurrence of these images had both fixed them in the public mind and whetted its curiosity. In them it sees a suggestion of nostalgia for the surroundings of your childhood, a fairy-tale atmosphere or the illustration of some folk legends of your native Vitebsk. It sees them as private symbols—using the term symbols to signify an image used as an analogy for an abstract idea,—a dove, for example, to represent peace. Your friend and admirer, Raissa Maritain, apparently also sees them in a similar light in her recent appreciation of your work. Yet the critic Florent Fels in *Propos d'artistes* once quoted you as stating very flatly: "In my composition there is nothing of the fantastic, nor of the symbolic."

COLORPLATE 14
COLORPLATE 11

CHAGALL: That was many years ago, 1925, still it is just as true as ever. There is nothing anecdotal in my pictures—no fairy tales—no literature in the sense of folk-legend associations. Maurice Denis described the paintings of the Synthetists in France about 1889 as plane surfaces "covered with colours arranged in a certain order." To the cubists a painting was a plane surface covered with form-elements in a certain order. For me a picture is a plane surface covered with representations of objects—beasts, birds, or humans—in a certain order in which anecdotal illustrational logic has no importance. The visual effectiveness of the painted composition comes first. Every extra-structural consideration is secondary.

Just as before the war of 1914, I constantly had the word literature, or "literary painting" thrown at me, now I am constantly said to be a maker of fairy-tales and of fantasies. As a matter of fact, my first aim is to construct my picture architecturally, just as in their day the impressionists did, and cubists did—along the same formal paths. The impressionists filled their canvases with spots of light and shadow. The cubists with cubic, triangular, and round shapes, I try to fill my canvases in some fashion with objects and figures employed as forms—sonorous forms like noises—passion-forms which should give a supplementary dimension impossible to achieve through the bare geometry of the cubists' lines or with the spots of the impressionists.

I am against the terms "fantasy" and "symbolism" in themselves. All our interior world is reality—and that perhaps more so than our apparent world. To call everything that appears illogical, "fantasy," fairy-tale, or chimera—would be practically to admit not understanding nature.

Impressionism and cubism were relatively easy to understand, because they only proposed a single aspect of an object to our consideration—its relations of light and shade, or its geometrical relationships. But one aspect of an object is not enough to constitute the entire subject matter of art. An object's aspects are multifarious. . . .

But please defend me against people who speak of "anecdote" and "fairy tales" in my work. A cow and woman to me are the same—in a picture both are merely elements of a composition. In painting, the images of a woman or of a cow have different values of plasticity,—but not different poetic values. As far as literature goes, I feel myself more "abstract" than Mondrian or Kandinsky in my use of pictorial elements. "Abstract" not in the sense that my painting does not recall reality. Such abstract painting in my opinion is more ornamental and decorative, and always restricted in its range. What I mean by "abstract" is something which comes to life spontaneously through a gamut of contrasts, plastic at the

Piet Mondrian (1872–1944), Dutch painter strongly influenced by Cubism; Wassily Kandinsky (1866–1944), Russian artist and theorist, best known for his role in the Munich Expressionist movement.

same time as psychic, and pervades both the picture and the eye of the spectator with conceptions of new and unfamiliar elements. In the case of the decapitated woman with the milk pails, I was first led to separating her head from her body merely because I happened to need an empty space there. In the large cow's head in *Moi et le village* I made a small cow and woman milking visible through its muzzle because I needed that sort of form, there, for my composition. Whatever else may have grown out of these compositional arrangements is secondary.

The fact that I made use of cows, milkmaids, roosters and provincial Russian architecture as my source forms is because they are part of the environment from which I spring and which undoubtedly left the deepest impression on my visual memory of any experiences I have known. Every painter is born somewhere. And even though he may later respond to the influences of other atmospheres, a certain essence—a certain "aroma" of his birthplace clings to his work. But do not misunderstand me: the important thing here is not "subject" in the sense pictorial "subjects" were painted by the old academicians. The vital mark these early influences leave is, as it were, on the handwriting of the artist. This is clear to us in the character of the trees and card players of a Cézanne, born in France,—in the curled sinuosities of the horizons and figures of a Van Gogh, born in Holland,—in the almost Arab ornamentation of a Picasso, born in Spain,—or in the quattrocento linear feeling of a Modigliani, born in Italy. This is the manner in which I hope I have preserved the influences of my childhood, not merely in subject matter.

SWEENEY: I know you have frequently stated "art is international, but the artist ought to be national." Nevertheless, on your return from Russia in 1922 after an eight years' sojourn there you came to the realization that your native land—the Soviet no more than Imperial Russia—had no need of you. You stated "To them I am incomprehensible, a foreigner." Does this mean that you regard racism as more important than nationalism and that you, as a Jew, were a foreigner even in Vitebsk?

CHAGALL: Race? Not at all. As a native of Vitebsk I was still as close to Russia and to the soil as the day I left. But as an artist I felt myself just as much a stranger to the official, aesthetic ideology of the new government as I had been to the provincial art ideals of the Russia I left in 1910. At that time I decided I needed Paris. The root-soil of my art was Vitebsk, but like a tree, my art needed Paris like water, otherwise it would wither and die. Russia had two native traditions of art, the popular and the religious. I wanted an art of the soil, not one uniquely of the head. I had the good luck to spring from the people. But popular art—which I always love for that matter—did not satisfy me. It is too exclusive. It excludes the refinements of civilization. I have always had a pronounced taste for refined expression, for culture. The refined art of my native land was a religious art, I saw the quality of a few great productions of the ikon tradition—Rublev's work, for example. But this was fundamentally a religious art and I am not, and never have been, religious. Moreover, I felt religion meant little in the world that I knew, even as it seems to mean little today. For me Christ was a great poet, the teaching of whose poetry has been forgotten by the modern world. To achieve the combination of refined expression with an art of the earth, I felt I had to seek the vitalizing waters of Paris.

I would like to say that my moves from country to country have always been dictated by artistic considerations. Son of a laborer, I had organically no other grounds for leaving my native land, to which I think in spite of everything I have remained loyal in my art. As painter and man of the people—and the people I consider the class of society most sensitively responsive—I felt that plastic refinement of the highest order existed only in France. Here is perhaps the source of my dualism and my climatic maladjustments through all these years. Still I would not say that I have been less able to acclimatize myself in Paris than other foreign artists.

Neither Vitebsk nor St. Petersburg offered me what I felt I needed as a young painter setting out on his career in 1910. Similarly, after an eight-year sojourn in

"I don't love you anymore, Lucille, and I'm dropping you off at your mother's house."

A cartoon of Chagall's painting *Over the Village* (1915). Drawing by Dedini; © 1988. Courtesy The New Yorker Magazine, Inc.

Russia between 1914 and 1922, I found the ideology of the Soviet provided no better place for my ideals of what an art expression should be. The revolution had not replaced the atmosphere which had proved so unsatisfactory to me in my early years in Russia with a more congenial one. The ideal it proposed to its artists was to become illustrators—to transport the ideology of the revolution onto the canvas. Its aim was a pictorial photography, not a poetry of forms with logic of associations relegated to a secondary level. My ideal was still a picture above all—without subject, without "literature," as always.

But again do not misunderstand me: there has never been a true art but that has not been addressed solely to an elite; and equally there has never been an art truly great which has not been addressed solely to the masses. The fact is, an elite which is truly elite keeps in mind its bonds with and roots in the masses. In the past the proprietor classes possessed not only the great works of art of their period but also possessed the faculty of immediately comprehending them. The masses held themselves apart. . . .

The year 1922 saw me back to the well-spring in Paris. And I can freely say today that I owe all I have succeeded in achieving to Paris, to France, of which the air, the men, nature were for me the true school of my life and of my art—the waters which fed the soil in which my art had its roots. In this way I found the international language in Paris and have scrupulously striven to maintain the strength of my root soil in Vitebsk.

LOUIS ARAGON

"The Admirable Chagall"

1982

Painting! A man has spent his life painting. And when I say his life, you must understand what I mean. Everything else is gesticulation. Painting is his life. What does he paint? Fruits, flowers, a king entering a city? Everything that is explainable is something other than life, that is, from what he understands by life. His life is painting. Inexplicable. Painting or talking perhaps: he sees like the rest of us hear. Subjects are painted onto the canvas like simulated sentences. Connected words. After all, the words make a sentence, there is nothing to understand; is it this way with music? Then why is it not so with painting? Let us start from the beginning. How does one begin to write about this unfinished world, this strange, unfamiliar country, this weightless land where there is nothing to differentiate a man from a bird, where the donkey lives in the sky and everything is a circus, and where we walk so well on our heads. No explanation is needed if color is used to emphasize a rooster on a flutist's arm and a naked woman is drawn in the shadow of his neck while in the distance the sun and moon bathe the village in gold. We are constantly before the clock. The second hand shows the path. The spectacle is *given:* men and women surrounded by visions of brutal beasts, characters from a travelling theatre company, a meaningless sabbath in Brocken, childhood obsessions, wandering souls, gymnasts from a topsy turvy world, jugglers accompanied by an invisible violin. People's fantasies in a world so full of lovers that it is hard to choose one. Without doubt, no painter has ever flooded my eyes with so much light, with nights that are so divine.

There is a Chagallian dialectic for which *The Midsummer Night's Dream* is the only precedent I know. No need to have rags adorn the actors who wear anything from sequins to feathers, and bouquets are somehow thickets that are compared to dancers. The older the painter became, the more he took a pagan pleasure in shavings of colors. The mirage is not at the end of a desert but in a shimmering vision mingling human beings and animals; nor do we know in which daydream the hand lovingly cuts up shadow and light and feels through the fingers a scattering of green and orange. The painter sometimes appears, palette in hand, at the bottom of the canvas, with an animal-like expression on his face reminiscent of Bottom. The whole world seems to be in front of him like the model of an imaginary parade where far-away visions and dreams become reality and the unconscious becomes the conscious. And everywhere, almost everywhere, it is the kingdom of touch, the caressing world of hands, mostly opened— who else has ever painted like this?

An ox walks by in the distance so slowly that the violin dies out and every embrace depends on the silence of love constantly being reinvented, as if it is always the first time, the same wonder felt at adolescence.

Wonder here hardly depends on understanding because everything I recognize increases rather than diminishes the sense of mystery. Peasants, clowns or lovers for one night. And the villages off in the distance that can also be Notre-Dame, the Eiffel Tower, or the Opera. Even Paris is the countryside, with its lights that could be lilacs. In the old days painters used to leave students and artisans free to add details to the secondary characters, thereby changing the perspective of their major works; these were all *postiches*. Chagall always rejects any hasty interpretation of his paintings that may make them non provocative.

One character starts running through the streets on his hands, another takes off through the sky, head cast downwards, face turned away; try to get a sensible and coherent story, at least so that a mythology can be defined. The painter tends to contradict the general composition through the detail and even upsets the balance of what the painting seems to say—for example, when animals are coupled with human beings, to which I dare you to attach any symbolic meaning or value. Time does not change this work that covers more than eighty years. On the contrary, nowadays, the logic of arbitrariness predominates, a challenge hurled at age, a mockery of time and of its power. Some will certainly say that some of Chagall's paintings contradict my observations and will insist on the coherence of the subject matter, particularly because in the great biblical works the painter seems to comply with the "story" as it is told, to respect and even illustrate it. But what does this prove, except that the painter is extremely versatile. Besides one mythology does not preclude another.

Certain paintings, having looked at them for so many years in a particular way, no longer strike us as either strange or irrational. Their *irreducible* quality eludes us. But this is precisely wherein lies their greatness, their poetry. Since a Chagall scene is hardly reminiscent of everyday life, it is impossible to give a common meaning to the individual elements. For this painter, the rigor of composition resides in his freedom. It is my belief that Chagall is dominated by the pleasure he gets from his painting, from the hegemony of colors, rather than by what he is trying to represent. I like him most of all when he seems to get lost or unraveled in apparent disparity. Also, he seems to play in a strange kind of kaleidoscopic way that always destroys the geometric balance just as the work of art is about to be finished.

With Chagall there is a bestiary to assemble, and if at times parents, horses and birds are all there, variations in their morphology are to be expected. I would like to take the example of a recent painting in which on a deep blue night the moon is black and the ground once again bears a Bielorussian village; someone is sitting under a raging sky and like a thunderbolt, lightning falls like a scarf on his shoulder . . . try and describe this! When it is really the indescribable, two birds, a naked child, a female figure laterally traced in white against a dark background, a pony, and this face lighting up the top of the canvas—does it belong to the body striped in brown, black, green and fresh blood? And below on the left, cast in light, is the pinkish head of a horse with a green body whose blue foot rests on the paleness of a moon-like face (or is it a stone?) while the other foot and its fine

COLORPLATE 87. *The Prophet Elijah.* 1970. Stone mosaic with colored glass. Approximately 23 ft. 6 in. x 18 ft. 9 in. (7.1 x 5.7 m).
Musée National Message Biblique Marc Chagall, Nice. Photograph © Réunion des Musées Nationaux.

COLORPLATE 88. *Goat and Figure*. 1962. Ceramic tiles. 30 3/8 x 20 1/4 in. (77 x 51.5 cm).
Collection Marcus Diener, Basel.

COLORPLATE 89. *The Lovers' Offering (The Dream of the Couple).*
1954. Ceramic vase. 17 x 6 ³/4 in. (43 x 17 cm).
Collection Daniel Malingue, Paris.

(Opposite top, opposite bottom, this page) COLORPLATES 90, 91, 92. *The America Windows*. 1977. Stained glass.
Approximately 8 ft. x 32 ft. 4 in. (2.4 x 9.8 m). Gift of the Auxiliary Board of the Art Institute of Chicago
in memory of Richard J. Daley. Photographs © The Art Institute of Chicago. All Rights Reserved.

COLORPLATE 93. *The Tribe of Levi*. 1960–61. Stained glass window. Approximately 11 x 8 ft. (3.5 x 2.4 m). Synagogue, Hadassah-Hebrew University Medical Center, Jerusalem. © Hadassah Medical Relief Association.

COLORPLATE 94. *The Tribe of Gad*. 1960–61. Stained glass window. Approximately 11 x 8 ft. (3.5 x 2.4 m).
Synagogue, Hadassah-Hebrew University Medical Center, Jerusalem. © Hadassah Medical Relief Association.

COLORPLATE 95. *Peace*. 1964. Stained glass window. Approximately 15 x 12 ft. (4.5 x 3.4 m).
Photograph: The United Nations, New York.

ankle seems to belong to the mysterious pregnant woman in the sky. Look at it! You will probably not see what I am observing, and bless your eyes if they see something else. I only wish to warn you against any tendency to impose on these nocturnal paintings or even on those bathed in sunlight an arbitrary mythology. Do not wake the painter up. He is dreaming, and dreams are sacred. Secret things. He will have dreamt his painting and his life. The world is his night just as he has made his day.

THE TAPESTRIES AND MOSAICS

GUY WEELEN

"Monuments of a Return to the Land of the Prophets"

1982

Guy Weelen, author and art historian living in Paris.

Impulsive, spontaneous, light-handed, quick-spirited painters do exist, but Marc Chagall is not one of them. A long meditation and often an inner unavowed drama always precede his work. Shut up within himself, overcome by doubts, he tries for a breakthrough, and, in order to go on any further, he must suddenly perceive a reality, but without disdaining or abandoning recourse to divination. As he himself admits, he recognizes this reality that is needed to trigger his painterly impulses by a sort of vibration, a sort of pigmentation of matter similar to the hoarfrost on the fields.

In 1965 the Gobelins studio began work on three large tapestries by Marc Chagall intended for the Israeli Knesset. . . .

This group of tapestries as well as the mosaic floor which, for mythological and metaphysical reasons, only Marc Chagall could have undertaken, express his faith and admiration before the extraordinary phenomenon of the resurrection of Israel.

The tapestries constitute a vast triptych. *The Exodus* (15'6²/₃" x 29'5²/₃") forms the central panel. The panel on the right is *The Prophecy of Isaiah* (15'6²/₃" x 17'7⁵/₈"), and on the left *The Entrance to Jerusalem* (15'6²/₃" x 17'7⁵/₈").

Taking into account the historical reality, the artist sought to unfold in this enormous woven fresco a large-scale organization of color and light, of radiance and rhythm where the revery of his spirit could express itself freely, but without doubt he also wanted to portray in abbreviated form the destiny of the Jewish people.

The most striking thing about these great sketches executed by a hand carried away and enchanted by the magic it gives birth to is that all three are celebrations of energy.

It is easy, with respect to Marc Chagall, to employ the words "dream" and "revery," and they have not been used sparingly. But all too often dream and

Chagall produced about thirty tapestries over his long career, most of which were woven at the atelier of Yvette Cauquil Prince. The three tapestries that hang in the State Reception Hall at the Israeli Knesset (Parliament) were woven at the State Gobelins studio in Paris and were paid for by the family of Baron Rothschild.

COLORPLATE 114

Chagall produced several mosaics for the Israeli Knesset in Jerusalem. They were unveiled together with his famous tapestries. Chagall's mosaics can also be found at the Chicago National Bank, at the Musée National Message Biblique Marc Chagall in Nice, and at the university in Nice.

The Prophecy of Isaiah. 1963. Tapestry installed in the Knesset (Parliament), Jerusalem. Photograph: Lauros-Giraudon/Art Resource, New York.

revery are considered to be opposed to action, and this seems to me to be an hierarchy of thought that is definitely outmoded. What we still refer to today as "dream" is so intimately connected with everyday reality that it provides a single, real image of man. How irritating to always hear dreams referred to as something mild, pleasant and ambiguous, and to have the images they secrete considered as the simple babblings of a man split in two. For Marc Chagall, energy and "dream" are one; they are the expression of the totality of man, and for this reason energy is not the opposite of the dream but its complement. Each instant bears the mark of engagement and decision, and it was for this reason that he chose his themes. *The Prophecy of Isaiah* is the triumph, the everlastingness of Jerusalem. *The Exodus* is, at one and the same time, ordeal, rupture and agony. *The Entrance to Jerusalem* is the resurrection of the earth recaptured, the jubilation of homecoming!

Every great work is open to a great variety of possible interpretations and conceals multiple treasures; its ambiguity is the result of its complexity. Ambiguity has always seemed a virtue to me, and even a cardinal one; it is a

290

reservoir of mystery and grandeur because, as nothing is fixed, everything can be, can happen. In its essence it is dynamism and the dynamic source of poetry.

The fantastic events that Chagall has tried to convey in wool are fleeting moments in history that have fundamentally affected man. Illuminating his destiny, they evoke the essential human truths. An ample gesture must stand behind such a design; a deep harmony must reign between the inspiration and its formulation.

Aware of the imperatives of his choice, Chagall established an overall compositional design; it is based on an enormous V supported by two strong points (Moses and David) that are connected by two large circles. In *The Prophecy of Isaiah* the compositional elements are distributed around a vast arena in whose center symbolic animals move. In *The Entrance to Jerusalem* the men advance in compact masses, whereas in *The Exodus* they traverse the surface in two intersecting diagonals. Internal dynamic bonds unite these three compositions and bring out a sense of tension which, rather than being broken, is continued by the two large figures: David playing the harp and Moses revealing the Tables of the Law to the people. Like caryatids, these two figures bear the weight of the architecture and their colorful vigor accentuates and controls the dynamic effect of the masses. Without hindering the eye's movement across the undulating lines and the bright motes of color, they reinforce the active vigor of the composition.

Once again, Chagall, master of his art, has instinctively embodied his plastic ideas. He detests using evidence, detests believing in the necessity of precision. He knows it and has doubts on this subject: "I'm not sufficiently precise, so-called precise," he has written. And he adds, not without irony: "But words are not precise!" Something else is involved, which he wants to attain, and he declares, "Divine fluidity, now that's truly precise: the fluidity of Monet, of Mallarmé."

In effect, to specify is to arrest, encircle, isolate, to find an affirmation only at the very end of the trajectory. This attitude is contrary to the very spirit of Chagall, for whom all things are interlinked and continually passing from one into the other, like communicating vessels. Hence, the comet in its lightning descent flaps wings like the cock perched on the roof, the bird pecks at the hours counted out by the old clock, and the streets of Vitebsk run through Paris as well as Jerusalem. In connection with this there is no need to evoke the fantastic: it is better explained in Chagall's own words: "I am against terms like 'fantasy' and 'symbolism.' Our whole inner world is real, perhaps even more real than the visible world."

Imagination is thus the key to the Chagallian conception of the world. Light, deceitful fantasy and imagination—which Baudelaire rightly considered to be "the queen of the faculties"—are two completely different things. Chagall's imaginary universe has its own coherence and internal logic which create a system of relationships and associations. Form and content combine in his work and produce new revelations. The V composition he chose with large open branches ending in circles is an attempt to unify, to fuse the various elements and forces; here, opposites, instead of being exalted, are abolished in the interest of the total composition. Moreover, Chagall is free, and to communicate his feelings he knows how to modify and diversify his means without being subject to any of them. . . .

The concept of a mosaic floor posed a new problem. To start with, we should note that the flooring can be one of the most beautiful architectural elements of a building; think of the floors of the cathedral in Siena, the small church of Torcello, San Marco and Santa Sophia. A mosaic floor is a sort of carpet spread out under the feet of emperors and kings; it goes very well with the haughty gait of a master striding from the brightness of a large open door toward a sanctuary; it provides delicate ornamentation for women's baths and for patios where family members come together and around which social life is organized. Its humble position below feet perhaps accounts for its being scorned or neglected, and yet

Entrance Tapestry. 1971. 89 x 91 5/16 in. (226 x 232 cm). Musée National Message Biblique Marc Chagall, Nice.

all grandeur, all feeling for pomp and ceremony, extols it. Precisely because something in us rejects the lowly paving-stone, it is honored by those who want to set up a ritual and impress the traveler. But the organization of such stones into designs and figures should never act as an obstacle to the person who walks across them. His eye must not be encumbered and his step must not be hindered.

Considerations of this kind were probably behind Chagall's making a very special decision. Rather than stretching a geometrically shaped garden under the feet of the visitor, he preferred to embed the elements in a mass of stones from the Negev that were of slightly different hues of the same color. As a result the huge State Reception Hall of the Knesset of Israel is sprinkled with unexpected mosaic forms. Furthermore, the floor can be visualized as having another, poetic aspect: couldn't what is involved here be a collection of broken and rearranged archaeological elements bearing the traces and wounds of time, the avatars of a long struggle, of battles throughout the centuries? It seems also that in establishing the coloration Chagall recalled the Greek and Roman mosaics he had had a chance to see during his travels, as well as those he saw in Israel . . . from the fifth and sixth centuries. . . .

Mythic, sacred themes are not suitable for mosaic floors, which are better served by free or geometric ornamentation, as many artists realize. But we know that Chagall, if he uses geometry deliberately, does not really want to indulge in it. He encloses within forms that tend to be elliptical images that belong to the everyday world. However, the commonplace in Chagall, as we have learned, is full of complexity, and consequently we discover many unusual aspects in it: trees weighed down with fruit; overflowing baskets of produce that recall the time when Palestine was an orchard and the animals of nomadic tribes grazed on the rich grass; baskets of fish like those which the fishermen of long ago used to haul in plentifully on the shore, just as they still do today; branches of flowers; scattered grain; a bird caught in a trap, which an anxious hand comes to free; goats cropping the fragrant herbs on the hillsides; mysterious signs; checkerboards with their ends cut off; stars shining in the feathers of a partridge. These simple rustic and bucolic scenes illustrate the work of the pioneers who retimbered the hills, made the abandoned terrain green again and with enormous effort were able to repeople these lands that for centuries had been worn away by the blazing intensity of the sun. Even the use of Eilat stone is symbolic. Once calcined, split and unused, today it is hewn, shaped and assembled under the feet of the visitor, where it unfolds like a prairie ripe with possibilities and future wealth, charged with the history of men.

MARC CHAGALL

At the Unveiling of the Tapestries in the Knesset, Jerusalem

June 18, 1969

From left to right: Israeli President Zalman Shazar, Chagall, Prime Minister Golda Meir, and Vava Chagall at the unveiling of the tapestries in the Knesset (Parliament), Jerusalem. Collection Jacob Baal-Teshuva.

Over forty years ago, I was invited by the French publisher Vollard to paint motifs of the Bible. Then, I was confused: I didn't know how to begin the work. I was so far from the biblical spirit, in a strange land. . . .

Fortunately for me, the Mayor of Tel Aviv, Meir Dizengoff, appeared before me like a flying angel. He invited me to come to Eretz Israel. Since then, I have grown close to the land and have created on biblical motifs; since then, I am new-born; I have become a different person. It is difficult for me to explain it in words. Why? I only know that, since then, I have always had the desire to express signs of devotion, however and whenever I can.

I have made many voyages through the land. And every time, it meant an even-greater closeness; and here and there I left a sign of it.

Finally, I am in the new building of the parliament of Israel in Jerusalem—the Knesset—on its floor and on its walls; I am in the Knesset with its dear Speaker Kaddish Luz, who has so inspired me.

But it is not for me to talk about myself and my work. My goal, as I said, was to get closer to the land, to the biblical homeland of the Jewish people, to the land where there is an understanding and a right to life—a creation in the spirit of that which hovers over every page of the Bible and hovers here in the air, in the fields, in the sky, and in the souls of the inhabitants. When the world, including our so-called "foes" (who are rather their own foes), understands this; when the world feels this—a new peace will come, as envisaged by our Prophets. But, in the meantime, the reality is tragic: the vision of peace is still a mirage.

Art of genius and its luminaries are so rare. . . . People prefer to be content with evil and injustice rather than to clutch onto love.

I pity our enemies, who waste their time and their lives on byways and try to burst through closed doors that are actually open. The straight road and the key to the doors is love, which is sown here at every step by our forefathers, by the people who returned here two thousand years later, from all the ghettos; returned to live with a renewed love and brotherhood with the surrounding Semitic peoples.

From my whole heart, I would call to friend and non-friend, whose soul is

The Offering. 1975. Mosaic. 261 ⁷/₈ x 224 ¹/₂ in. (665 x 570 cm). Chapel of Sainte-Roseline, Les Arcs, France.

shining, to open their eyes and stretch out a hand to give content to our short life, elevate our life, and create at the height of the genius of nature.

Some may not understand my fragmented words, but perhaps you will sense the pulse of life throbbing in them and the breath of truth permeating them: that our would-be enemies would reject their weapons of annihilation, for they destroy first of all their own souls.

My voice echoes the voices of my parents and forefathers: the world must listen to the voice of that people who gave content to life—and thereby the world will endow itself with content.

There is no art or creation in a life without love. Love lives in this land, and everything that comes with love is great and sublime.

Let my work here, whatever it may be, serve as an expression of my soul's devotion to the land—this land of justice and biblical peace.

MARC CHAGALL

Letter to the President of Israel

1969

Dear friend Zalman Shazar,
You have to be a Shakespeare or a poet of our Bible to be able to express what I would like to tell you—
Fate put you at the head of our biblical land—today when humanity wants even less to recognize our spirit and right to life—
I kiss you and wish you and all of Israel happiness—to live through and live to see.

Marc Chagall

THE BIBLICAL MESSAGE

MARC CHAGALL

"The Biblical Message"

1973

Ever since early childhood, I have been captivated by the Bible. It has always seemed to me and still seems today the greatest source of poetry of all time. Ever since then, I have searched for its reflection in life and in Art. The Bible is like an echo of nature and this is the secret I have tried to convey.

With the ebb and flow of my powers, throughout my life, although I sometimes felt I was someone else altogether, that I was born, one might say, between heaven and earth, that the world is for me a great desert in which my soul wanders like a torch, I did these paintings in unison with this distant dream. I decided to leave it in this House so that men may try to find a certain peace in it, a certain spirituality, a religiosity, a meaning to life.

To my way of thinking, these paintings do not illustrate the dream of a single people, but that of mankind. They are the result of my meeting the French publisher, Ambroise Vollard, and of my trip to the Orient. I thought I would leave them in France, a kind of second birthplace for me.

It is not up to me to comment on them. Works of art should be able to speak for themselves.

People often talk about what way, and in what forms, and in what Movement color should be placed. But this color thing is innate. It does not depend on the manner nor the form on which you place it. Nor does it have anything to do with mastery of the brush. It is outside of all Movements. The few Movements which have endured throughout history have all possessed that innate color . . . the movements are forgotten.

Are not painting and color inspired by Love? Isn't painting only the reflection of our inner self, and in that sense it goes way beyond mere mastery of the brush. It has nothing to do with it. The color and its lines contain your character and your message.

If all of life moves inevitably towards its end, we must during ours, color it with all our colors of love and hope. Within this love are found the social logic of life and the basis of every religion. For me perfection in Art and in life comes from this Biblical source. Without this spirit, the mechanics of logic and con-structivity in Art, as in life, cannot bear fruit.

Perhaps the young and the not-so-young will come to this House in search of an ideal of brotherhood and love such as my colors and my lines have dreamed it.

Perhaps they will also speak the worlds of this love which I feel for everyone. Perhaps there will be no more enemies, and like a mother bringing a child into the world in love and pain, the young and the not-so-young will build a world of love with new coloring.

And everyone, regardless of their religion, will be able to come here and speak of this dream, far from evil and confusion.

I would also like to be displayed in this place works of art and documents of high spirituality by all peoples, so that people may hear their music and their poetry as dictated by the heart.

Is this dream possible?

But in Art as in life, everything is possible provided it is based on Love.

DORA VALLIER

"From Memories to Myth"

1982

Dora Vallier, French author, critic, and art historian. She was the wife of the late French writer Louis Aragon.

In 1930, Chagall proposed to Vollard to illustrate the Bible. Their agreement involved a certain number of engravings for a deluxe edition. Thus, it was on the fringe of his other work. However, once it was undertaken it became the center. Before starting the engravings, Chagall painted a series of gouaches on Biblical themes. He felt a need, he explained (as Franz Meyer tells us in his exemplary book), to find "the color" of the Biblical world—a quest that led him to the very sites of sacred history, and it was only on his return from Palestine that he began his engravings. But when they were completed and finally edited he executed, in 1955 and over a period of several years, seventeen large paintings which repre-sent Biblical scenes. This periplus, as a whole, constitutes the *Biblical Message* that Chagall has just bequeathed to the French Musées Nationaux.

An occasion has become an event. This dilatation of an initial idea that even-tually pushed Chagall's work to the foreground took place because, as in every instance of Chagall's work, it was a conquest of the past. And wasn't the road that was to lead the painter back to his origins already traced in the account of his life that he had written well before illustrating the Bible? The true commentary on his

From *The Story of Exodus: Moses in Egypt.*
1966. Lithograph. 19 5/8 x 14 1/2 in.
(50 x 37 cm). Private collection.

works is found in those pages which, placed beside the *Biblical Message*, illuminate it and, like a shutter, close all around him to preserve the freshness and the secrecy.

Once again Chagall has remained true to himself, and to the very end. The Biblical world, object of his research, urged him in the opposite direction, the unique core of his entire work: his childhood which he was able to recapture from the most distant dimension of childhood—that of the sacred. Distance and closeness, thus intermingled, have exchanged their characteristics: man's fate bound to God has, for Chagall, assumed a familiar aspect. The myth has catalyzed the memory. A daring alchemy that presupposes an unshakable candor. A very personal solution in which the voice of the heart, always preponderant for Chagall, has prevailed.

ANDRÉ VERDET

"Eternity Recaptured"

1982

André Verdet (b. 1913), French poet and critic, who has lived for many years in Saint-Paul-de-Vence, and interviewed and wrote extensively about Chagall.

On Friday morning, January 12, 1973, Marc Chagall was at the work-site on the Cimiez hill in Nice where the Biblical Message Foundation was in the process of being built. He visited the various rooms that, since his gift was dedicated in July, 1973, have received his works. He spent a particularly long time in the music and conference room in front of the three stained-glass windows constituting *The Creation of the World* and on the patio in front of the large mosaic, whose image will be reflected in the water of one of the pools. The stained-glass windows and the mosaic had been completed. Their setting is an integral part of the architectural scheme, which was carefully planned and took into consideration their long-range destiny and the spiritual light that emanates from them. . . .

It seems germane to recall here that in the mind of the great Chagall this project can in no way be likened to a "museum," as one usually conceives of such an edifice today. Rather, it is a "sensitive, spiritual place" open to winged meditation and subtle revery, "a place," Marc Chagall would say, "where a certain presence imposes respect.". . .

The true spiritual starting point of the *Message* goes far back in time, no doubt to Marc Chagall's stay in Palestine from February to April, 1931. Ambroise Vollard had commissioned him to do some etchings for a Bible. The artist had just illustrated Gogol and La Fontaine. He departed for Palestine because, as he said, "I wasn't seeing the Bible, I was dreaming it." Contact with the landscape of the Holy Land, with that sort of luminous and fluid streaming of the legendary centuries, gave him both a revelatory shock and the dazzling confirmation of the meaning of his preceding works related to biblical motifs. Here, under the lovely Palestinian sky, he discovered the poetic and at the same time the spiritual element of those works in which nostalgia for the fabled land soared toward mystical regions.

He had seen the trace and heard the echo in his past works. . . . And here he was face to face with a land in which history continued to live and be incarnated, from a distance certainly but still present through its myths, among the most ancient of human civilization. . . .

The biblical stories are integrated in the historical process of the Afro-Mediterranean civilizations. They profoundly nourished Chagall, who has furnished us with a plastic version that is only related to his visionary art. He interprets, makes them his, while respecting the spirit, the law I might say, of the Scriptures. Having forgotten the pictorial tradition that was connected with them, rejected conventional iconography and the irritating anecdotal aspect, he imparts to them youth and freshness, charm and a new force and does so in such a way that contemporary man, touched in his heart and soul, becomes attentive to their ontological meaning, their moral resonance on the plane of the complexity of human destinies.

The Word is painted. Painted, it attains an epic grandeur, often verging on the sublime, but at the same time it remains familial, grazed by fantasy and winged grace.

From *The Story of Exodus: The Parting of the Red Sea.* 1966. Lithograph. 19 ⁵/₈ x 14 ¹/₂ in. (50 x 37 cm). Private collection.

BENJAMIN HARSHAV

"Jewish Art and Jesus Christ"

1994

Benjamin Harshav, Chagall scholar and J.H. Blaustein Professor of Hebrew and Comparative Literature, Yale University.

Chagall was not an ideologue; and though at some points in his life he was close to programmatic Jewish art circles, he never joined them. Through the years, he maintained contacts with both Jewish cultural circles and French intellectuals. Even in his most "chauvinistic" statement, "Leaves from my Notebook," published in Moscow in a Yiddish journal in 1922, he states, "Beginning with the Renaissance, national arts began to decline. Boundaries are blurred. Artists come—individuals, citizens of this or that state, born here or there (blessed be my Vitebsk)—and one would need a good registration or even a passport specialist (for the Jewish desk) to be able to 'nationalize' all the artists." He is proud of

The Resistance. 1963–68. Oil on canvas.
24 ¹/₈ x 19 ⁷/₈ in. (61 x 50.5 cm). Private
collection.

what the "little nation" of Jews has achieved: it gave the world Christ and Christianity, Marx and Socialism, and it will "show the world some art." But he refers to Art in general, measured by international standards, rather than "Jewish art." Indeed, there was no identity crisis here since in the minds of young intellectuals on both sides of the Modern Jewish Revolution, general culture and Jewish culture coexisted in one consciousness.

Because Christianity was central to the European cultural tradition, it attracted many Jews in the modern period: Edmund Husserl, Gustav Mahler, Alfred Doeblin, Roman Jakobson, and many others converted to Christianity. Chagall was not one of them, since he was deeply connected with a Jewish folk sensibility; but culturally, the Christian world was a tangible reality in his work and life. His friends in the interwar period, Raissa and Jacques Maritain, actively propagated conversion of the Jews. Raissa, herself a Russian Jew who converted to Catholicism, also wrote a book about Chagall. Hence the many fusions and confusions of Jewish, Russian, and Christian elements in Chagall's paintings; they interact, coalesce, and represent each other, just as other modular individuals—man and animal, or man and woman—do. He presents the sacrifice of Isaac in the form of a Michelangelo *Pietà,* or he portrays the Holy Family with a bearded, "old," little Jewish child; he paints himself as a Christ child along with his parents in the famous *Golgotha.* Some Jewish critics were puzzled, even outraged by the use of Christian motifs in the works of a Jewish artist like Scholem Asch or Chagall. But Christian art was the mainstream of the European art tradition and was part of Chagall's intellectual world: as Buddha and Zen Buddhism may appear in the writings of a Christian writer, so did Martin Buber discuss Buddhism along with Hasidism in his writings; and such, too, was the openness of modern Jewish literature in Hebrew and Yiddish.

Golgotha *refers to* Calvary, *colorplate 7.*

A special case is the figure of Jesus Christ. His image was part of the modern gallery of Jewish literature. Dr. Yosef Klausner, a native of Russia, editor of the flagship of Hebrew literature in Europe, *Ha-Shiloah,* and the first professor of Hebrew Literature at the Hebrew University in Jerusalem (between 1925 and 1949), devoted many years to the study of Jesus of Nazareth and his time. Similarly, Uri-Tsvi Grinberg, the Expressionist poet who wrote in Yiddish and Hebrew and who edited the avant-garde Yiddish journal *Albatros,* used the figure of Jesus prominently in his work. There can be no doubt that Chagall knew *Albatros,* for it was a major organ of the *Khalyastre* (Happy Gang), a group of Yiddish Expressionist poets, who also published the journals *Khalyastre* and *Literarishe revi* in Paris, with many illustrations by Chagall.

Grinberg had been a frontline soldier during World War I, had deserted, and lived in hiding. After experiencing a pogrom in his hometown of Lemberg (Lvov), he became an ardent Zionist who firmly believed (already in 1924, in Berlin) that the earth was burning under the feet of the Jews in Europe, and that one day they would be gassed. In 1924 he left for Palestine, where he became a prominent Hebrew poet and extreme nationalist. In 1922 he wrote a Yiddish "concrete" poem in the form of a cross, which was entitled "Uri-Tsvi Before the Cross / INRI." Chagall painted a similar image, *The White Crucifixion,* with the same letters I.N.R.I. above the cross, and below, he added an Aramaic version of the text in Hebrew letters, "Jesus of Nazareth King of the Jews." In "Uri-Tsvi Before the Cross" and in the long poem "In the Kingdom of the Cross," Grinberg addresses Jesus as "our brother," symbol of Jewish suffering, hanging on crosses all over Europe for two thousand years. I will quote a few lines pertinent to Chagall:

COLORPLATE 45

> At the churches
> Hangs my brother
> Crucified
> Frozen
> From his covered member
> Girls get pregnant. . . .

Why am I one of the suffering caravan, not hanging next to you on a village pillar at a crossroad, sun drying me, night weighing on me? . . .

Brother Jesus, a Jewish skin-and-bones shrinks (two thousand years after you Old!) . . .

Brother Jesus. You had two thousand years of calm on the cross. Around you, *no longer world* . . . At your feet: a heap of cut-off Jewheads [allusion to the pogroms].

Torn *talises* [Jewish prayer shawls]. Pierced parchments. Blood-stained white sheets . . . Ancient Jewpain. Golgotha, brother, you don't see. Golgotha is here: all around. Pilate lives. And in Rome they sing psalms in the churches . . .

The Jews! The Jews!
When poisoned gas enters the temples
And icons suddenly scream in Yiddish . . .
On the wound-ridden body a torn *talis*—the body
Feels good in a Jewish *talis*—Oh, good in a *talis:*
The wind cannot blow sand on the dripping wounds. . . .
Oh-Ho, I am king in a wound-and-blood *talis!* [Emphasis added.]

Such was the Jewish context of Chagall's *The White Crucifixion,* which included Jesus wearing a *talis,* as well as the context of similar images in later paintings responding to the Holocaust. Of course, unlike Grinberg, Chagall did not paint it with an Expressionist scream. Just as Chagall borrowed images from Yiddish literature, so did his painting evoke responses from inside Jewish culture. Here is a comment about the painting entitled *Flayed Ox:*

COLORPLATE 51

Look closely at the red, flayed calf, hanging as a crucifix over the whole city. As the true crucified, the father of all the crucified in the world, since the evil of a living creature wielded its power over a living creature. See how the red of its blood screams, see the brutal cut in its body split in two, see the purity of its face licking from the bowl—

Does another crucified like this exist among all the crucifieds?

Weren't we all stunned, trembling in our childhood, when we saw the neighbor butcher slaughter our beloved calf? Isn't Fayerberg's "The Calf" authentically Jewish for all time? And is there a more authentic feeling of pity for the lot of the powerless? And a stronger scream of rage at the brutality of the heartless? And isn't Chagall here like Fayerberg? . . .

Look closely and see the zenith of human Evil, emanating from an idyll that is clear purity and beatitude.

This was written in Yiddish after the Holocaust by the President of Israel Zalman Shazar, a Hebrew scholar and former Israeli Minister of Culture, who was born in Byelorussia two years after Chagall. Given their shared cultural background, the calf may be more appropriate than the ox in the painting's title.

Naturally, Chagall had ideological hesitations about crossing religious boundaries in his paintings. As a young man of twenty, before leaving for St. Petersburg to study art, he went with his mother to Lubavitsh to see the head of the Chabad Hasidic sect and ask for his advice; characteristically for that time, the Rebbe told him he must judge for himself. And half a century later, Chagall wrote to the first Israeli President Chaim Weitzmann, invoking the traditional authority of the Rebbe, and asked for advice from "the highest Jewish authority" about whether to accept a commission for a Christian church. According to Chagall, who felt apologetic toward his Jewish friends, Weitzman, too, answered that Chagall must decide for himself. And he did.

CHAGALL
AND ISRAEL

MARC CHAGALL

"My Land"

1946

Only that land is mine
That lies in my soul.
As a native, with no documents,
I enter that land.

It sees my sorrow
And loneliness,
Puts me to sleep
And covers me with a fragrance-stone.

Gardens are blooming inside me,
My flowers I invented,
My own streets—
But there are no houses.
They have been destroyed since my childhood.
Their inhabitants stray in the air,
Seek a dwelling,
They live in my soul.

That's why I smile sometimes
When the sun barely glimmers,
Or I cry
Like a light rain at night.

There was a time
When I had two heads,
When both faces were covered with a film of love—
And evaporated like the scent of roses.

Now I imagine
That even when I walk back
I walk forward—
Toward high gates,
Beyond them, walls are strewn about,
Where worn-out thunders sleep,
And broken lightning———

Chagall was himself a poet and published a volume of his poetry with his own illustrations in 1975. He said, "Some have reproached me for incorporating poetry into my paintings, but show me a single masterpiece that has not got some poetry in it."

Former mayor of Jerusalem Teddy Kollek with Chagall in Jerusalem, February 1962. Collection Ida Chagall, Paris.

BERNARD BERENSON

Imaging Chagall

December 1, 1956

Bernard Berenson (1865–1959), renowned art historian, critic, and connoisseur, especially of Italian Renaissance art.

Marc Chagall comes from Vitebsk but has nothing Jewish about him in looks, in manner, in any peculiarities. Yet he paints almost nothing but ghetto life—and in a semi-naïf, rather childish fashion, does it with enough feeling to "put it over." His wife looks as little Jewish as he, only she is dark, slight and with a sari and a wart on her forehead would pass muster as a high-class Hindu. Whence these curious types appearing in Jewry? The Hindu I cannot trace at all. The Egyptian-like Doro Levi or Anna Maria Cicogna with their skulls so overdeveloped behind the ears, must go back to the far, faraway days, when Israel was in Egypt. In my own face and features I trace a Germanic something, not infrequent among Central and Eastern European Jews. To go back to Chagall, I enjoyed his simplicity, his candor. He, though a famous painter, seemed in no way inclined to talk about himself, no touch of the average painter's self-adulation and fathomless conceit.

JACOB BAAL-TESHUVA

"Chagall in a Reminiscent Mood"

1962

"I feel as though the tragic and heroic resistance movements in the ghettos and the Israeli war of independence are blended in my flowers and beasts and my fiery colors."

So spoke Chagall, greatest living Jewish painter, on the occasion of the dedication of his twelve stained glass windows in the synagogue at the medical center of Hadassah in the hills of Jerusalem. Chagall's windows, depicting the twelve tribes of Israel, highlight the artist's career as he nears his 76th birthday.

"All the time I was working, I felt as if my father and my mother were peering over my shoulder—and behind them Jews, millions of other vanished Jews of yesterday and a thousand years ago," said the artist. "The air and earth of Vitebsk, my birthplace, and of thousands of years of exile, find themselves mingled in the air and earth of Jerusalem. Not only my hands directed me in my work, but the poor hands of my parents and of others, and still others with their mute lips and their closed eyes, seemed to gather and whisper behind me, guide me as if they also wish to take part in my life. . . ."

It is not too often that Chagall speaks about his work, about himself and what inspires him to create. It was moving to hear him describing his windows.

He wanted to give the windows a magical quality, he said, to make them vibrate, live. He worked out every figure, every color, in such a way that the glass would fuse every ray of light as he wanted it. "There is the light of the sky in these windows, and the participation of the good Lord," he said. "They have completely transformed my vision. They gave me a shock, made me reflect. I don't

COLORPLATE 96. *The Painter and the Dove*. 1978. Oil on canvas.
45 1/2 x 31 5/8 in. (115.5 x 80.5 cm). Private collection.

COLORPLATE 97. *The Painter and the Bridal Couple*. 1978. Acrylic on canvas.
23 ⅝ x 19 ⅝ in. (60 x 50 cm). Private collection.

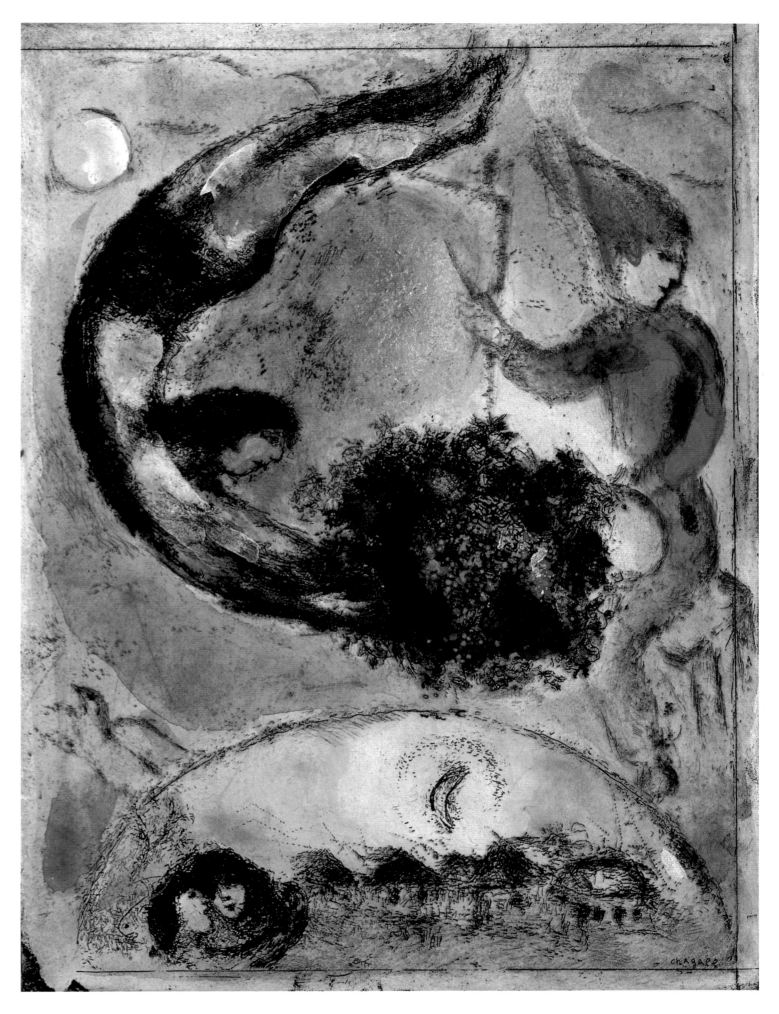

COLORPLATE 98. *The Offering*. 1944–45. Hand-colored etching. 9 7/8 x 7 3/8 in. (25 x 18.8 cm). Private collection.

COLORPLATE 99. *The Prodigal Son*. 1975–76. Oil on canvas. 63 3/4 x 48 in. (162 x 122 cm). Collection Ida Chagall, Paris.

COLORPLATE 100. *Don Quixote.* 1974. Oil on canvas. 77 ¹/₈ x 51 ¹/₈ in. (196 x 130 cm).
Collection Ida Chagall, Paris.

COLORPLATE 101. *Paris Landscape*. 1978. Oil on canvas. 51 ^{1}/$_8$ x 63 ^{3}/$_4$ in. (130 x 162 cm). Private collection.

COLORPLATE 102. *View Over Paris.* 1969. Gouache on paper. 21 $^1/_2$ x 28 $^3/_8$ in. (54.5 x 72 cm). Private collection.

COLORPLATE 103. *The Dream*. 1978. Tempera on canvas. 25 ¹/₂ x 21 ¹/₄ in. (65 x 54 cm). Private collection.

Self-Portrait. 1954–55. Watercolor, pen, and ink on paper. 24 x 16 ¾ in. (61 x 42.5 cm). Private collection.

know how I shall paint from now on, but I believe something is taking place. I am still under the influence." He wanted to convey a sense of the mystery and spirituality of Israel in these glasses. "I still have no theory for my way of working." He did not try to follow any theory. God created man without a theory—art is best created without a theory. "It is only in our power to work for art," he said, "and God does the rest."

Because the windows are installed in an oriental country, he said, the orient always suggested to him an extraordinarily beautiful woman. Israel he thinks of as an oriental queen. "This synagogue should be in the queen's crown, and I want my windows to be the jewels of her crown."

Chagall has been described as a "poet in color." But I think the best description was that of controversial novelist Henry Miller. Miller called Chagall "a poet with the wings of a painter."

I first met Marc Chagall eleven years ago. He is shy, soft spoken. Despite his advanced age (he will be 76 soon), I was impressed by his vitality, his energy. And by his Jewishness. His inspiration, despite the art critics, has been unequivo-

Pour Jacob Baal-
Teshuva
en bon souvenir

LE PLAFOND
DE
L'OPÉRA DE PARIS

1966   Marc Chagall

A drawing by Chagall (drawn on the title page of a book) made for the author, Jacob Baal-Teshuva, 1966. Courtesy Jacob Baal-Teshuva.

cally Jewish. Unlike that of other famous Jewish painters—Modigliani, Pissarro or Soutine, for example. Almost every one of Chagall's paintings or drawings exudes Jewishness. . . .

My last meeting with him was a rare experience.

⟐ The artist spoke a polyglot of Yiddish and French. Though he would not venture opinions on other artists, he could not refrain from saying something about contemporary art.

"There is bad art or good art. New developments in art generally bring upheaval, revolution. But the developments taking place today only amount to a mishmash. Of course we are going through a cultural crisis—but a crisis is not a lasting phenomenon. After depression comes renaissance. It seems to me that the fault peculiar to our century is that it has failed to nurture genius. For me every child contains something of genius,—only later it is spent, lost. Today's youth is experiencing an eruption that presses upon its consciousness, and thus upon the quality of the things it creates. . . . An artist needs tranquility. . . . Maybe, too, the youth of today is healthier, more naive, more spontaneous, acting more through the heart. . . . I don't like clever, barren art. . . . I do not deal in art. For me art is the justification of an artist's existence, never his trade, only his raison-d'etre."

I asked him the usual—to which of the old masters he feels closest.

"My masters were my parents. My home. My street. We were nine children at home—my father, a worker, always worked hard. When I used to look into his face—*that* was my art academy. The most important thing is to look at and observe people. . . . I never imagined that I would come to study in Paris—but I began to see things in color and line. There I saw the great masters. When I looked at a Giotto, Rembrandt or Goya, I thought to myself, these pictures resemble my father."

"And the Russian subjects that show up in your paintings—how about *them?*" I asked.

Interior of a Synagogue, Palestine. 1931.
23 x 28 in. (58.4 x 71 cm). Private collection.

"Though I am not a nationalist, I have an attachment to Russia, always remained faithful to my native home, my family, my land. I avoided falling into assimilation. At my age, you know, one must be able to find a homeland in himself. I did not leave Russia for political reasons. Only that in Vitebsk there was no color. In France I found color, and only then was I able to illuminate Vitebsk in my pictures. If I had an exhibition in Russia, the ordinary Russian people, people like my father, would be able to express their views which for me are more important than those of the critic. I have always thought about such people. . . ."

I asked him why he wouldn't settle in Israel since his Jewish feelings are so basic. France is "home" to him, he said and, moreover, he feels a deep gratitude for the French people, who have treated him so well all these years.

He described his first visit to Israel (1931) as a "shock." He had gone there at the invitation of the then mayor of Tel Aviv, Meir Dizengoff. "It was that visit which inspired me to start the set of illustrations for the Bible commissioned by Ambroise Vollard."

It was 28 years later—in 1959—that a committee of three Hadassah women visited the artist in Paris and asked him to make the windows for the Jerusalem synagogue. They did not suggest any subject. But since there were to be twelve windows, the idea of the twelve tribes of the ancient Hebrews seemed logical to him.

The Western Wall. 1926. Ink drawing on paper.
16 ½ x 13 in. (41.9 x 33 cm). Musée National
d'Art Moderne, Centre Georges Pompidou,
Paris.

He had to confine his composition to animals, fish, birds, and so on—*in accordance with Jewish law, which forbids anthropomorphic imagery.* Though he did not find the time to reread the Bible before making the rough sketches, his memory did not deceive him. "I had the Bible in me, in my heart, my head."

MARC CHAGALL

Letter to President Weizman

1962

President Chaim Weizman, the first president of the state of Israel.

This is actually a summary of the letter, apparently made in English by Ida Chagall from Chagall's associative Yiddish letter. It was appended to Chagall's letter of March 22, 1950, to his friend in New York, Yiddish writer Yosef Opatoshu.

I write to you as our fathers in Russia used to write to their Rabbis for help in solving problems of conscience.

I have been asked to execute mural paintings in a 16th-century chapel in Vence, which is a historical, cultural, and religious center on the Riviera. I have not yet accepted. . . .

Of course I shall be left entirely free to paint whatever I wish and if I accept I intend to do Biblical scenes such as appear in some of my paintings, strictly in my own manner and from my own point of view, symbolizing the suffering of the martyred Jewish people.

To decorate a chapel might give me the chance to do work that is only possible on large walls, instead of having to limit myself to relatively small canvases destined to hang in private houses. To decorate walls in public buildings has long been my dream. If it were possible to decorate a synagogue my dream would be completely fulfilled.

If I decide to decorate this chapel I would not want the people of Israel to think that in my heart or mind—not to speak of my art—I have anything in common with non-Judaism. With my ancestors I shall always be bound to my people.

On a more temporal basis I do not know whether I should decorate a Catholic church at a time when the Vatican is not favorably disposed to Israel. At the same time, I wonder if the presence of a Jewish painting in a church might be good propaganda for our people.

In other situations I have solved similar cases myself. I refused my friend Jacques Maritain's request to donate a picture to the Vatican's museum of modern art. I refused to exhibit in German museums after the war, in spite of the official invitation of the French Cultural Services. An exhibition that has recently taken place in Düsseldorf was organized without my consent and consisted of pictures from German and Dutch collections. I refused to be present at the opening of my exhibition in London at a time when British policy was unfavorable to our interests.

But today I have neither the strength nor the capacity to reply, and all the more because I have been asked to do work in other churches and in other towns.

But with the renaissance, after 2,000 years, of the spiritual and political center of the Jewish people, I cannot help turning with all my doubts toward its most eminent representative.

MARC CHAGALL

At the Celebration in Jerusalem

1962

Chagall's relationship with Israel was very complex and at times strained, though he was always a welcomed guest and even an honorary citizen of Jerusalem. Despite his professed love and affection for Israel, he did not leave any paintings to museums in Israel upon his death.

How did the air and earth of Vitebsk, my hometown, along with thousands of years of Diaspora, blend with the air and earth of Jerusalem?

How could I have known that it was not only my hands and colors that would lead me in my work, but also the dear hands of my father and mother, and of others and yet others, with their mute lips and closed eyes, who whispered behind me as if they wanted to take part in my life?

It seems to me that your tragic and heroic resistance movements in the ghettos, and your war here, in this country, have merged with my flowers and animals and fire-colors. . . .

Insofar as our age refuses to see the whole figure of the world and is content with a very small part of its skin, my heart aches when I observe this figure in its eternal rhythm, and my will to go against the general stream is strengthened.

It seems to me that the colors and the lines flow out, like tears from my eyes, though I am not crying.—And do not think I am talking here in a moment of weakness. On the contrary, the more years I pile up, the more certain I am of what I want and what I say.

I know that my life's path is eternal and brief. And I learned, back in my mother's womb, to walk that path more out of love than out of hatred.

The thoughts have nested in me for many years, since the time when my feet walked on the Holy Land, when I prepared myself to create engravings of the Bible. They strengthened me and encouraged me to bring my modest gift to the Jewish people—that people that lived here thousands of years ago, among the other Semitic peoples.

And what is now called religious art I created when I recalled also the great and ancient creations of the surrounding Semitic peoples.

I hope that, thereby, I stretch out my hand to the neighboring peoples, their poets and artists, to whom human culture is dear. I saw the mountains of Sodom and the Negev, and the shadows of our Prophets, in their garb the color of dried bread, shine from those mountains. I heard their ancient words. . . .

In their words they marked the path for behavior on the earth and pointed out the moral essence of our life.

I draw hope and courage from the thought that my modest work will remain on their-your land.

Jew with Torah. 1925. Gouache on paper mounted on board. 26 3/4 x 20 in. (68 x 51 cm). The Tel Aviv Museum of Art. Donated by the artist in 1931.

MARC CHAGALL

On the First Day of the Six-Day War

June 6, 1967

Would that I were younger, to leave my paintings and brushes, and go, fly together with you—with sweet joy to give up my last years.

I have always painted pictures where human love floods my colors.

Day and night I dreamed that something would change in the souls and relationships of people.

I have always thought that, without human or biblical feelings in your heart, life has no value. Now the Semitic nations have arisen, jealous of our hard-earned piece of bread, our burning national ideal, our national soil. They want to show that, like other nations, they are also anti-Semites. They want to choke us as did the Pharaohs of old. But we crossed the sea of the ghettos, and our victory was eternalized in the [Passover] Hagada.

We now stand before the great world trial of the human soul: will all dear visions and ideals of two thousand years of human world culture be blown away with the wind?

History again puts the torch and sword in our hand, for the world to tremble when it hears our prophetic voice of justice.

Thousands and thousands of simple people here and everywhere are with you. Only "leaders" with no heart are with our enemies.

Perhaps I am of an age to bless you, and, instead of crying, to comfort you.

I want to hope that the land of the great French Revolution, the land of Zola, Balzac, Watteau, Cézanne, Baudelaire, Claudel, Péguy, will soon raise its voice to stop the world shame.

I hope that America with its democracy, the land of Shakespeare, and also the land of Dostoevskii, Moussorgskii—the land of my birth—will begin to scream that the world must stop its "manners" and give the people of Israel one chance—to live free and create freely in its own land.

Anyway, no one will be able to create freely anymore if the nations let consciences go to sleep. The last drop of talent will evaporate and their words will remain hollow.

To let Israel and the Jews be choked—means to kill the soul of the whole biblical world.

No new "religion" can be created without this drop of the heart's blood. And we will see if we are worthy of continuing to live or of being destroyed by the atomic bomb.

My word of consolation is in my eyes, which you cannot see now.

And my blessings are embossed in my windows of the Twelve Tribes, now hidden in Jerusalem. . . .

Chagall putting the finishing touches on *Loneliness* (1933), which he donated to the Tel Aviv Museum of Art in 1953. Photograph © Lipnitzki-Viollet.

MARC CHAGALL

Poems of Dedication

TO ISRAEL

Should I pray to God, Who led my people to the fire,
Or should I paint Him in image of flame?
Should I get up from my place a new Jew
And go fight along with my race?

Should my eyes lament without a halt,
So the tears drown in a river?
I won't let my grief approach
When I swim to your shore.

And when my weary foot gropes on the sand—
I shall lead my bride by the hand.
For you to see her—the holy bride in the sky,
As I will dream with her our last dream.

1950

The Eiffel Tower. 1923–24. Pen and ink on paper. Approximately 10 x 8 in. (25.4 x 20 cm). Museé Nationale d'Art Moderne, Centre Georges Pompidou, Paris.

THE SHIP

Two thousand years—my Exile,
My land is just a few years old.
Young as my son David.
I crawl on my knees with spread-out hands
And seek the stars and the Magen-David.

The Prophets swim past me,
Moses shines to me from afar.
I have long been enraptured by his beams
And by the wind blowing from him.

All those years I counted the tears,
Sought you in the sky, on the earth,
Two thousand years have I waited
For my heart to calm down and see you.

Like Jacob, I lay sound asleep,
I dreamed a dream:
An angel raises me on a ladder,
Extinguished souls sing around me.
About the new land Israel,
About two thousand years of our Exile,
And about David—my son,
They sang sweeter than Mozart and Bach

When will you come, my hour,
When I shall go out like a candle,
When will I reach you, my distant one,
And when will my rest come?

I don't know if I'm walking,
I don't know who I am,
I don't know where I stand,
My head and my soul—where they are.

Look, my dear mother,
At your son going down,
Look, my dear crown,
How quiet and deep my sun sets.

1960

ALEKSANDR KAMENSKY

A Conversation with Chagall

June 10, 1973

Aleksandr Kamensky (b. 1922), a leading Russian critic and art historian and author of Chagall: The Russian Years 1907–1922, *published in 1988.*

KAMENSKY: Marc Zakharovich, you have experienced so much, seen so much and created so much that one could interview you for a whole week without finishing. I would like to limit this interview to what concerns the Soviet people . . .

CHAGALL: I don't like interviews. What I think, I usually write down. And I leave the critics to their own opinions . . .

KAMENSKY: Well let's not consider this conversation as an interview . . . Marc Zakharovich, you have lived through wars and revolutions: Hitler, Mussolini, Hiroshima, Babi Yar, Auschwitz. You have had a difficult life; you left your country, your friends and loved ones; your works were burned in an *auto-da-fé* at Mannheim. Yet despite all these dramas you have been able to preserve a sense of beauty and happiness. Even your tragic subjects assert that the world is good in itself and that its horror is only a deviation from the correct order of things. Am I right in seeing this in your work?

CHAGALL: That isn't a question. It's a whole speech. You have said some fundamental things . . . The world is good if you love it. I love love. Love helps me to find colour. I can even say that it is love itself which finds colour and that I only report that discovery on canvas. It is stronger than me. That is how I see life. It is beautiful, terrible. Strange also, probably because I look on it with the eyes of love. Hitler, Auschwitz—that was terrible. It's the past, but humanity is still threatened today. They want to take love away. But love has always existed, and colour also. This has been the message in my work since the beginning. It is within me. It is stronger than me.

KAMENSKY: For you, the word "colour" is not a technical or aesthetic term. You give it a much broader meaning. Is this a precise concept?

CHAGALL: Of course. Colour is purity. Colour is *art. Pure art.* Or its fundamental intonation . . . But one must undoubtedly be born with colour. If I love Vitebsk so much it is not only because I was born there but because it was there that I found my colour . . .

Yes, you must be born with colour. For colour is a quality.

KAMENSKY: Do you mean quality in the French sense of the term? That is, a positive value?

CHAGALL: If you wish. Although a word is always richer than a term.

KAMENSKY: In the twentieth century values are far from being appreciated. And yet you have been recognized even by those—critics, painters or theoreticians—who oppose lyricism or tradition. How can you explain this contradiction?

CHAGALL: Are you saying that I have not had enemies? But I have, and more than one. You yourself mentioned the *auto-da-f*é at Mannheim. But I also had enemies amongst painters. Kazimir Malevich, for example, whom I invited to teach at the School of Art in Vitebsk. And even before, in 1911 to 1913, in Paris, Delaunay and Metzinger accused me of creating *de la littérature*. They said that I belonged to the past and that I would soon be forgotten. How many times has that same thing been said of me.

KAMENSKY: Yet you are not afraid of appearing anachronistic. You have not been afraid of solitude.

CHAGALL: I have never felt myself to be alone. Some painters were very close to me in spirit, in their colour. For example Matisse, Braque and Gris.

KAMENSKY: But many others have depicted a cruel world without a soul, a world opposed to that seen in your work.

CHAGALL: I myself have also often seen evil and cruelty. But I have simply fought against them. I don't really know if I have succeeded. And I would not like to oppose anyone.

KAMENSKY: Then you accept it when people compare you to painters who have nothing in common with you?

CHAGALL: Perhaps it is because in their work there is a colour, a quality, a "chemistry" close to mine.

KAMENSKY: As in abstract art for example?

CHAGALL: Yes. Abstract art also has its own purity. For example the work of Mondrian or Paul Klee.

Piet Mondrian (1872–1944); Paul Klee (1879–1940).

KAMENSKY: Don't you think that Mondrian and yourself belong to different movements?

CHAGALL: Movements! There are painters and that's it. Movements—they are theoretical conceptions. And the great painters have always been above movements. Sometimes this division into systems has annoyed even the great painters. Delacroix accused Courbet of naturalism. In the debate he won, but as far as colour is concerned it was Courbet who was the winner. Twenty-five years ago I was mocked because I appreciated the colour of Claude Monet. And now he is lauded to the skies as the founder of abstract art. But do we like Monet because he belonged to this or that school? He was a great painter who had a keen sense of colour. And what does it matter how he is defined. What is important is to understand his strength, his colour.

KAMENSKY: OK. But it would be difficult to write a history of art without at least the minimum of classification. Let us leave that to the specialists. However, you have been described as one of the founders of Surrealism. Even as one of the classic artists. What do you think of that?

CHAGALL: Let us leave that word "classic." Only time will tell. Surrealism? Do you really need a label? I have never understood why I have been described as a Surrealist, and I do not like the word. It is true that I wished to get rid of a certain heaviness, to get away from slavish copies of reality. I wanted to make colour into the mediator between psychic and spiritual elements. The result irritated the older generation as well as the moderns. I have been accused of creating literature. So? It's only a word. As long as there is colour. And poetry. For me the greatest work of poetry is the Bible.

KAMENSKY: The whole of the Bible? The Old and the New Testament?

CHAGALL: Of course. They are inseparable . . . In fact on 7 July, in Nice, I am going to open the Museum of "Chagall's Biblical Message." I have given them over four hundred works devoted to the illustration of the Bible. And I have produced stained glass windows for several churches.

KAMENSKY: But Surrealism?

CHAGALL: I have said everything on that subject. I am frankly totally indifferent to the definition. In order to speak of art you must talk in concrete terms and not clutter your thoughts with abstract concepts. Of course today's painters have a different language to those of the past. But reality itself is no longer the same. In order to see it you need new colours. I belong to no particular movement. What I need is colour, purity and love, nothing else. That is not a movement, it is a conviction.

KAMENSKY: You often reveal the illogical character of events, or rather you make them depart from the usual logic.

CHAGALL: Perhaps. But in what way is that a movement? Each painter has his own way of viewing the world. It is a matter of an artistic logic, a poetic logic.

KAMENSKY: In your pictures you don't treat them in a linear fashion. It is more of a poetic convention.

CHAGALL: That's always the case in art.

KAMENSKY: But in the past people have sought to stick close to reality.

CHAGALL: Not always . . . I have often dreamed of finding the feeling of the unity of the world that the ancients had. To see the world as an indivisible whole, to embrace both the beginning and the end at once, what purity! That is why I love icons so much. I owe a lot to icon painting. It is an art full of spirituality, unembarrassed by devices. For devices kill purity.
Time. I have always wanted to penetrate the mystery of time. When I began to depict my character's memories and thoughts as concommitmant my pictures were considered to be bizarre. But is not memory a form of time? The past is inseparable from man. And his thoughts. They form a whole. And it is this whole which I paint. It helps me to understand man. *Homage à Apollinaire* is the first work in which I painted time. Guillaume Apollinaire and Blaise Cendrars were my friends. They mentioned my pictures in their poems and helped me to under-

stand myself better. Later Eluard wrote a long poem inspired by my paintings. And the poem ended thus: *Notre naissance est perpétuelle* ["Our birth is perpetual"]. It's true. We begin again and again. Each day brings new hopes. On 7 July I will be eighty-six years old. I would still like to be able to do many more things.

KAMENSKY: You could say that in each of your pictures time is able to contract or expand. It seems to me that each of your works is a stage set, often even a mystery.

CHAGALL: Perhaps. But I don't want to be theatrical. I love the theatre. But the theatre and theatricality are two different things. Theatricality is only artifice. It means a loss of purity. Yes I love the theatre. And the circus as well. It is in the circus that eccentricity and simplicity blend most naturally. You say that my works recall the theatre. You should rather say the circus. Not in its correct sense, you understand. But you find there the same search for colour and purity.

KAMENSKY: Apart from the theatre you have explored areas other than that of easel painting.

CHAGALL: That's right. I have done stained glass windows, mosaics, frescoes, ceramics. I painted the ceiling of the Paris Opéra.

COLORPLATE 71

KAMENSKY: You say that easel painting is bound to disappear.

CHAGALL: That's utterly false. Drawing and painting, like the symphony, the novel or poetry are eternal forms which touch the depths of the soul. For me the difference between stained glass and fresco is purely technical and spatial. Whatever I do I am always a painter. Nevertheless there is a different approach: stained glass or fresco are more decorative. Easel painting gives more space for contemplation and reflection. Nothing can replace it.

KAMENSKY: But their psychological and aesthetic functions change. In the same way as, with them, everything which forms our vision of the world changes.

CHAGALL: Yes, and? Things changed in the past. But great artists and great works retain their value despite changes.

KAMENSKY: Feelings also change. You who have so often depicted love, where do you stand with regard to this evolution?

CHAGALL: Let people love as they wish. There are no rules for love. For me, any man is an artist in love, even if he does not know how to paint or write. How sad it would be if the artistic principle which lies at the basis of love were to disappear. Art must help love. Art and love are intrinsically linked.

KAMENSKY: And the art of loving art?

CHAGALL: That is necessary to human nature. Sometimes, unfortunately, the public is mistaken. In this sense, criticism can be useful.

KAMENSKY: Have critics helped create a better understanding of your work? Have they helped you personally? Whom have you liked best?

CHAGALL: Much has been written about me. People have written foolish things, but also serious things. I have much appreciated the studies by Tugendhold, Efros, Benois, Venturi and Meyer.

KAMENSKY: Abram Efros was not only your biographer. He also helped you in concrete terms.

CHAGALL: Efros was the first to notice me. And more, he helped when I left Vitebsk for Moscow. It was he who invited me to work in the Granovsky Theatre.

KAMENSKY: I think that the Pushkin Museum is planning to organize a major retrospective of your work.

CHAGALL: Yes, I've heard about that. That would be truly marvelous. I've been very aware of the reception I have been given here. But I can't hide the fact that I have the impression that my work is little known to the Soviet public. Such an exhibition would enable us to remedy that.

KAMENSKY: The Museum would also like your works to hang beside those of Matisse and other great painters.

CHAGALL: What works exactly? It would be strange if the works that I painted in Russia were to be exhibited beside those of European painters. On the contrary they must be placed in museums devoted to early twentieth-century Russian art.

KAMENSKY: And your later works? It would be foolish to present twentieth-century art without Chagall! There would be a link missing in the chain!

CHAGALL: You are reasoning like a historian. For me I would like to say that I have always considered myself as a Russian painter. When I finally left Russia in 1922 I had the impression of being an uprooted tree, suspended in the air. I have suffered a lot. But I never broke my links with Russia. Of course I owe a lot to France. It was there that I got help and encouragement. But I have always drunk from the Russian spring. And I sincerely thank those who have helped me to return to my native land in my eighty-sixth year. I dreamed of it for a long time. And this dream has at last been realised.

* * *

11 July 1973
St. Paul

Dear A. Kamensky,
Excuse me for addressing you thus (I have a poor memory). Thank you for all you have done for me. I have received your long article. I am entirely in agreement with you. Thank you. You write better than you interview; you are very sensitive. I was so pleased to make your acquaintance; I am aware of your passion for art history. How could it be otherwise?

I was so happy to be in my native country, to see so many wonderful people. The landscapes enchanted me. I am sorry that I was not able to paint them.

I would like to thank you once more for your sympathy and love for me.

My wife sends her regards.

Yours truly
Marc Chagall

REMEMBERING CHAGALL

ALEXANDER LIBERMAN

From *The Artist in His Studio*

1958

Alexander Liberman (b. 1912), renowned Russian artist and photographer, whose works in many media, including monumental sculptures, have been widely exhibited. He lives in New York where he is editorial director of Condé Nast Publications.

The short, stocky man who descended the long flight of steps that joined the studio with the terrace was Chagall. He was dressed all in blue; a thin crisscross of red checkered his blue shirt; a thick, rough leather belt held his baggy blue linen trousers.

Chagall's face was tanned and weatherbeaten, his strong, marked features surrounded by thinning unruly locks of gray hair. His well-muscled, compact body gave a sense of youthful, dynamic vitality, of earthy male vigor. The intimate welding of the extremes, the physical roughness with the spiritual, contributed stature and dimension to his presence.

He smiled when he saw us, a quick, self-conscious smile, his head slightly tilted to one side, like a bird examining a new object from all angles. The sadness of his eyes added, by contrast, intensity to his smile.

His voice, very soft and husky, had the dim hoarseness of many Russian voices. He seemed to speak with the tips of his lips. In whatever language he uses—French, English, German—strong indestructible Russian accent colors and modifies the sound of each word. He sat down with a sigh. Vava poured the tea. Often during our conversation I noticed the sighs that seemed momentarily to ease some inner pain.

He laughed often; he laughed as though he enjoyed laughter. He seemed to find it, as in the sigh, a physical release. He has an acute sense of humor, a curious ability to extract fun out of the incongruities of life, like a protective device quickly interposed in order to avoid the underlying sadness. Perhaps, like Figaro, he makes "haste to laugh . . . for fear of being obliged to weep."

As I watched, the rich texture, the variety, the complexity of this man's nature became apparent. He is intensely alert, curious about people and places. Curiosity, the desire to find out, is a sign of interest in life, and interest in life is a sign of youth. He punctuated and interrupted the conversation with direct, down-to-earth questions. Having asked, he awaited the reply with a preformed expression, as though in advance he knew the answer.

The most mobile, revealing lines on his face are the wrinkles on his brow. A high forehead is plowed by five or six sinuous furrows that undulate simultaneously. His emotions may be measured by the intensity and the direction of these exterior ripples. Surprise, interest, suffering, joy, all have their stylized counterparts in the movements of his brow.

With his ability to ask, he has the parallel gift of listening. Few people listen; an artist must. As Chagall listened, his face took on a sad, meditative expression or suddenly, as if kindled by a spark, his eyes lit up, his mouth opened slightly, as though to facilitate the penetration of meaning. His eyelids opened wide, his eye-

brows pushed up, as if to clear the path of sight. At those moments his face was the face of a believing child to whom some miraculous fairy tale was being told. This ability to believe the unbelievable, to see the magical, the wonderful, and the unseen, is a gift shared only by the poet, the artist, and the child. Chagall, now seventy-one, has preciously protected and sheltered the spontaneity of his perception. When the child that is within all of us grows up, then we look, think, and are our real age.

"When people tell me how young I look," Chagall said, "I say, 'Yes, yes, I am stupid.' One must be a little bit stupid and then a little bit smart to retain his original purity."

After tea we went into his studio, a long white room. In front of his own handiwork, a new Chagall appeared, a much graver, sterner man. A craftsman surrounded with the tools of his trade, he went about his work in a more matter-of-fact way.

Most artists are quiet in the act of creation. They become absorbed; they withdraw from their environment. Chagall sat down at a large drawing table by the single large, low window. From the incredible clutter of pencils, pens, brushes, paints, he selected a brush and meditatively started to draw. Drawing is the most direct expression of a painter's thought. The black line that slowly unwound on the white sheet of paper was a sinuous arabesque, an undulating expression of a sensuous and supple mind. The curve, the curl, the wound-up spring are images of pent-up vitality, of potential growth.

Slowly under my eyes the curve became a woman's body, the outline of the image that is always first in Chagall's mind. As in music, the line that he had drawn was his main theme. Around it he could play melodic variations. His face suddenly close to the paper, he added tiny dots, black galaxies on the milk-white paper. He would squint, draw back his head, add a minute mark, squint again, and

Chagall in his studio. Courtesy Jacob Baal-Teshuva.

with a subtle, barely perceptible flourish contribute a final dot—half smiling, as though amused by his own subtlety.

Of some painted tiles in the studio he said, "What noble materials for the artist to create with: earth and fire. To be worthy of them one must be pure, simple." There is a yearning in Chagall for deeper values, away from the pleasing. He finds that taste is playing a much too important role in art. "Too often art equals taste. Cheese has taste," he added. He spoke of painters whose refined and subdued color harmonies are in good taste, adding contemptuously, "A woman dressed in the colors of their paintings would look smart."

Above all, he admires the great colorists. Monet: "I adore him, he is the greatest." Bonnard: "Now here was a great painter, and *du sérieux*." He passed short judgments on his contemporaries. Braque: "Great painter, very French." Mondrian: "Good taste, charming." Klee: "I adore him." Modigliani, Soutine: "Great painters." Matisse: "He doesn't give a damn for anything or anybody. He is so sure of himself." Giacometti: "He feels the profound forces of nature. He counts."

Two large canvases stood on easels along the greater length of the main studio. The paintings loomed even larger under the low ceiling; enormous, fantastic

328

COLORPLATE 104. *Bouquet of Flowers*. 1937. Oil on canvas. 39 x 28 in. (99 x 71 cm).
Courtesy Scharf Fine Arts, New York.

COLORPLATE 105. *Bouquet of Flowers with Faces*. 1966. Oil on canvas. 39 ³/₈ x 31 ⁷/₈ in. (100 x 81 cm). Private collection.

COLORPLATE 106. *Village with Two Bouquets*. 1975. Oil on canvas. 23 5/8 x 28 3/4 in. (60 x 73 cm). Private collection.

COLORPLATE 107. *The Village on Holiday*. 1981. Oil on canvas. 51 3/8 x 76 3/4 in. (130.5 x 195 cm). Collection Ida Chagall, Paris.

COLORPLATE 108. *The Paris Sky.* 1973. Oil on canvas. 39 3/8 x 28 3/4 in. (100 x 73 cm). Private collection.

COLORPLATE 109. *The Bridal Couple Over Paris*. 1972. Oil on canvas. 51 ¹/₈ x 37 ³/₄ in. (130 x 96 cm).
Collection Ida Chagall, Paris.

334

COLORPLATE 110. *Idyllic*. 1980. Oil on canvas. 31 $^7/_8$ x 23 $^5/_8$ in. (81 x 60 cm). Private collection.

COLORPLATE III. *The Painter.* 1976. Oil on canvas. 25 ⁵/₈ x 21 ¹/₄ in. (65 x 54 cm). Private collection.

scenes swirled kaleidoscopically in oceans of solid color, yellow and blue; float-ing, dancing figures ignored the laws of gravity.

The bouquets of flowers in his paintings resemble gay fireworks in the star-studded sky; the little upside-down huts reel away from our vision as we are pro-jected into space away from the earth. Man and animal inhabit this eerie land-scape. But man looks like man only when he loves. Chagall's lovers he in tender embrace, wrapped in a deep ultramarine shadow, while a fish with a man's hand screechingly fiddles. The violin, the instrument that most easily touches our emo-tions and nerves, is usually present; this is a man-made sound, pathetic against the "music of the spheres."

Chagall, practically alone among artists, has painted love. He said, "Love is all; it is the beginning." He has tried to represent love as the original creative impulse, and the great consolation of existence. He translates into visual terms the yearning of lovers. . . .

Like a human being, a Chagall painting reveals its rich complexity only if one has lived with it and in it, in somewhat the way the artist has during its creation. One must look at his paintings closely to experience their full power. After the impact of the overall effect, there is the joy of the close-up discovery. In this inti-mate scrutiny, the slightest variation takes on immense importance. We cannot concentrate for a long time; our senses tire quickly and we need, after moments of intense stimulation, periods of rest. Chagall understands this visual secret bet-ter than most painters; he draws our interest into a corner where minute details hold it, and when we tire of that, we rest, floating on a calm space of color, until the eye lands on a new small island of quivering life.

This ability to concentrate on a small area is particular to Chagall. The minute scratching of the needle on the copper when he etches, the deposits of ink from the thinnest nib when he draws, the slight variations of brushstrokes when he paints, are all one pattern. In anything that Chagall creates, the smallest touch, mark, stroke, scratch have meaning.

We left the studio to go back to the house. It is like a Chagall museum. In every room, on every wall, hang rare early Chagalls, miraculously saved from Russia, direct contacts with his youth and the sources of his art. If memory fades, if intensity weakens, he has only to look at his early canvases to be recharged with his own emotional energy. . . .

After my visit to Vence, I met Chagall again at his daughter's house in Paris. He told me that he was still working on his monumental task of illustrating the Bible, which in 1923 Vollard had asked him to do.

One of the major creative efforts of our time, this illustrated Bible, when finally published in 1956, placed Chagall among the greatest etchers. He has etched more than three hundred plates. By a miracle, a conscientious craftsman hid the Bible plates during the German occupation. Chagall, at sixty-nine, finished the work he had started over thirty years ago. For over thirty years he lived constantly with the Bible. He was like a tree, his roots underground in this then unseen, unpublished work; the leaves, the fruit, the branches were the color-drenched canvases that the world knew as Chagall.

These unseen roots of the creative man explain so much in Chagall's art. Until the publication of his Bible it was as though the world saw a play in which the actors spoke but their voices could not be heard. The meaning of Chagall is in the Bible. And again his history proves there is no great art without faith.

Because of his background, Chagall could feel emotionally and physically a part of the Bible. His Moses is not the elderly Italian noble of Michelangelo or the athletic Greek statue by Blake, but a familiar to Chagall, a patriarch of the Jews. It is a curious plan of fate that, after all his wanderings, Chagall should have settled in Vence. For the landscapes that he saw in his mind as a child, through readings of the Bible, are the landscapes of the Mediterranean land where he now lives. Chagall in his essence belongs to this Mediterranean, the sea of our culture, the sea of the Bible. He has been to Israel, he has been to Italy, to

Greece, bringing back from each voyage precise drawings, notations that confirm and revivify the visions of his memory.

That day in Paris, when we left Ida's house, we drove through the streets on our way to the engraver's. Chagall kept exclaiming, "Look at the light. Look at the light of Paris; a stone from Connecticut would be beautiful to paint in the light of Paris.

"Countries have their own colors, which are preordained. There are countries where there is an absence of color; others have just a trace of color; in others still, the color is completely photographic. No one knows why. It is an unsolved problem."

The engraver's atelier was a small two-storied building in a narrow street, far from the vibrations of traffic. Inside, the walls were covered with the prized works that had been produced there. Next to etchings by Léger, Segonzac, and Chagall hung second-rate works. It seems as though without second-rate art there would be no great art; the abundance of art in Paris, regardless of quality, is a fertilizer to art in general.

Only in Paris can one still find a few craftsmen with manual ability equal to that of the artist. One of the reasons why Paris has attracted artists is because at some moment in the execution of their works of art they need that skilled manual help. Painters, sculptors, etchers, designers can still find assistance among that élite of the working classes, the master craftsmen.

We went upstairs to a little room where a window opened onto a sunny garden. On a small table, white gauze stretched on a frame screened the distracting view and equalized the light. Chagall took off his vest. In a workman's shirt, he attacked the dull copper plate lying flat on the table. He picked up a proof and pointed out, using musical terms, "There must be the same black accents everywhere; 're-echoes,' that's the word.

"Black and white is a color. If you do not see color in a black and white picture, it is dead. In Rembrandt, Goya, and Daumier you can see the color in black and white, less so in the others. Matisse has a beautiful black and white because he was a colorist."

To be able to see the barely visible scratches, he put on thin-rimmed glasses, quickly hiding them with the vanity of a man refusing to submit to the image of age. Again, as in his studio in Vence, the subtlest nuances acquired meaning. The eye and the mind must learn to concentrate fixedly on minute detail, while constantly retaining the grand overall conception. This mental gymnastic is part of the infinite difficulty of art, the system of checks and balances where the tedium of execution slows down the impetuous flight of creation.

In the presence of his *chef-d'oeuvre,* the real Chagall emerged, a great and profound religious painter, in the tradition of Rembrandt. When Chagall finished his morning's work, his last fervent plea, his passionate cue to the engraver, gave the key to his conception: "It must sing, it must cry; it is the Bible."

ANDRÉ MALRAUX

Chagall's Poetic Creativity

1972

André Malraux (1901–1976), author, art historian, and the former Minister of Culture of France. He commissioned Chagall to paint the ceiling of the Paris Opera.

I leave to other experts the task of analyzing Chagall's creative art in the particular fields of ceramics and sculpture. Here I want to speak of Chagall's inner dialogue with himself.

No other artist of our time has been so misunderstood, primarily because, in these days in which the figurative is rejected, Chagall and his themes cannot be wholly divorced from each other. What matter that he is the greatest *imagier* of the century; this is a century that abhors the maker of images. If Chagall has gained acceptance today it is because he is considered to be an exception. What weight should we attach to the "images" of Matisse, Braque or Picasso, when they themselves deny their importance? Perhaps this is less true of Picasso who is aware that the work of his youth formed the building blocks of his future genius.

Chagall's work abounds with imagery. So too does that of Rouault, but his subjects were directly inspired by the world of the Bible; those of Chagall are taken from the outer fringes of Judaism. He illustrated the Bible, you will say? Yet everything that he depicts, whether in close-up or at a distance, belongs to a popular Bible that he himself has lovingly invented. But the Ox and the Ass, constants of Christian art over several centuries, do not appear in the Gospel stories of the Nativity. Chagall was the first artist who dared to create apocryphal prophets seen through the apocryphal creation of the Old Testament. Just as the artists of Assisi showed us how, in prayer, the Ass crossed its ears and the Ox its horns, so Chagall created a world not present in the Scriptures—rabbis walking the earth, lovers flying through the air and wandering clocks . . .

A childhood world? The Ox and the Ass would not have survived across the centuries had they been but creatures of the child's world. And Chagall's images would not have spread throughout the western world had they been no more than fairy-tale figures.

We should not allow ourselves to be led astray by this innocent wonderment; an art such as this must not be judged by its touch of the fantastic, but by the fantastic skill of its creative painting which exudes poetry. What other living artist could have painted the ceiling of the Paris Opera as Chagall did? Yet if his painting creates poetry, the poetry itself inspires the painting.

COLORPLATE 71

Indeed, I am very conscious of Chagall's poetic creativity (who else is there like him . . .). Had he done no more than bring to life the vibrant purity of a world inspired by the Bible and conceive the Ox and the Ass of the Prophets, he would be a great artist. Yet I fear that this side of his work may come to form a screen between him and his public. Though Chagall, like Hieronymus Bosch, Piero di Cosimo, and many others, is indeed a poet, he is, above all, one of the great colourists of our time. He might never have painted a rabbi or his triple-coloured canvases across which ghostly figures pass. But his creative power is the same in the works of his youth and in *Ma Vie*; between these works it is not his creative poetry that has changed, but the colours.

It was not until late in his career that he took up the challenge of colour, by which I mean the passionate urge that links the last Monets with the last Titians, and others too many to enumerate. I simply want to distinguish his genius from that of Rembrandt, of Caravaggio, or of Vermeer. What shall I call it . . . orchestration perhaps? He is a Grunewald, not a Fouquet. The two approaches have been distinct for three hundred years now. We are told that Chagall found his talents as a colourist through his work with stained glass. And yet the luminosity of stained glass stems from its transparency; Chagall had to invent his own, and transparency does not give unity to a painting. . . .

Chagall's world of the imagination (an allusive one, since he never offers us the phantasmagoric world of, for example, a Hieronymus Bosch) is often derived from plastic elements—his lovers are not forced into the form of an arabesque, the arabesque is transformed to become the couple. Imagination is a constant factor in Chagall's work that can be traced from the Jews of Vitebsk right up to his latest and greatest works. Yet, to my mind, this imaginative streak belongs less to the realms of the picturesque than to what Chagall himself simply calls Love. Though the canvases of his youth are vital and moving, they are not of the same stamp as the great paintings of the Maeght Foundation. Had he died at the age of forty, we should not be speaking of him in the way that we do today. Chagall has established a dialogue with colour comparable to that established by the Venetian artists in about 1550, at the time when Titian brought the sovereign right of picto-

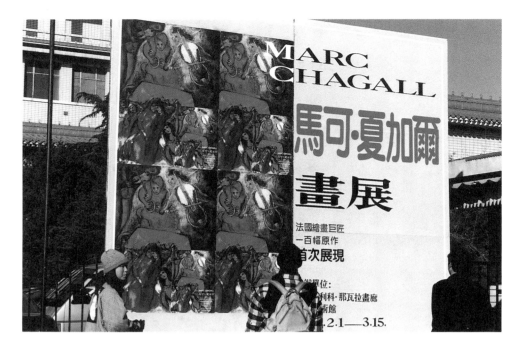

Billboard for Chagall exhibition in Beijing, China. Photograph: Anne Pfeffer. Courtesy Galerie Navara, Paris.

rial lyricism (the *Callisto* in Vienna) into confrontation with the amber shades of his earlier days. Many of Chagall's canvases, and the ceiling of the Paris Opera, form an illustrious image that counts among the finest poetry of our day, just as Titian belongs to the finest poetry of his day. . . .

Were we to look at Chagall's latest paintings with less attention to their figurative elements and with more of an eye to their allusive aspects, his contribution to painting would stand out more clearly—as it does when we see his recent works displayed together. His present colour technique has no precedent; the colours of the great artists of the preceding generation, such as Bonnard for example, were said to be merely part of the painter's vision. During the whole of that period to which the label "impressionism" can be applied—except in Ensor's extravaganzas which are not impressionist—a certain range of colours (a "palette" as painters say) remained constant and accepted, in Van Gogh just as in Bonnard, and even among the Fauvists. . . . Cubism was monochrome, as too were Chagall's early works. Most of Picasso's great works, even *Guernica*, were camaieux. . . . In Chagall's great canvases, colour continues to evoke forms, just as earlier an arabesque evoked the couple in the sky. At times colour is completely liberated, with no outward sign of the control which is, of course, there. Of all the artists we are considering, Chagall is the most lyrical; by this I mean, of course, that, as has been said of Delacroix in his preliminary sketches for paintings, he is the one who endows colour with an unreality similar to the mysterious interplay of music—great raspberry-coloured splashes, canvases in which blue confronts red as in the stained glass windows of Chartres . . . As we look at Chagall's latest works, who springs to mind but the Stravinsky of the *Rites of Spring*? It is often the mark of an artist of genius that he manages to escape from the colour reference of his period. But what distinguishes Chagall's most striking (and often most recent) paintings from his notable earlier works? Above all, they are different in that in them Chagall confronts harmony with a certain dissonance very much akin to that found in modern music. On leaving an exhibition of his stained glass work, or his retrospective held at the Grand Palais, Paris, we have the feeling that all his previous works, no matter how varied, form part of one great family.

ANDREI VOZNESENSKY

"Chagall's Gala"

1987

Andrei Voznesensky, famous Russian poet of the younger generation. He lives in Moscow.

I congratulate you on home-coming, Marc Chagall, genius of the age, blue patriarch of world painting!

At last we have lived to see his genuine resurrection.

At long last his masterpieces are being viewed in the exhibition rooms of the Pushkin Museum by his country-people, for whom he painted. In a true sense Chagall never really separated from his country. Be it Paris, New York, Saint-Paul-de-Vence, his country always kept blossoming on his magic canvases. His Eiffel Tower stands on chicken's legs, as if coming out of folktales of his land.

He called Paris his second Vitebsk.

I remember him returning briefly to Moscow in 1973. He had come by invitation of the Ministry of Culture. His hotel room was piled with baskets of flowers and ceremonial gifts. But the blue-eyed master of genius, his mane of hair snow-white like the frost patterns on the window, sobbed over a simple nosegay of cornflowers—it was the colour of his childhood in Vitebsk, the humble, enchanting flower whose radiance he splashed over the stained-glass windows of the whole world from Tokyo to the Metropolitan Opera House in New York.

It was then that I wrote a poem for him.

CHAGALL'S CORNFLOWERS

Your face is all of silver like a halberd,
your gestures light.
In your vulgar hotel room
you keep pressed cornflowers.

Dear friend, so this is what you truly love:
Since Vitebsk, cornflowers have wounded
and loved you—those wildflower tubes
of squeezed-out
         devilish
           sky-blue.

An orphaned flower of the burdock family,
its blue has no rival.
The mark of Chagall, the enigma of Chagall—
a tattered ruble note at a remote Moscow station.
It grew around St. Boris and St. Gleb,
around guffawing speculators with their greasy fingers.
In a field of grain, add a patch of sky.
Man lives by sky alone.

Cows and water nymphs soar in the sky.
Open your umbrella as you go out on the street.
Countries are many, the sky is one.
Man lives by sky alone.

How did a cornflower seed chance to fall
on the Champs-Elysées, on those fields?
What a glorious garland you wove
for the Paris Opéra.

In the age of consumer goods there is no sky.
The lot of the artist is worse than a cripple's.
Giving him pieces of silver is silly—
man lives by sky alone.

Your canvases made their escape
from the fascist nightmare, from murder,
the forbidden sky rolled up in a tube,
but man lives by sky alone.

While God failed to trumpet
over the horror,
your canvases rolled up in a tube
still howl like Gabriel's horn.

Who kissed your fields, Russia,
until cornflowers bloomed?
Your weeds become glorious in other countries,
you ought to export them.

How they hail you, when you leave the train.
The fields tremble.
The fields are studded with cornflowers.
You can't get away from them.

Chagall at home in his studio, Saint-Paul-de-Vence. Courtesy Alexander Liberman.

When you go out in the evening—you seem ill.
Eyes of the unjustly condemned stare from the field.
Ah, Marc Zakharovich, Marc Zakharovich,
is it all the fault of those cornflowers?
Let not Jehovah or Jesus
but you, Marc Zakharovich, paint a testament
of invincible blue—
Man Lives by Sky Alone.

A year ago, after I had recited these lines in New York's purple-seated Carnegie Hall, I was given a letter written in a very fine hand. It was signed *Bella Chagall*.

On the next day, dressed with a student's simplicity, she told me about her grandfather's last moments. He died in his own home amid the greenery of Saint-Paul. Marc Zakharovich was in his wheelchair and passed away as he was being taken by lift up to the second floor. He died with a faint smile on his fine, beet-root lips; he died soaring up to the sky, flying.

JOHN RUSSELL

From *The New York Times*

"Farewell to Chagall, The Great Survivor"

April 7, 1985

John Russell, art critic and author. He was the chief art critic for The New York Times, *to which he still contributes articles.*

It was difficult, when talking to Marc Chagall, to remember that he had been born in 1887, had more than once played a considerable part in the heroic age of modern art, and had had his troubles not merely with the upheavals of the 20th century but with the upheavals of the late 19th century as well. He had the gift of immediacy in conversation, as if the here and now mattered more to him than the ancient memories that an awed stranger would often try to revive.

When he came to England at the age of 81, for the inauguration of a memorial stained-glass window that he had designed for a little country church outside Tonbridge in Kent, he did not carry on like a grand old man who was doing us a favor by being there. He behaved as if this were the first great success of his life, and as if there were no limits to the pleasure that he had in being surrounded not only by new-found English friends and patrons but by the incomparable craftsmen from Rheims who had built the window.

Do not think, however, that he forgot the business angle. By the end of the afternoon, when all around him had been reduced to an amiable near-stupor by good food, good wine and good company, Marc Chagall, alert as ever, had landed an order for four more windows. (I would doubt, moreover, that he had discounted the price.) And, sure enough, in his 92nd year four more windows were delivered. They do not look in the least like an old man's work. Fresh, apt, restrained and unfeignedly poignant, they have a direct and delicate fancy and are absolutely at home in the English countryside. (They will, by the way, be on view at the Philadelphia Museum of Art from May 12 to July 7 as part of the full-scale Chagall retrospective that was initiated by the Royal Academy of Arts in London.)

Self-Portrait. 1955. Brush and ink drawing.
15 ¹/₂ x 12 in. (39.4 x 30.5 cm). Private collection.

In life, as in art, this was Chagall the great survivor, the man who had rebuilt his career over and over again and ended it, not far short of his 100th birthday on March 28, in an almost all-enveloping glow of adulation. He had his detractors—more so, perhaps, than any other major figure of our century—and undeniably he recycled some of his ideas not once, but many times, too often. For many years he had the reputation—not least among those who delighted in his earlier achievement—of having turned into an amiable but rapacious manufacturer who flooded the market with work that was high on sugar but very low indeed on urgency, necessity and daring.

It was harmful to him, and to his reputation, that much of his finest work had remained in the Soviet Union, where it was accessible only to a handful of privileged people (and not always even to them). Chagall in his native country was his own whole self. Not only was he born and raised there, but he was formed as an artist by his experiences in childhood and boyhood. His repertory of themes and images was complete, almost, by the time that he left Russia for Paris in his middle 20's. Many years later, he wrote to a friend that "the title of 'Russian painter' means more to me than any international fame . . . In my paintings there is not one centimeter that is free from nostalgia for my native land."

His imagery was bred into him. As a member of a Hasidic family, living within the Pale of Settlement in the town of Vitebsk, Chagall grew up in a world of ancient legends that were intensely alive to him. They fed him, nurtured him,

344

powered his imagination and made it possible for him to overturn, in his art, the political degradations that came his way.

If his lovers flew high in the air above an archetypal Russian small town, it was not because he thought they looked pretty. It was because he could represent them as free from the regulations that prevented them from leaving town without a special permit. (Chagall himself could only go to art school in St. Petersburg by pretending to be a domestic servant in the house of one of his patrons.) If his prototypical fiddler on the roof played away all his life long, it was not because he was rehearsing for a Broadway musical. It was because, halfway between earth and heaven, he was fulfilling the ancient role of the violinist in Jewish life. (It is also likely that Chagall had in mind the exploits of an Estonian, Eduard Sormus, who in 1905 had fired street demonstrations with the sound of his violin. "It is with my violin," he said, "that I shall free the proletariat.")

Chagall by the summer of 1914 was the acclaimed young artist of the day both in Paris and in Berlin. He had everyone on his side—poets, painters, collectors and dealers. Russia may have formed him, as a man and as an artist, but Paris made him. It was in Paris that Guillaume Apollinaire and Blaise Cendrars introduced him to the perfected cosmopolitanism of the Western European poetry of the day. It was in Paris that Robert Delaunay showed him how to graft his imagery onto a pictorial architecture that had epic scale. It was in Paris that he came to know the heroic age of European modernism at first hand, and never was anyone a quicker study.

It was through Apollinaire that he got to be known in Berlin, through the advocacy of Herwarth Walden—dealer, editor and artistic impresario. And it was from Berlin that he went to Vitebsk in the summer of 1914 for what he thought would be a brief visit. Caught by the outbreak of World War I, he stayed there until 1922, thereby enjoying—though that was not, in the end, the right word—a second Russian period no less momentous than his first one.

Chagall never failed to refer to the Russian revolution of 1917 as an event of primordial importance in his life. How could it be otherwise, when the revolution transformed his status, alike as an artist, and as a citizen? As a Jew, he had full citizenship for the first time, and after a period in which the hideous institution of the pogrom had been in full operation. As an artist, he suddenly found himself a big somebody in a town where he had until then been a little nobody. The year

1918 saw him become commissar with power to organize every aspect of artistic life in Vitebsk and its neighborhood, together with the right to intervene in all matters pertaining to the theater.

He gave himself over completely to the task. No project was too grandiose for him, and no detail too paltry. He got the best artists to come and teach in Vitebsk. ("Men from the capital for the Province!" was his call to arms, and people listened to it.) During the first years of the revolutionary era he did, moreover, a great deal of his finest work. To be part of what seemed a glad new day was intoxicating to him. To be able to validate the ancestral culture of the Jews—as he did in murals and decors for the new Jewish Theater in Moscow in 1920–21—was the consummation of his hopes and ambitions.

It should have been paradise, but it wasn't. Chagall was eased out of Vitebsk by the very artists—above all, by Kasimir Malevich—whom he had been so keen to welcome. Not only did they ease him out, but they won over precisely the young people to whom he had devoted himself. The new freedom and full civil status of the Jews in Soviet Russia did not last long. When Chagall left Russia for Western Europe in 1922, after teaching in colonies for orphans of the war, it was as a saddened and defeated man. He never forgot it, either. More than 50 years later, when he paid his last visit to New York, he astonished some of his fellow guests at the home of his dealer, longtime champion and close friend Pierre Matisse, by saying to them, "I know about Kandinsky, but who was Malevich? Can anyone tell me?"

In this sense, and in literal fact, Chagall left much of the best of himself behind him in the Soviet Union. Nor did he ever get over the loss of his native country, which he was to visit only once more (in 1973, and briefly). But he went on to give pleasure of an undemanding sort to millions of people the world over, and for those who take the trouble to seek it out there is over and over again in his work a residue of the original, tough, poignant and searching Marc Chagall—and nowhere more so than in the illustrations for his autobiographical *My Life* and for Gogol's *Dead Souls*. It should also be said that in the late stained-glass windows and, remarkably enough, in some of the paintings of his very last years, he was able to restrain and renew himself to remarkable effect. In those achievements it is not the mass market synthesizer we hear, but the solo violinist of Vitebsk.

ANDRÉ VERDET

"Farewell to Marc Chagall"

1985

Marc Chagall loved flowers. He delighted in their aroma, in contemplating their colors. For a long time, certainly after 1948 when he moved for good to the South of France after his wartime stay in the U.S., there were always flowers in his studio. In his work bouquets of flowers held a special place. They were a source of inspiration for this genial Russian painter, born of poor parents in Vitebsk in 1887. Usually they created a sense of joy, but they could also reflect the melancholy of memories, the sadness of separations, of solitude, if not suffering or tragedy.

His wife Vava, of the beautiful iconlike face, was with him when he died in his villa "La Colline" at St. Paul de Vence, the proud medieval town which looks like a long stone boat that juts from a hilltop overlooking the Mediterranean. That same afternoon the artist was still at work, as if an eternity of life remained before him.

On the morning of Monday, April 1, during the funeral service the gladdening spring sun shone out over the village. Doves hovered in the sky as if giving a fond signal of farewell. A part of the cemetery was transformed into a dazzling garden of countless flowers, the homage of hundreds upon hundreds of people, well-known and unknown, gathered there from around the world.

Chagall was one of the last great painters to span the twentieth century. He was to change Modern art with an ineradicable hand. His fantastic vision of a world in which animals are the customary partners of man was all his own, unclassifiable and inimitable. It unfolds in a realm where the present merges with immemorial concerns which transport us beyond our earth, beyond our sky, to enable us by his interpretations of myths and Bible mysteries to grasp at the ungraspable of the world.

Although this mystical painter was nourished by Hebraic culture from his earliest childhood and drew on works of Christian inspiration as well as of pagan Greece, both Apollonian and Dionysian, he could only have followed one religion, that of loving and love. He was for me a great friend. I remember a visit to "La Colline" some time ago. He had taken a painting from his studio and placed it against a tree trunk next to plants and flowers. He said, "If my painting holds up in nature, if it doesn't disturb the harmony, then it is real, and perhaps one day I could put my name to it."

Charles Marq and Chagall, c. 1975.
Courtesy Charles Marq.

CHARLES MARQ

"For the Record"

1987

Charles Marq, painter and master craftsman of stained glass windows. He worked with Chagall on all of his stained glass windows and was the first director of the Musée National Message Biblique Marc Chagall in Nice, France.

Painting has no need for commentary, and Marc Chagall's perhaps less than that of others, in spite of appearances.

He was a painter before even learning that one could be a painter and transform one's entire life into a painting.

He was a painter in his vision of art which he communicated to those around him, without theory and without words, but by means of that gift he had of bringing his assistants to another region, another place, where the Other Reality can appear.

It was not about *his* art, for, as he said, "I do not know Chagall," and these were not the words of an artist; his self-awareness was totally engulfed by the awareness he had of Creation, an awareness both total and specific, of men, women, animals, plants and flowers, of heaven and earth.

This cosmic consciousness made of him a *good* man, as in the beginning of Genesis, the Creator at the end of the day knew that it was good, that it was very good.

He was a painter in his ability to touch the material, making it into a talisman: making a stone precious, making the glass [into] light, making the blue [into] sky and man into an angel.

As in the spring each leaf from a tree is always new starting from the first day, each touch by Chagall is always a new substance, hitherto unknown.

Astonishment and joy at seeing the painter in his studio infusing dullness with new life and the stained glass window with the light of dawn.

CHARLES SORLIER

In Memorium

1985

I met Chagall in early 1950 during the production of his first color lithograph for the Maeght Gallery in Paris, which held a special exhibition of the artist's works upon his return to America. I was quite impressed by this interview with a painter whom I already deeply admired without for one moment imagining that one day I would have the good fortune of meeting him face to face.

I must certainly have grabbed his hand too enthusiastically, for his first words were, "You're going to break my fingers!" Despite this violent metacarpal reaction, a very deep friendship developed between us. I was to become his assistant, not only as his sole interpretive engraver, supervising the printing of his original lithographs; I was also to be present for the installation of monumental works such as the ceiling at the Paris Opera, the murals at the Metropolitan Opera in New York, the tapestries at the Knesset in Jerusalem, as well as supervising costumes and theatre sets among other things.

Chagall also created a large number of stained glass windows, working this time with Charles Marq, the best master glassmaker in France, if not the world.

He considered "his two Charles" as his spiritual sons.

We called him "The Boss."

Fernand Mourlot was the one who injected new life into the art lithograph after World War II. His print-making studio became famous because of the outstanding reputations of the artists who came to work there. Their names stand out as the greatest masters of the twentieth century.

The place was frequented by painters and sculptors but also writers: Colette, Carco, Reverdy, Aragon, Eluard, Cocteau and Prevert. Under the aegis of the Mourlot print studio, the blending of text and image often yielded magnificent results. While there, Chagall produced *Daphnis and Chloe, The Circus, The Exodus, The Odyssey* and *The Storm.*

COLORPLATE 78

From 1950 to 1952, Chagall went regularly to the studio, which was then located at 18 rue de Chabrol near the Gare de l'Est, not to produce lithographs but to learn the trade. He studied like a young apprentice eager for knowledge. He practiced every possible technique with equal amounts of stubbornness and dedication. No craftsman could ever feel as proud as I do for having held the hand of such a gifted student.

As a beginner, he executed many plates on both stone and zinc, essentially in black, repeating successive stages, torturing the flat surface with scrapers, learning to use wash and "toad skin" in order to find out just how far is too far, for the art of lithography has its limits and involves technical constraints which must be well understood.

Thus he came for months on end and worked assiduously, printing only an occasional proof from his first attempts for the good and simple reason that he was not entirely satisfied with them.

From the outset, his fellow printers adopted him as one of their own. Whenever Marc started working, Master Chagall would wait patiently for him in the cloakroom.

It sometimes seemed that an angel would come down to visit him. I remember seeing him do a drawing entitled "Shadow and Light" in front of the cameras during the taping of a television program. The producer, Daniel LeConte, had asked me if the artist would agree to work under such conditions and I had answered that he should not entertain any illusions to that effect. However, just in case, I had a stone and some equipment prepared.

Chagall puts the finishing touches on his canvas *Jacob's Dream* before hanging it up for exhibit at the opening of the Musée National Message Biblique Marc Chagall in Nice, July 7, 1973. Photograph: AP/Wide World Photos.

Chagall arrived, glanced at the set designed to ensnare him, and grumbled, "Not that, of all things!"

He sat down elsewhere. The cameraman prepared to film the interview. Suddenly one of the assistants yelled out in colorful but highly concrete terms: "———, they forgot the sound tape."

At that time, sound and image had not yet been synchronized. The person responsible for this careless mistake slipped out to go to the studio for the forgotten equipment. Chagall grumbled his displeasure at this unfortunate foul-up. The minutes crept by. Like all creators, "The Boss" felt he was wasting his time by remaining inactive. The work table suddenly beckoned as a refuge. Once he had his lithographic stone in front of him, he caressed its smooth surface for a long time.

He liked having a tactile relationship with things and used exactly the same approach with a blank canvas.

Without a model and apparently without preconceived ideas, he began to draw while the cameraman, delighted with this stroke of luck, did not miss a frame.

He began with the couple on the sixth day, with the animals from a Chagallian Eden coming to join them, and the Angel, the one which had entered his head, placed itself quite naturally on the composition. For about two hours he worked without seeming the least bit bothered by the technicians, the cameraman or even the sound engineer, who had returned with a tape recorder. Forgetting all this agitation, Chagall alone was communicating with his imaginary world.

Chagall was goodness and kindness incarnate. Once you got to know him, it was impossible not to like him. Meeting him and knowing him as a professional, as a friend and as a human being, transformed my life in every respect.

Chagall's last color lithograph (untitled), 1985.
Collection Jacob Baal-Teshuva.

Charles Sorlier was the last public person to
see Chagall before his death. They were
working on the lithograph which became
Chagall's last, and which he never signed.
The artist's signature appears in facsimile.

For me, he remains "The Boss." Our thirty-five years of friendship never wavered until that fatal day, Friday, March 29, 1985, when I saw him for the last time "As into himself eternity changes him."

I had spent the whole day of Thursday the twenty-eighth in his company. He made a small lithograph in my presence, which he gave me along with two other plates he had already done in black, as well as a proof, a circus scene, for which he asked me to prepare the color plates and to send him the "zincs" as quickly as possible. He also signed the final corrected proof of a lithograph which was to be his final gift to the Association des Amis du Message Biblique. He remained as generous as ever right up to the end.

We parted at around seven in the evening without an excessive show of affection. I still had a few days to spend near him, and he knew I would be back the next day. I did not feel that the kiss we exchanged was a definitive farewell.

When the hotel desk clerk came at about 8:30 that evening to let me know I was wanted on the telephone, I suddenly felt a terrible premonition. Between two sobs, Vava, the painter's wife, told me simply, "Chagall is dead."

I felt as though I had been struck by lightning. I felt no shame at letting the tears flow. I had just been orphaned for the second time.

I feel it is important to look again at Chagall's last drawing, for this sketch is his farewell to life. It depicts the artist in front of his easel. A bird comes out of his head and takes flight. His left hand no longer holds a palette. The metaphors he used all his life take their place one last time in this work and transform it into a message.

How can one not think of *The Tempest*, which he illustrated, Shakespeare's final comedy, at the end of which the poet, in the person of Prospero the Magician, frees the Angel Ariel (the bird)—"Then to the elements be free"—and then breaks his magic wand (the palette) before taking leave of the public:

> Now my charms are all o'erthrown,
> And what strength I have's mine own,
> Which is most faint . . .
> . . . release me from my bands
> With the help of your good hands
> Gentle breath of yours my sails
> Must fill, or else my project fails,
> Which was to please.

To anyone who sees this as a mere coincidence, I would say that the theme of the artist's next-to-last drawing is the "Arrival in the Promised Land."

Chagall was a thief of fire and a clairvoyant. I am convinced that for a few days he alone *had known*.

On the morning of the funeral, the little village of Saint-Paul was invaded by a crowd. The sky had dressed in Chagall blue in honor of the event. Busloads of tourists, so numerous during the Easter season, brought a flood of visitors. German, Japanese, Italian and American—a mixture of races attended the ceremony, as though achieving that Universal Brotherhood which meant so much to the Master. The shopkeepers paid homage to him all along his final route by hanging reproductions of his work in their windows. Family members and guests of honor were to be cordoned off from the crowds by the police, but they were overcome by a human wave impossible to contain. I was not able to gain entry to the tiny cemetery. There the lowliest peasant rubbed elbows with the high and mighty to accompany Chagall to his eternal reward.

He is very happy.

I did not use the wrong verb tense in the above sentence, for only those with barren minds can believe that the Master is dead. He is simply walking around this world in the state of levitation which was peculiar to him.

He was supposedly buried on April first. When I realized that, I suddenly understood that the nightmare we had been living through all that time was in fact only a joke in very bad taste.

> The Boss is eternal.
> He is always nearby, inspiring me and judging me.
> Chagall with two wings.

Chagall at home in Saint-Paul-de-Vence, just before his ninetieth birthday. Photograph: AP/Wide World Photos.

COLORPLATE 112. *The Kidnapping*. 1990. Tapestry. Approximately 9 ft. 8 in. x 11 ft. 8 in. (2.9 x 3.5 m).
Private collection. Courtesy Yvette Cauquil Prince, Paris.

COLORPLATE 113. *The Big Circus*. c. 1993. Tapestry. Approximately 10 ft. 4 in. x 19 ft. 8 in. (3.1 x 6 m).
Private collection. Courtesy Yvette Cauquil Prince, Paris.

COLORPLATE 114. *The Exodus*. 1965–68. Tapestry woven at the Gobelin Works. Approximately 15 ft. 6 in. x 29 ft. 8 in. (4.7 x 9 m). Collection of the Parliament, Jerusalem, Israel. Photograph: Giraudon/Art Resource, New York.

COLORPLATE 115. *The Harlequins*. 1993. Tapestry. Approximately 10 ft. 5 in. x 17 ft. 4 in. (3.1 x 5.2 m). Private collection. Courtesy Yvette Cauquil Prince, Paris.

COLORPLATE 116. *Life*. c. 1990. Tapestry. Approximately 11 ft. 10 in. x 16 ft. (3.6 x 4.8 m).
Private collection. Courtesy Yvette Cauquil Prince, Paris.

COLORPLATE 117. *The Creation of Man.* 1956–58. Oil on canvas. 118 1/8 x 78 3/4 in. (300 x 200 cm).
Musée National Message Biblique Marc Chagall, Nice. Photograph © Réunion des Musées Nationaux.

COLORPLATE 118. *Noah and the Rainbow*. 1961–66. Oil on canvas. 80 3/4 x 115 1/8 in. (205 x 292.5 cm).
Musée National Message Biblique Marc Chagall, Nice. Photograph © Réunion des Musées Nationaux.

COLORPLATE 119. *Abraham and the Three Angels.* 1958–60. Oil on canvas. 74 ⁷/₈ x 115 in. (190 x 292 cm).
Musée National Message Biblique Marc Chagall, Nice. Photograph © Réunion des Musées Nationaux.

(Following spread) COLORPLATE 120. *Jacob's Dream.* 1958–60. Oil on canvas. 76 ³/₄ x 109 ¹/₂ in. (195 x 278 cm).
Musée National Message Biblique Marc Chagall, Nice. Photograph © Réunion des Musées Nationaux.

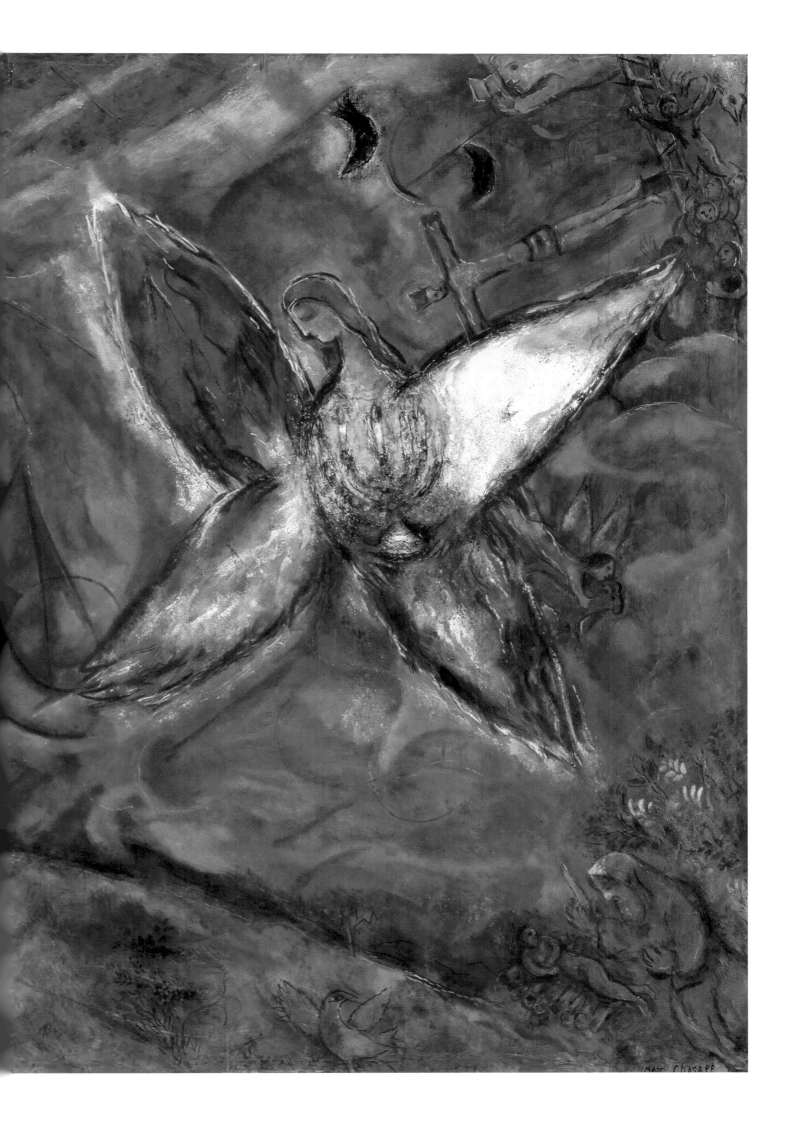

COLORPLATE 121. *The Smiting of the Rock*. 1960–66. Oil on canvas. 93 x 91 ²/₃ in. (236 x 232 cm).
Musée National Message Biblique Marc Chagall, Nice. Photograph © Réunion des Musées Nationaux.

COLORPLATE 122. *Moses Receiving the Tablets of the Law*. 1958–60. Oil on canvas. 93 ³/4 x 92 ¹/8 in. (238 x 234 cm).
Musée National Message Biblique Marc Chagall, Nice. Photograph © Réunion des Musées Nationaux.

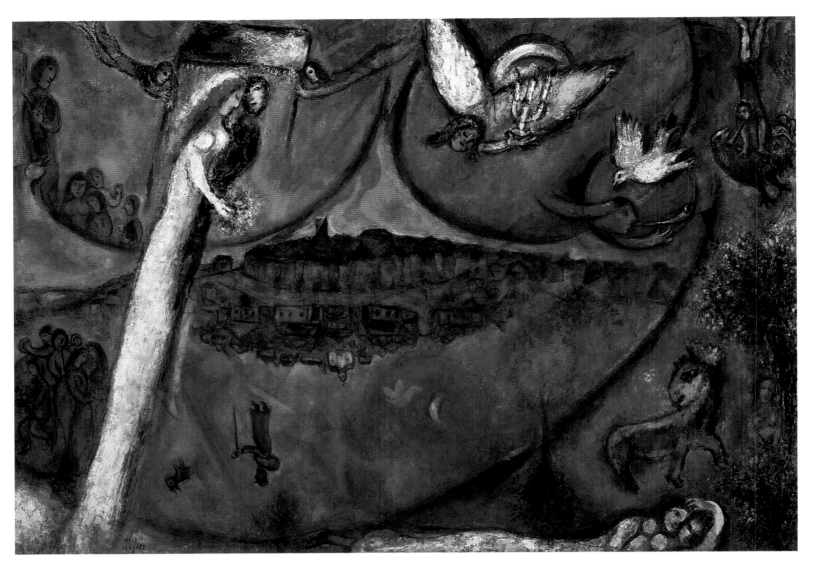

COLORPLATE 123. *The Song of Songs III*. 1960. Oil on canvas. 58 5/8 x 82 5/8 in. (149 x 210 cm).
Musée National Message Biblique Marc Chagall, Nice. Photograph © Réunion des Musées Nationaux.

INDEX

Page numbers in italic denote illustrations.